BREAKING GROUND

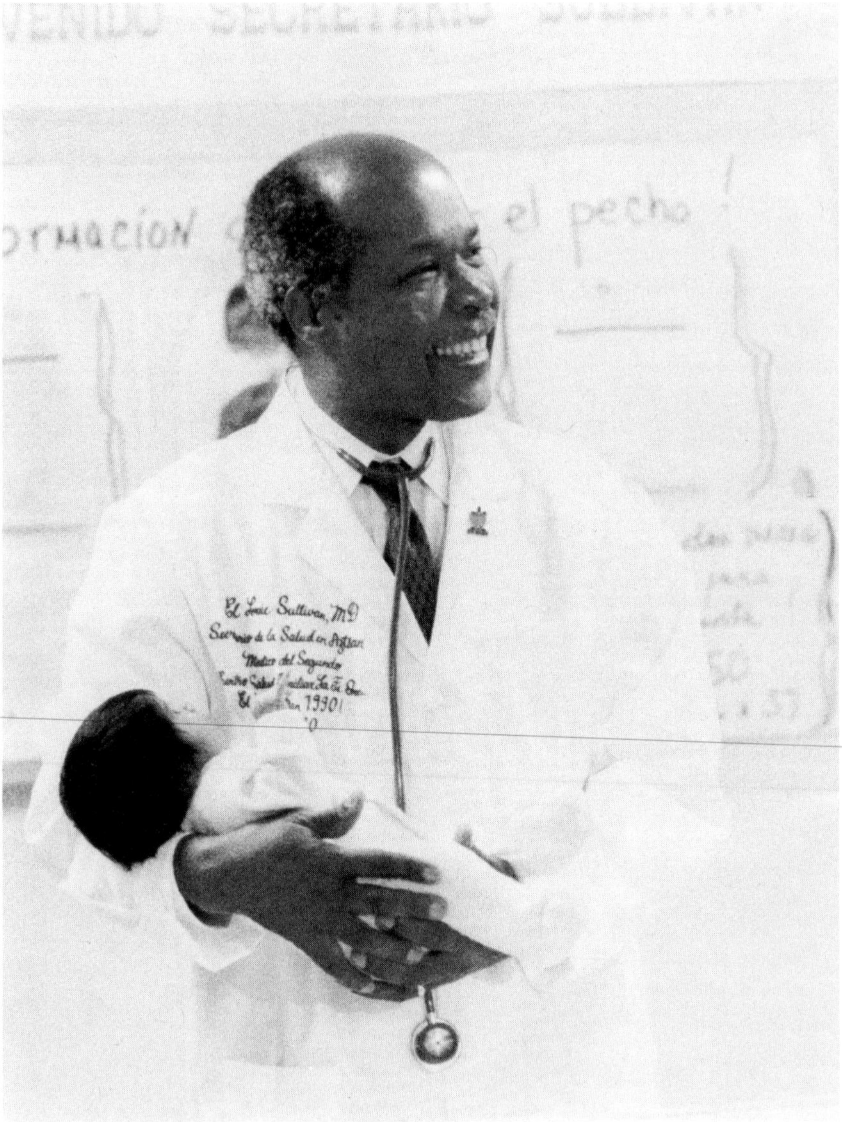

ormacion
el pecho

Breaking Ground

MY LIFE IN MEDICINE

Dr. Louis W. Sullivan

with David Chanoff *Foreword by Ambassador Andrew Young*

THE UNIVERSITY OF GEORGIA PRESS   ATHENS & LONDON

A Sarah Mills Hodge Fund Publication

This publication is made possible in part through a grant from the
Hodge Foundation in memory of its founder, Sarah Mills Hodge, who devoted
her life to the relief and education of African Americans in Savannah, Georgia.

Published by the University of Georgia Press
Athens, Georgia 30602
www.ugapress.org
© 2014 by Louis W. Sullivan and David Chanoff
All rights reserved
Designed by Erin Kirk New
Set in Adobe Garamond Pro
Manufactured by Thomson-Shore
The paper in this book meets the guidelines for
permanence and durability of the Committee on
Production Guidelines for Book Longevity of the
Council on Library Resources.

Most University of Georgia Press titles are
available from popular e-book vendors.

Printed in the United States of America
14   15   16   17   18   C   5   4   3   2   1

Library of Congress Cataloging-in-Publication Data

Sullivan, Louis Wade, 1933–
Breaking ground : my life in medicine / Dr. Louis W. Sullivan with
David Chanoff ; foreword by Ambassador Andrew Young.
pages cm
Includes index.
ISBN 978-0-8203-4663-2 (hardcover : alk. paper) —
ISBN 0-8203-4663-2 (hardcover : alk. paper)
1. Sullivan, Louis Wade, 1933– 2. African American physicians—Biography.
3. Physicians—United States—Biography. 4. United States. Department of
Health and Human Services—Officials and employees. 5. Morehouse School
of Medicine. I. Chanoff, David. II. Title. III. Title: My life in medicine.
R695.S85 2014
610.92—dc23 [B]
2013029150

British Library Cataloging-in-Publication Data available

Frontispiece: Visiting Brown Hospital, El Paso, Texas, 1990,
as U.S. secretary of Health and Human Services

I am privileged to dedicate this publication of my life's story to my wife, Ginger, who has shared so much of this with me, with unconditional love and support in all my endeavors. I also dedicate this to my parents, Walter W. Sullivan Sr. and Lubirda Priester Sullivan, who gave me life, a strong legacy, inspiration, and a clear value system. The core of who I am emanates from these beloved persons who are so important to me.

CONTENTS

FOREWORD

When Louis Sullivan was a child in rural south Georgia, the nearest black doctor was forty miles away. Dr. Joseph Griffin was famous in that part of Georgia and revered by the African American community. At the age of five, young Louis decided he wanted to be just like Dr. Griffin. When he grew up he would be a doctor, taking care of people who had no one else to take care of them.

Louis Sullivan did become a doctor. He never fulfilled his youthful desire to practice medicine in one of the small Georgia communities that are still, today, seriously lacking in health care. But he turned that early dream into a career that has protected and enhanced the health, not just of the poor and underserved, but of all Americans.

Widely acknowledged as one of the most effective and influential secretaries of Health and Human Services in that department's history, Sullivan was a leader in the war against AIDS and smoking and catalyzed the ongoing national effort to make the fight for good health something each of us can take responsibility for in our own lives. He has helped teach America that above all else health care means staying well, which is largely in our own hands, not sick care, which we have to leave to doctors and hospitals.

Today everyone knows that exercise, eating properly, and not smoking enhance health, but we forget that not so long ago these concepts were not considered truths, but unproven, easily ignored assertions. As secretary, Sullivan was instrumental in changing our national mindset about how the way we live our lives affects how we do, or do not, keep ourselves healthy.

Sullivan changed the face of American health care in other ways as well. When he took office as the country's second black HHS secretary (and the only African American in George H. W. Bush's cabinet), research relating to the health of women and minorities was shamefully neglected. At NIH Sullivan established the Office of Research on Women's Health and the Office of Research on Minority Health (now the National Institute of Minority Health and Health Disparities). To help ensure that programs addressing the health needs of women and minorities were not neglected and shunted aside he appointed highly qualified women and minorities to leadership positions in what had previously been a male-dominated and essentially lily-white government health establishment. In doing so he helped break the glass ceiling that had relegated the talent of the nation's women and minorities to secondary and less than fully productive roles.

Sullivan's commitment to the health of America's neediest was incorporated in the health reform legislation rolled out by the elder Bush administration in early 1992. When Sullivan took office as HHS secretary, thirty-seven million mostly poor Americans did not have health coverage. Sullivan's overarching concern as secretary was to remedy that. The health care reform plan devised under his direction provided coverage and at the same time attacked escalating health costs. As a plan developed by a Republican administration and encompassing the Democratic push for universal coverage, it would have allowed the country to avoid the vicious partisan conflicts that characterized both the Clinton and Obama health care reform efforts.

In a career that has spanned the gamut from clinician to biomedical scientist to public health leader, Lou Sullivan's signature accomplishment has without doubt been the Morehouse School of Medicine, the nation's first predominantly black medical school in more than a century. As Morehouse School of Medicine's founding dean and longtime president, Sullivan built an institution from which many graduates go on to practice in inner cities and rural communities where the need is greatest. Recently ranked the number one medical school in the country in terms of social mission, Morehouse exerts an influence far beyond its size in addressing the nation's critical need for primary care physicians.

I am proud to have played a role in the early years of the Morehouse School of Medicine when in 1975, as the congressman from Atlanta, I introduced the dean of this new institution to my fellow members of Congress, who subsequently provided financial and moral support to the school's growth and development.

Lou Sullivan has always believed that addressing the health requirements of the country's neediest—its minorities and poor—will bring the greatest benefit to society as a whole. That was the theme of his tenure as secretary, and that has been the impact of the medical school he founded. In this book he writes with clarity, passion, and humor about the life he has led and the issues that dominate our current health care debates. Now in his early eighties, Sullivan remains one of the medical world's wisest and most inspirational public voices.

ANDREW YOUNG

CHAPTER I

Blakely, Georgia

In the little town of Blakely, Georgia, my father, Walter W. Sullivan Sr., buried the black people. It wasn't that the white undertaker, Mr. Minter, would deny blacks his services. But in that place at that time even death was segregated. At the white funeral home African American loved ones would have to go in around back. And black customers would take their last ride, not in Mr. Minter's hearse but on his flatbed mule-drawn wagon. It was not a dignified ending, which was why, before my father came to town, deceased African Americans were often buried by a black mortician in Albany, fifty miles east—a considerable inconvenience for family and friends.

My father wasn't always a mortician. Before that, he was a life insurance salesman for the Atlanta Life Insurance Company. Atlanta Life was founded in the first years of the twentieth century by Alonzo Herndon, a former slave who became one of the South's first black millionaires. After he was emancipated, Herndon worked as a farm laborer, then learned to cut hair. His barbering customers were all white, many of them lawyers and businessmen, and Herndon absorbed enough knowledge from their talk to start up several businesses, including Atlanta Life.

Atlanta Life became the economic engine for Atlanta's black businesses, including financial institutions that financed homes, other real estate, and commercial start-ups. But early on in the Great Depression people stopped buying life insurance almost before they stopped buying anything else. Atlanta Life was in trouble, and my father, along with the other agents, was going broke. He needed something different.

He wasn't particular; any job would do. So he went searching door-to-door, from one business to the next. Because he always believed in making a neat appearance, he wore a tie and jacket and his straw hat. He was penniless, but he looked good. After one fruitless interview (they were all fruitless) a lady stopped him on the street. "Mister," she said, "can you spare a dime?"

"I'm sorry," he answered, "I don't have a dime. I'm trying to find a job."

"Well." She looked him over. Given his appearance she wasn't sure she believed him. "Well then, you need to get out of those fancy duds and beg like the rest of us."

With nothing available and a family to feed, my father thought about his situation, and what he thought was that as a life insurance agent he had paid off many death claims. No one was buying insurance now, and he wasn't paying claims anymore. But people were still dying. And everyone who died needed to be buried. Somehow—we're not sure how it happened—he went into partnership in a funeral home business in Albany, Georgia. Then, when he and his partner had a falling out, he went looking for a place to open his own funeral parlor, and he found Blakely, a farming town of ten thousand people or so in south Georgia's red clay peanut and cotton country.

Blakely had no black funeral parlor; in fact there wasn't one in all of the surrounding Early County. It seemed like an ideal location, so in 1937 my father moved us there: my mother, Lubirda; my five-year-old brother, Walter Jr.; and me.

I was four, a year and a half younger than Walter, but I remember our first house well. It had four rooms, which served as both our home and the funeral parlor. The living room did duty as the viewing room, where the departed were laid out for final visits. Then there was the kitchen, where we ate our meals; a bedroom, where all four of us slept; and a fourth room, where the caskets were stored and where Dad did the embalming. In that house we were never far away from death. There was plenty of air, though. The house was built sometime in the nineteenth century, and the old clapboards had long ago loosened up, leaving spaces in our walls. In bed at night Walter and I would stare up at the stars through the many open knotholes in the ceiling planks.

When Walter and I started school, we read by kerosene lamps, and though Dad was eventually able to put in running water and a toilet, we never did have electricity in that house. But we were never hungry. At times people were unable to pay for funerals, and instead they'd slaughter a cow or hog or bring vegetables to us, so we always had food on the table.

While Dad did everything he could to get the business up and running, Mama held the family together and brought in money from her job as a teacher. Among other things, she did all the cooking, apparently for good reason. Throughout her life she was almost never ill, but at one point when we were young she had something that put her flat on her back, which seemed very strange and worrisome to us. Dad said, "Lu, you stay in bed and rest. I'll get breakfast." I remember the results of his efforts, which sent Walter and me straight to her bedside. "Mama," Walter wailed, "look at these biscuits!" We showed her the biscuits; they were like bricks. A moment earlier she had been lying motionless with her eyes closed, but when she saw the biscuits, she cried, "My babies. My poor, poor babies," and she got right up out of bed and went in the kitchen to fix breakfast.

Eventually Dad had enough money to buy a larger house around the corner and to put up a separate building next to it as his funeral parlor. From a young age Walter and I were his part-time work crew, helping in whatever way we could. Walter helped more than I because he was older and because, in his old-school way, my father was grooming his firstborn to take over the business. Walter was going to become a funeral director. I, however, had decided to be a doctor.

I had come to this decision because of Dr. Joseph Griffin, who lived and practiced in Bainbridge, Georgia, forty miles south of Blakely. Dr. Griffin was a household name among Georgia's blacks, together with Dr. Eugene Dibble of Tuskegee and George Washington Carver, also of Tuskegee, the man who revolutionized the peanut industry and a great deal more in the South's agricultural life. There were so few black doctors and scientists that everyone knew who they were.

Dr. Griffin was famous, but my father knew him personally, and from the age of five I did too. The reason we did is that neither Blakely nor any of its surrounding towns had a black doctor or a black hospital. If you were sick enough that you needed medical attention, you could do without and let nature take its course; you could go to one of the local root doctors, folk healers who dealt in roots and herbs, potions and magical spells; or you could go to the white doctor, but that meant going around back and sitting in a separate waiting room, which people considered demeaning. It meant you were acquiescing to the so-called universal presumption of black inferiority. That was a constant black people had to put up with in Blakely, as they did all over the South, but they didn't like it; it was an affront.

The other option was that you could go to Dr. Griffin, who treated patients at his twenty-five-bed hospital in Bainbridge. Having Dr. Griffin take care of you was more in keeping with your dignity. It was also something of a statement of independence, tinged with defiance. It meant there were some things, at least, that you would *not* put up with if you could help it.

Since so few people had transportation, my father would take them in his hearse, which doubled as an ambulance. Often I went along. In later years I used to think how these patients must have felt—sick enough to make the long trip to Dr. Griffin and picked up for that trip by the undertaker in his hearse.

At the hospital Dr. Griffin would appear in his green scrubs and surgical cap, a larger-than-life figure. The hospital smelled of ether, a pungent, mysterious aroma that made me think something magical was happening in his examination room or operating theater, which I was never allowed into. I'd see patients in the recovery room, though. Then I'd see them later, when they were well enough to be discharged and my father and I would pick them up. So from an early age I was completely taken by how a doctor could help very ill people get better. What an impression that made. I wanted to be exactly like Dr. Griffin. In our community no one was more respected or looked up to. I knew without a doubt that I was going to be a doctor.

When I told this to my mother, she said, "That's just wonderful, Louie. Walter will be a fine funeral director, and I know you'll be a great doctor." I was five. That was all the confirmation I needed.

The question was, coming from Blakely, how would I ever get to do that? In Blakely, when I was growing up, getting an education was an uphill struggle if there ever was one, at least if you were black. Not many years before this no schools for blacks existed in Blakely. Classes for black kids were held in church basements, abandoned buildings, former barracks, anyplace there was space. Even when black schools were built, resources were minimal. Desks and chairs were secondhand. Books were outdated hand-me-downs from the white schools, something that was typical not only in Georgia but all over the South. Blakely's black schools, such as they were, ran only seven months a year because so many kids were needed on the farm for planting in the spring and harvesting in the fall. In addition, they only went up to the eleventh grade. Given the poverty and the demands for their labor, twelfth-grade black students would have been few and far between.

For Walter Sullivan Sr. and Lubirda Sullivan this was not an acceptable situation. My mother was a teacher, a graduate of Clark College, who later went on to get her master's degree at Atlanta University. My father had attended Claflin College in South Carolina, although he had had to drop out after two years, when his father died and he was needed to run the family farm. He was one of eleven, the youngest boy; when their father passed, his brothers all had families and work of their own, so he was the one called on. The farm was a subsistence operation in Alachua, Florida, so it's a bit of a puzzle how my father managed to get himself to college and how he supported himself while he was there. But he was an energetic, enterprising man, so it's not a complete surprise. He was determined to get himself educated, which he only managed to do halfway. But now that Walter and I were in the picture, he, along with my mother, was going to make sure we got the best education available.

That meant, first of all, that we were not going to go to school in Blakely. In fact, that was an easy decision. Though Mama had a teaching degree, she was never able to get work in Blakely, which was one of the ways the town's white establishment had of retaliating against my father for being an uppity, provocative troublemaker. Instead, Mama worked in different surrounding communities: Bluffton, Donaldsonville, Colquitt, and Cuthbert in Randolph County, where she eventually became supervisor. She drove to these places, some of them thirty or forty miles away, and Walter and I went with her. Wherever she was teaching, that's where Walter and I went to school.

Before junior high the two of us were shipped off to Savannah, where mother had grown up. There we stayed with our grandfather and our two aunts who lived with him, all of whom served in loco parentis while we were in school there. Granddad Priester was a postman and part-time Methodist preacher. Aunts Ruth and Izet were secretaries for Guaranty Life, another black-owned insurance company.

Walter and I were used to the close oversight of our mother and father, and our lives in Savannah weren't very different, except now instead of two parents we had four (our third aunt, Mildred, lived nearby). Just as at home in Blakely, there was a lot of love. The discipline was similar too. In Savannah the house was close to a marsh where Walter and I liked to play. One day we were down there, and I heard my grandfather calling me to come and do something, but I was having too much fun and pretended not to hear him. A little later when our aunts came home he told them about it, and Aunt Ruth told me to go out and cut a switch from one of the bushes. It was the custom in our family to make the children fetch the instruments of their own destruction. I knew exactly what to look for by that time, a switch that wasn't too scanty, in which case you'd incur further wrath, but that wasn't too stiff either, which would really hurt. After Aunt Ruth had tanned my legs to her satisfaction, she called my mother in Blakely to tell her I had disrespected Granddaddy. When my mother heard, she said, "Whip him again." There was a great deal of love in our family, but they had a low tolerance for disrespect.

Walter learned as many lessons along those lines as I did, maybe more. Granddad was a lay preacher—all the Priesters were strong Methodist churchgoers. On Sundays we all had breakfast together before church, and one Sunday Granddad felt the spirit move him as he said grace over the food. We were thankful for all our blessings, he said, enumerating many of them. We were thankful for the food we were about to eat, for the health of our bodies and the refreshment of our spirits, the different foods on the table before us, and also many of the foods we were blessed to enjoy at other times, which he also counted off. We praised God for these things, as we praised him for so much more that we had in our lives. Granddad went on and on. I had my hands folded and my head down, wondering when and how he was going to wind this up, when I was startled to hear Walter say, "Enough, Granddaddy, enough."

I could hear the gasps around the table. I don't know if Granddad looked at Walter; I had my eyes shut tight. In any event he went on. When he eventually came to an end, he asked Walter to step outside with him. I don't think Walter has interrupted a prayer again in the intervening sixty-five or seventy years.

Prayers could be long in the Priester house. Prayers and preaching could be long in church too. At one point my mother was teaching in a four-room schoolhouse in Bluffton, a tiny village fourteen miles north of Blakely. One Sunday we had attended services in Blakely, but in the afternoon we were also expected to be at church in Bluffton. The Bluffton church was so far out of the way that it only had a circuit preacher once a month, who administered communion once a year, a special time when several preachers gathered for the ceremony. That particular Sunday was communion day, and Bluffton's teachers were expected to attend.

As we drove up, we saw tables laden with food outside on the church grounds. Several watchers were stationed by the tables to shoo flies away—it was December but still warm. The dishes looked and smelled delicious, and Walter and I were hungry after our earlier devotions. As the service wore on we kept sneaking glances out the church's open door to the tables outside, getting hungrier and hungrier.

The circuit preacher, though, was deep into his topic, the spirit upon him. After the first half hour he was just getting warmed up. After an hour he seemed to be almost in a trance, and his preaching was getting stronger and stronger. Finally the two other preachers sitting on the dais stood up and pulled him down into his seat. But even then the spell wasn't broken. "You may sit me down," he shouted, "but you cannot shut me up!" and he kept on preaching from his seat. Eventually a group of ladies surrounded him, fanning him with their big church fans, trying to cool him down. By the time we got to the food it was almost dark.

Church was a big part of our lives. We attended Wesley Chapel AME, just up the street from our house. Mama was the pianist, and Daddy was a steward. But church was a big part of pretty much everyone's life. Work was too. Many of the families around Blakely were sharecroppers, and children worked the fields alongside their parents. People lived without much ready cash and often with none. Kids were always scraping for a few extra pennies, trying everything they could think of. They dug worms, picked early cotton for farmers, and sold a few eggs to the "rolling stores"—the grocery buses that went out to the rural areas. More than a few helped their fathers at night, which was when they made moonshine. Seven- and eight-year-olds carried large sacks of sugar out to the forest stills in the dark, scared to death of revenuers and even more scared of ghosts. In school the next morning they'd stare blankly, practically comatose, or fall asleep at their desks. Their teachers would send them home sick, although it's probable most of them knew exactly what was going on.

Walter and I worked hard too, though not out in the fields picking cotton. Daddy did decently in Blakely, but he started with extremely meager resources, and it was always a narrow margin operation, especially during the Depression.

Life in the black community revolved around church: Sunday services, weddings, baptisms, funerals. This was when people would come together, when they would put on their finery. Black funerals were significant social events, and if someone prominent had died, an especially large congregation would gather. There my father would be, in charge of the arrangements. My brother and I would assist, passing out fans embossed with "The Sullivan Funeral Home," helping push the casket, taking care of the flowers. And there was my mother, playing piano. It was a real family affair.

Because Walter was older and because he was supposed to take over the business, he was more my father's right-hand man than I was. Sometimes we'd get a call in the middle of the night that someone had died and had to be picked up.

I'd wake up to my father's voice: "Walter, get up, boy. We've got to go get so-and-so." Walter would drag himself up, jostling me—we slept in the same bed. I'd be laughing under the covers, which I knew he knew. Off he'd go, and I'd nestle back to sleep.

But plenty of times I'd go out too. We'd get to the departed's house with our big oblong basket. We'd lift the body onto its side, slide the basket under, lay it in, then put a sheet over it. Back at the funeral parlor daddy would prepare the body, extracting the blood and stomach juices and injecting embalming fluid. Afterward the hairdresser or barber would come in, and finally the make-up would go on.

None of this was particularly traumatic—other than the one time we were called to pick up the body of someone who had been killed in a fight. We were able to get there quickly, a little too quickly as it turned out. The man's throat had been cut. Blood was gushing from both jugulars, but he was still alive and still conscious. When he saw my father, he managed to gasp, "Walter, you don't have to bring me to the hospital. Just take me straight to the funeral home."

Neither Walter nor I ever felt strange or fearful being around dead people. We were used to it. Death was simply another part of life. The business never appealed to me, though. Families were so sad, invariably distraught, sometimes even hysterical. One of the ironies was that my father would be back in the embalming room humming a tune as he worked. Meeting with the families, he was always sympathetic and deferential. But it was obvious that he was happy with what he was doing. He was making a living for us, and he was rendering an important service.

Undertaking was a satisfying vocation, and a serious one, for which he was suited temperamentally. But he had a sense of humor too. At one funeral a bereaved widow just could not stand to see her husband go without her. At the graveside she kept crying and hollering. She wanted to go into the grave with her husband, she just had to go. People were trying to hold her and talk to her. But she was inconsolable. She wanted to go down with him. She made so much noise that finally my father went over and said quietly, "It's all right, sister. It's all right. Let me help you." He took her arm and walked her to the edge of the grave. They stood there for a minute looking down, then she walked back and said nothing more about it.

In those days it was the custom during the interment for the funeral director to sit on a chair at the head of the casket while the preacher delivered a final eulogy. The preacher's job at that point was to say the words that would get the departed soul admitted to eternal bliss. Whatever the person might have done in his life, the preacher would try to get him or her through the pearly gates. One memorable funeral deep in the countryside was for a man who had lived a checkered existence in which women had played a big role. Recounting the departed's life, the preacher said, "We've gathered here today to bury Brother So-and-So. Brother So-and-So is survived by wife number one, Mrs. So-and-So, who could not make it today. He is also survived by wife number two, Mrs. So-and-So, who is sitting over there on the right. Also by wife number three, Mrs. So-and-So, who is sitting on the other side over there. Also wife number four, Mrs. So-and-So, who could not make it today. Brother So-and-So is also survived by wife number five, Mrs. So-and-So, who is sitting down here in front."

Walter and I were listening to this trying to choke back our laughter. It was hot, ninety-five degrees, and the gnats were swarming. The preacher went on, "We don't know if Brother So-and-So made it"—he swatted at some gnats. He looked at the widows. "But if he made it, he made it. And if he didn't, well . . . we just won't talk about it any more."

Many of those funerals were out in the countryside. The Sullivan Funeral Home served all of Early County. When Walter got old enough, Daddy sometimes let him drive the hearse. On one occasion Walter was driving and backed the hearse up to a little backwoods church. We took the casket out and brought it inside. But as the funeral went on, it started raining hard. Early County is red clay land, and when we took the casket back out, we found ourselves sloshing around in viscous red mud.

When we got the casket back in the hearse, my father said to Walter, "Boy, you want me to take it?"

"No, Dad," Walter said. "I got it, I got it."

"Are you sure?"

"Yes, Daddy. I got it."

On those roads down there the ditches could fill up fast with water, and next thing we knew the back wheels were spinning in the ditch. We didn't hear our father curse much. But that was one time we heard him loud and clear. We had our suits on, and we were trying to push the hearse out, but it would not budge.

After a lot of fruitless straining one of the locals said, "Brother Sullivan, Brother Jed lives over there beyond that hill. And he's got a team of mules." Forty-five minutes later the parishioners were treated to the sight of the Sullivan Funeral Home director driving a team of mules, pulling our hearse out of the ditch.

Daddy was known by black people throughout the county because of his work. But he was also known for the activism, or agitation, he injected into Blakely's racial picture. South Georgia was the heart of Jim Crow country, an extremely harsh place, second only to Mississippi in the number of lynchings, which were still happening when I was growing up. People alive now remember times when black men were arrested, taken to jail, and never seen again.

We came to live in Blakely in 1937, only one standard lifetime removed from slavery. Attitudes hadn't changed much either. Blacks had no part in government, in law enforcement, or in any civil institution. Ku Klux Klansmen occasionally walked down the street in their white sheets and conical hats with their faces uncovered so everyone would know who they were. White and black children didn't go to school or church together and generally had little to do with one another. For black adults subservience was the order of the day, along with the frustration and (mostly) suppressed anger they lived with. Of course cross-racial friendships were around; my father had a number of white friends. But equality was definitely not in the air, and there were no signs it would be any time soon.

This was the atmosphere that greeted my father when we arrived in Blakely. Walter Sullivan Sr. was not an aggressive man, but he was not someone who took things lying down either; he did not turn the other cheek. He was a small man, only five feet four or five feet five. He may have weighed 120 pounds dripping wet. But if a fight came, he was absolutely positive that he was the one who was going to do the licking and the other guy was the one who was going to get licked.

He came from that kind of family. They had been in bondage in Rocky Mount, North Carolina, but when the Civil War was over they left that place. They hated the slave master who had owned them so badly that they wanted to get far away from there. So the whole group piled into a wagon and headed south, toward Florida. They also hated their owner's name—Spence, which had become their name. The family story was that they took the name that was on the first mailbox they saw when they started their journey south, which was how we got to be Sullivans.

I don't know what my father's activities might have been before Blakely, but soon after he got there he began aggravating the white community. The first thing he did was establish an NAACP chapter. The National Association for the Advancement of Colored People had been founded twenty-seven years earlier in part to fight for equal protection under the law and the right to vote, neither of which was available to blacks in Blakely. Then my father inaugurated an annual Emancipation Day parade on January 1, with bands, floats, and church services, kicked off by a march that started from our funeral parlor.

The parade first headed down Church Street, then crossed the railroad tracks that demarcated the black and white sections of town. In white territory now, the parade headed up toward Courthouse Square, a classic southern central square with the big courthouse at its center and the city's shops arranged around it. The parade marched around the square, the band playing as loudly as it could, then stopped at the platform Dad had set up, complete with microphones and a PA system. This was, among other things, my father's way of announcing loud and clear to everyone concerned: "This place is ours as well as yours!" He might as well have been shouting it out at the top of his lungs. Then the speakers would give speeches about what emancipation meant, how we were working toward full equality, how we had to do away with unfair voter registration laws, how we had to have the right to make our voices heard. If that wasn't enough, he then started actually getting people registered, standing up to the voting authorities and challenging their administration of the absurd so-called tests that were imposed on blacks trying to register.

"I remember when he got me registered," my brother Walter once said. "The lady was about to ask me one of the stupid questions they would ask at that time. She didn't see my father. There was just a window, like in the old post offices. You'd have to stick your head out and look around to see anybody other than the one who was in front of you. So she didn't see him. Then, just as she was starting to grill me, he stuck his head around, and she said, "Oh, shucks. Here. Just sign this!"

By the time Walter registered—this was in the early 1950s—my father had been at it for fourteen or fifteen years. The white establishment was still trying to keep blacks from voting—the civil rights laws were not passed until 1964. But by then they had had plenty of experience with my father, and they didn't want any more of it than necessary.

"Uppity" didn't even begin to describe the impression my father must have made. Here was this troublemaker coming in from the outside and stirring things up. A big city man—they held Atlanta against him—and a Republican (my father always had been and always would be a Republican; Abraham Lincoln, the Great Emancipator, was his icon), they held that against him too. None of this went over in the least with the white community.

Maybe the best illustration of Dad's true nature was what happened the day they shot my dog, Spot. The Blakely police chief, Mr. Dallas, enjoyed shooting dogs with his BB gun. He usually shot dogs who might have been strays or who had no license, not that he could really tell. He didn't catch them to check; he just shot them from a distance to watch them run off yelping. It was a kind of hobby of his. He thought it was hilarious.

Spot was a white mutt about the size of a boxer, with big brown spots, a wonderful playmate and protector. I loved that dog. We had a license for him, too. One day I was sitting on our front lawn with him when Dallas came riding along slowly in his cruiser. Next thing I knew, he had stopped, poked the barrel of his gun out the window, and shot Spot, who howled and took off. I was about thirteen at the time.

When this happened I ran down to the street, yelling, "Why did you shoot my dog? Why did you shoot my dog?" Dallas got out of the car, pointed his gun at me, and said, "Why? You want me to shoot you too?"

I completely lost my mind. I was absolutely insane with rage. I wanted to kill him. "You just stay here!" I yelled, and I ran back into the house, headed toward my parent's bedroom where I knew my father kept his pistol, under his clothes in the top drawer of the chifferobe. I was going to grab it, run outside, and shoot Dallas. I was so angry I was crying. Tears were streaming down my face.

I was groping around for the gun when my mother burst in. She had heard the front door slam and had come to investigate. When she saw what I was looking for, she grabbed me and started yelling for help. In another moment someone else had me in a bear hug, the iceman, who had been in the process of delivering ice to our funeral parlor next door. A few seconds later he was joined by a neighbor from across the street. It took them all a while to calm me down, or at least to stop me from struggling.

Not long after that my father and Walter arrived. They had been out in the country visiting a bereaved family and drove up to see this commotion, with neighbors gathering, me crying, the iceman still holding me, the whole scene a chaotic turmoil. The only one who wasn't there was Dallas. He had driven off when all the noise started.

It took some time for my father to sort out what had happened, but then he got a stone cold expression on his face and told Walter to come with him; he had something to do.

Here's Walter telling what happened next.

We got back and saw this commotion. Louie was being restrained by two gentlemen—one lived across the street, the other was the iceman, who had apparently been delivering ice. When we drove up, Mama was crying. Daddy said, "What are you guys doing?" They told the story. The iceman had to go about his business, so my father asked Mr. Hollinger, the man across the street, if he would stay there with Louie and our mother until he got back.

Then he said, "Come on, boy. I need you to drive me somewhere." I had just gotten my license a little while earlier, and I sometimes drove my father around on his business. We had been out in the countryside, and my father had taken his pistol along, which was lying between us on the front seat. In many ways Early County was hostile territory; you could never tell what might happen. The pistol was still in the car, which was why Louie couldn't find it in the chifferobe.

We got in the car. I said, "Where are we going?" Daddy said, "We're going to the jail." I drove to the jail. He said, "C'mon with me." And he put the gun in his belt. Inside, the chief was in the back, talking to two or three of his deputies. My father stopped a quarter way into the room and hollered, "Dallas!" so loud and with such authority that everybody was startled for a moment. "Dallas! Come up here! I need to see you!"

This was unthinkable, a black man talking to a white man this way—this was 1946. He came up, and when he did my father pulled his gun out of his belt and stuck it right in the middle of Dallas's forehead. He said, "I understand you had a few problems at my house today. Is that correct?" Dallas was so shocked and so nervous, with that gun between his eyes, he couldn't get a word out.

My father said, "Let me tell you one thing. If you have any problems with my boys or my wife, you don't do or say a thing to them, you come and see me. DO YOU UNDERSTAND?"

"Yes."

"OK. I hope you do. Because the next time I'm going to blow your brains out!" He stuck the gun back in his belt and walked out. I was like a bowl of Jell-O.

The next Saturday I was down by Courthouse Square getting something I had been sent for. People used to come in from the country and gather there on weekends, so there was a crowd around. I passed by Dallas and another white fellow. And I heard the other man say, "Who's that boy?"

Dallas said, "Don't you know? That's that crazy nigger Sullivan's boy." You see, whenever someone had trouble with a black person that person was supposed to be "crazy." It was obvious he didn't have good sense.

———————————

The reason Walter used to drive my father around was that several years before this Daddy had been shot, which had left his right arm only semiuseful. The bullet had gone through his neck and damaged his brachial plexus, the nerves that control the arm. It had then gone through and come within an inch of his heart, so he was lucky to have survived it at all. After some time he had regained partial use of the arm, but the injury inhibited him in various ways. He was right-handed, so he had to compensate. He had learned to write with his left hand, but driving tired him out.

The day he was shot, my mother, Walter, and I had driven to Albany to go to the bank and do some shopping. My father did all his banking in Albany. He didn't patronize the Blakely banks; he didn't want people in town to know about his business. There was always the chance it would give them some kind of leverage over him.

As we drove up to our house we saw a crowd of people on our front lawn. We thought, what in the world is going on here? Often if there was a funeral, family and friends would stand around for a while in front of the funeral parlor, which was right next to the house, but this was obviously different.

When we went in, Daddy was in bed, heavily bandaged, with blood seeping through the gauze. He had been shot by Ray Johnson, a black man who lived across the street from us. That puzzled us. Daddy got along with almost everyone in the black community. It was possible that he and Johnson may have had a little argument of some sort, but certainly nothing that would have caused Johnson to shoot him.

The mystery deepened when Johnson went on trial and was sent to jail for attempted murder but was released two months later, which was suspicious. After he got out he told Daddy that white men had paid him to do it. The background to this was that several years after we arrived in Blakely and Daddy had established his business, another black funeral home opened up almost across the street from us. Daddy had already made himself a thorn in the side of the white establishment with his NAACP and voter registration activities and Emancipation Day parades. He was sure the second funeral home was financed by whites, the idea being to undercut his business and drive us out of town. Ray Johnson was associated with the other funeral director. There was never any inquiry into what had really gone on, but we knew the truth of it.

That was the last, though, of any violence directed at my father. I think that after a while they just decided to live with him. Besides that, he was a central figure in the black community and did have white friends as well. Racism was alive and well in Blakely, but nobody really wanted to set things off. That had something to do with the fact that there were no repercussions when my father threatened Dallas with his gun. That could have been a declaration of war, but nobody wanted to start one. Besides, everyone thought the chief was being stupid and obnoxious, going around shooting people's dogs.

My father never backed down from confrontations, but he didn't go looking for them either. Mainly, he was concerned about running his business and raising his family. One of his ideas for Walter and me was that if we had a little business of our own to run during the summers it would keep us busy and out of trouble and also teach us some important lessons. What he had in mind was an ice cream parlor. Not only would that be good for us, it would also provide a place for Blakely's black youngsters to get together socially and have a good time. There was nothing like that for them in town. Adults out for some relaxation could go down to one of the juke joints, but young people weren't allowed in those.

The result was that Daddy put up a brick ice cream parlor on the other side of the funeral home. The parlor was a substantial affair, with room inside for a soda fountain and tables, with a cement patio outside. Walter and I ran the place, serving ice cream and soda, cleaning up, keeping the books. Mama helped us churn the ice cream on the back porch of our house, which was just a few yards away. At first we did that by hand, but the parlor was a big hit almost immediately, so we bought an electric ice cream maker. But we still couldn't keep up with the demand; people would be waiting around for us to make more. After the first month we started buying our ice cream from a company in Dothan, Alabama, about twenty-five miles to the west.

Our customers weren't just teenagers; plenty of adults and little kids would come by too. Sometimes the men would order a Coke, then drop a Bayer aspirin or Standback Headache Powder in the bottle and shake it up. I assumed that it made the soda fizzier, but later on Walter (who became a PhD chemist instead of a funeral director) heard that aspirin precipitated the precursors of cocaine in the Coca Cola. Supposedly, the men were getting a minor high at our soda fountain. It's also possible they just thought they were. They did, though, sometimes order a "dope" instead of a Coke, which puzzled us at the time.

One day while we were working at the fountain we heard that there had been a fight between a young black man named Hubbard and some whites in another part of the neighborhood. Word spread that this Hubbard had been attacked by several whites, had beaten one of them, then had run off. Hubbard's father just happened to be sitting on the patio with some other men right then, and as the excitement grew a pickup truck with four or five white men crowded on passed by slowly. The men looked at the knot of people in front of the parlor, then drove on.

Before long a rumor started that the Klan was getting ready to come by later on. No one knew if that was true, but it might have been. My father talked with Hubbard's father and some of the other men, and they arranged to sit out in front there, armed. Daddy didn't share anything about those arrangements with Walter or me, but I learned later that there was an informal black mutual protection group in Blakely. I only wish he were still alive so I could ask him about that.

In any event, when word got around that we might be visited again, Daddy called Chief Dallas. He told Dallas there had been an incident and that a truck full of men had ridden through in front of our place. "I understand the Klan intends to drive through our section of town," he said. "I don't know if you know anything about that, if you've heard anything. But you'd do me a big favor if you'd tell them that we're ready for them. So if they want to come, everyone should be prepared for whatever might happen." The upshot was that nobody else rode through that night, including the police chief.

＝＝＝＝＝＝

Given my father's disposition, Walter and I did not grow up in an atmosphere of fear. But concern was a constant in our household and so was defiance. Except when there was some incident, we didn't think much about this kind of thing. It was simply the norm we lived with, the everyday condition of life in Blakely. But racial matters were a burden. They weighed heavily on the business of surviving and trying to raise a family. All of the town's blacks experienced it that way.

My father and mother were absolutely intent on our getting the best education possible, but I think they also wanted to protect us from the harm that environment did, psychologically if not physically. Every black parent felt the same; they tried their best to protect their children from the damage growing up in segregation brought with it, with all its continual humiliation and intimidation. But we were a lot luckier than most. With my father's business and my mother's teaching, they had the ability to do something concrete about it.

They had sent Walter and me to school in Savannah when we were ten and eleven. Then, when we were ready for junior high, they decided we should go to Atlanta. The schools in Atlanta were much better than any school we could have attended locally. And Atlanta was a big city, with a large and, in some ways, thriving black community—a place where black political leaders such as John Wesley

Dobbs were fighting for civil rights and where church leaders like Martin Luther King Sr. (Martin Luther King Jr.'s father) led dynamic, socially and politically engaged congregations. Benjamin Mays was there, the president of Morehouse College and a figure of national stature. W. E. B. Du Bois had taught for years at Atlanta University. His great debate with Booker T. Washington over the direction of black education took place while the city was his home. Atlanta was alive with black political, social, intellectual, and business activity, as different from Blakely as it was possible to be. In Atlanta Walter and I would not just be getting a better education; we'd be immersed in a different universe.

In 1944 Walter and I moved to Atlanta, but we didn't go alone. Our mother came with us; she had decided to enroll at Atlanta University for a master's degree in education. She also started looking into funeral homes there, the thought being that they might possibly buy one and move the family to Atlanta permanently. She had never been happy in Blakely, and our father was hardly wedded to the town either. In the end, though, the idea didn't move forward. Daddy was an obstinate person. They were so anxious to run him out of Blakely that he decided to stay. He was going to go when he went, on his own terms and nobody else's. As a result, he and Mama stayed in Blakely for another thirteen years, mainly, at least as Walter and I saw it, to prove a point. He was a loving, protective father but also a stubborn, stubborn man.

When Mama finished her degree and left Atlanta, Walter and I stayed. She had made arrangements for us to board with Mrs. Maude Brown, a motherly woman who lived right across the street from Booker T. Washington High School, where we were going to enroll. Mrs. Brown's daughter, who lived with her, was a physical education teacher at the high school. Mama had met Mrs. Brown through a friend. She had hosted students before, and Mama had confidence that she'd be leaving us in good hands, which turned out to be true. Mrs. Brown was an excellent cook and also a disciplinarian who set strict curfews for us. If one of us was a few minutes late getting back she'd open the door slowly, give us a look of profound disappointment, and say, "Oh, I am *so* sorry." I don't know how guilty either of us actually felt, but we did make an effort to be on time; we also knew that Mrs. Brown was in regular telephone contact with Mama about the behavior of her boys.

In front of Booker T. Washington High was a statue of Washington himself, lifting the veil of ignorance from a slave rising from his knees. The school had been founded in 1924, the city's first secondary school for blacks. The statue was dramatic, but it was a faithful representation of what happened within the school's doors. The teachers there were to a person dedicated to eliminating ignorance and substituting knowledge and the habit of thinking. They taught the love of learning for its own sake, let alone that it would prepare us to be more successful and more competitive as we moved on. At Washington High students lived in an environment of encouragement and high expectations. We needed the strongest education possible so that we could go on to become doctors and lawyers and businesspeople. The atmosphere was one of striving to raise the race up and to raise us up as individuals. Our teachers there saw themselves as crucial enablers of our success, a role they undertook with great seriousness.

I liked nearly all my subjects, although chemistry and biology were at the top of the list, along with Latin. I knew I wanted to be a doctor, and I was told Latin would be helpful because so much medical terminology is derived from that language. I loved English too. Adolph Phillips, my English teacher, had a beautiful tenor voice. He'd read us poetry and occasionally break out into song. He had us mesmerized, reciting a Langston Hughes or Countee Cullen poem in his dramatic fashion. He made poetry come alive. Then he'd get us to do it. Some of those poems we learned to declaim weren't just beautiful; they conveyed messages that struck home. One I still recall by Arthur Hugh Clough went like this:

And not by eastern windows only,
> When daylight comes, comes in the light;
In front the sun climbs slow, how slowly!
> But westward, look, the land is bright!

How slow was the climb our grandparents and parents had been making? But we were sure the land ahead actually was bright.

Then there was "If," by Rudyard Kipling, which spoke to the black experience if anything did.

If you can keep your head when all about you
Are losing theirs and blaming it on you;
If you can trust yourself when all men doubt you,
But make allowance for their doubting too:
If you can wait and not be tired by waiting,
Or, being lied about, don't deal in lies,
Or being hated don't give way to hating,
And yet don't look too good, nor talk too wise.

At Washington High Walter and I were both in the marching band. My mother, the church pianist, had started us on piano lessons early. I got to be fairly proficient, playing Rachmaninoff and Chopin. I loved it, but in Atlanta it conflicted with after-school sports, so I gave it up, to my later regret. But I had also picked up the trumpet, and I started playing in the band. Walter had taken a similar path, only with the trombone instead of the trumpet. In fact he was lead trombone, which meant he set the tempo. The trombones were the first line of marchers—their slides meant they had to be first, and Walter was first of the first.

We had quite a few talented musicians in that band, some of whom went on to professional careers. We wore blue uniforms with white trim, white belts, and shoulder straps, with white lariats on our left shoulders. We had drum majorettes prancing up in front, twirling their batons. We high-stepped to the music—nothing like the dancing and intricate maneuvers marching bands do today, but pretty good for back then. We had a great time.

While we were in school there my father got to know the band director, Earl Starling, and the two of them made arrangements for the band to come to Blakely to march in my father's annual Emancipation Day parades. We were a big hit there, and Daddy got to show off his two sons, which gave him no end of pride.

Unfortunately, one year there was some kind of conflict, and the band couldn't make it. But that didn't stop him. "Well," he said, "that's too bad. I guess that means you two are the band!" We couldn't believe it, but he was unmovable. So there we were on Emancipation Day, Walter and I, me playing trumpet, Walter the trombone, marching through town heading up the parade in our band uniforms: a line of decorated cars, a couple of floats, with a trumpet and a trombone leading the way, playing John Philip Sousa marching songs.

Walter and I were so embarrassed we kept our eyes riveted straight ahead, afraid that people were laughing at us—it felt so ridiculous. But the people in Blakely thought it was just fine. The town had a black high school, also Washington High, but they didn't have a band. They had no money for instruments. My father had successfully sued the county to force Blakely to upgrade the black schools, but the suit hadn't covered band instruments.

After high school there was no question, of course, that I was going to college. But there *was* a question about where. I had done well. I had been elected president of my class, and at graduation I was salutatorian. Among the better students at Washington High, many of the boys were going to Morehouse College and most of the girls were going to Spelman, Morehouse's sister school. I was eager to go to Morehouse myself. My best friends had applied there, and Morehouse's reputation put it at the top of the South's traditionally black colleges. Many of my teachers and counselors talked about what a great school it was. But there was a problem.

The problem was that Morehouse had been founded back in 1867, under the sponsorship of the American Baptist Home Mission Society. The school's first home had been in the Springfield Baptist Church in Augusta before it moved to Atlanta. By the mid-twentieth century it no longer had a formal Baptist affiliation, but the Baptist tradition was still strong there. Benjamin Mays, Morehouse's famous president, was, among other things, an ordained Baptist minister.

We, on the other hand, were Methodists, from a long line of Methodists. Grandfather Priester was an assistant Methodist minister, my mother a Methodist church pianist, my father a Methodist steward. And Morehouse was just one of the five schools that made up Atlanta's consortium of black institutions of higher learning, another of which was Clark College. Also a good school, Clark had been founded by Methodists. Mama had done her undergraduate work at Clark, and Walter had enrolled there the year before.

My parents just naturally felt that Clark was my destination, so when I told them at dinner one night that I wanted Morehouse, it caused a bit of a shock.

"Morehouse?" my father said. "Why that's a *Baptist* school!"

"Dad," I said, "it was started by Baptists, but they severed their ties a long time ago."

"But we've always been a *Methodist* family!"

"Dad, I'm not going to church. I'm going to college."

"Wait a minute"—this was from my mother. "Walter, he wants to go to college. Morehouse is an excellent school. Why not?"

That was how, in September 1950 I found myself among the two hundred freshmen in Morehouse's new entering class.

CHAPTER 2

Morehouse College

If you visit Morehouse College today, your guide will stop at a memorial occupying a place of honor at the head of the school's main quadrangle. A bronze figure stands there, keeping watch over the campus. In front of the figure are a semicircular marble plaza and a large marble headstone. If it's the season for student tours, you may have to wait to get a close-up look, due to the groups that will be stopping there ahead of you. This is the last resting place of Benjamin Mays, Morehouse's sixth and most renowned president. Underneath the marble, Mays's wife of forty-three years, Sadie, lies next to him. The erect bronze figure is Mays himself, dressed in his academic robes. The epitaph engraved on the headstone reads, "Born to rebel against ignorance, oppression, and social injustice."

Behind the memorial, at the quadrangle's western end, sits Graves Hall, a four-story red brick structure with a Victorian roofline. Built in 1889, Graves Hall was the first building on the Morehouse campus. The president's office and apartment were there originally, along with students' rooms and classrooms. Together with the memorial, the historic Graves Hall constitutes Morehouse College's most hallowed ground.

In 1950, when I started at Morehouse, Graves Hall was a freshman dormitory. I lived in it my first year. Nowadays Mays's statue looks out over the campus. Back then the flesh and blood Mays presided. He was, very simply, an out-of-proportion human being. I don't mean his size, although he was tall and imposing; I mean his accomplishments, his intelligence, his dynamism, and, especially, the immense moral force of his convictions. You could not escape the power of Mays's presence, not that you wanted to. If you were an African American youngster just embarking on manhood, Benjamin Elijah Mays was just exactly what you needed.

Mays's character and values defined Morehouse as an institution. His spirit still pervades the place, forty-plus years after he left the presidency. He inspired a crucial generation of black leaders at Morehouse and elsewhere, including Andrew Young, Julian Bond, Maynard Jackson, and Walter Massey. Martin Luther King Jr., a Morehouse graduate himself, called Mays his "spiritual mentor" and his "intellectual father." I was as in awe of him as any other student. He was a hero to young people who needed heroes like they needed lifeblood.

"The tragedy of life," he told us in his ringing voice, "doesn't lie in not reaching your goals. The tragedy of life lies in not having goals to reach." "Every man and woman," he said, "is born into this world to do something unique. What is it that *you* were born to do?"

There might have been three or four hundred of us packed into the chapel, where he spoke to the assembled student body every Tuesday morning. But somehow his words seemed directed precisely at me. What were *my* goals? What was it that made *me* unique? "Whatever you do in life, you should do it so well that no man living, no man dead, and no man yet to come could do it any better."

We listened to that voice and those words and took them to heart. It's hard to exaggerate what that meant—"no man living, no man dead." It meant we ourselves were capable of doing whatever we wanted to do better than anyone else possibly could. Anyone! We had that in us. What we needed to do was set our sights, get down to work, and not let distractions get in our way.

This was not just pat, run-of-the-mill encouragement, as it might possibly sound in some commencement addresses today. Mays's listeners had grown up in a world that told them at every turn that they were inferior, unworthy, destined to always be second rate and second class. Even if you did not believe that in your heart—I certainly did not believe it—still it was there, lodged somewhere in the back of your brain. *They* were up there, and *you* were down here. "You want to make it in the world? It's not enough to be as good as whites; you have to be twice as good." How many times had we heard that mantra from our parents and teachers? But just how were you supposed to do that? How were you going to realize your potential so that you could compete against anybody for anything?

Mays was telling us that we could do it, and he was telling us how to do it. He was bucking us up with the confidence we needed and maybe didn't have. He was even insisting it was our *responsibility* to do it. And it was hardly just his words that were conveying this to us; it was the man himself.

Mays was born on a sharecropping farm outside a small town in South Carolina called, simply, 96, near Greenwood (his birthplace is now a national historic site). His mother and father had been born into slavery; he was their eighth child. His earliest memory was of men on horseback with rifles humiliating his father on the front porch of their house. Mays spent his youth picking cotton for pennies a pound. The elementary school he went to operated four months a year, November through February; he and his classmates were needed out in the fields the other eight months. But he was driven to educate himself. Against his father's wishes he found a way to attend a boarding high school at Virginia Union College in Richmond, Virginia; then he enrolled at Bates College in Lewiston, Maine. The young Mays believed that whites up North—Yankees—were smarter than whites down South. The way he saw it, if he could compete with northern whites, that would prove beyond any doubt that Negroes were *not* inferior. "Yankee superiority was the gauntlet thrown down," he wrote later. "I had to pick it up."

Mays graduated Bates Phi Beta Kappa as class valedictorian and went on to earn a PhD in theology at the University of Chicago, which forever put behind him the fear he had while he was laboring out in the cotton fields that maybe God had for some unfathomable reason indeed made black people less capable than white people. In his talks at the Morehouse chapel he didn't hold himself up as an example. He just was an example. He had his expectations, and you, whether you were a freshman or a senior, wanted with everything in you to live up to them.

Mays was a member of the first postenslavement generation, as was my father. That generation came of age after the bloom of Reconstruction had withered and died and most blacks found themselves again in near-slavery conditions, their voting rights taken away, their tenuous livelihoods dependent on the whites who owned the land they farmed and ruled the communities they lived in. Fear and subservience marked their relations with their white neighbors—for good reason. "Cringing and grinning and kowtowing" was the painful way Mays described it.

But amid all that were many who were, for whatever reason, simply fearless; I'd put my father in that category. Some others, by sheer power of determination and intellect, forced their way into the system and excelled. Mays was a prime example of that, and at Morehouse he gathered around himself others of the same makeup, college dean Brailsford Reese Brazeal, for one. Students did see Mays outside of chapel, but not regularly. Dean Brazeal we saw all the time.

Brazeal was a Morehouse graduate who had gotten his PhD at Columbia in economics. He was head of the economics department in addition to being dean. Edward Jones, chairman of modern languages, had received his PhD from Cornell. He was another orator, known for his memorable quotes. "It's better to light a candle in the dark than to curse the darkness" was his. "Stop complaining about what's been done and get down to the business of doing something yourself," he told us. "Get out and make something of yourself. Be competitive. Force yourself into the mainstream."

Then there was James Birnie, chairman of biology, who became my premed adviser. He had earned his doctorate in endocrinology at Syracuse University and was an assistant professor there before coming to Morehouse. No one pushed harder to get us out into the big world, beyond the walls that had closed us in our entire lives.

That was a daunting prospect. But they had done it themselves, sons of former slaves as most were, under far more daunting circumstances than we faced. They were true groundbreakers. We had them to emulate. If they had done it, coming from where they did, why couldn't we? That might have been the essence of Morehouse. This wasn't just a good, rigorous liberal arts college we had landed in; it was a moral environment suffused by a powerful social purpose.

Not everything at Morehouse was quite on that level of profundity. Dean Brazeal was bent on preparing us for life outside, which in part meant acquiring the necessary social skills. How, for example, do you introduce yourself to a young lady? What was the proper, gentlemanly way to do this, as opposed to the uncultured approach we might have picked up in our previous lives?

"Hello, I'm Louie Sullivan. I'm a freshman at Morehouse. Could you tell me your name, please?" That was the right way to address a person of the opposite sex. There was a proper way to attire yourself too: a sport or suit jacket, of course, and always a white handkerchief in your jacket pocket and a second handkerchief in your pants pocket, to blow your nose if necessary. This was part of clothing decorum. You also wanted to have that second handkerchief available for your young lady date if for some reason she suddenly broke out into tears.

I was never clear on why your date might do that, but something must have stuck because I still habitually wear a handkerchief in my jacket pocket. I think a lot of Morehouse men of my vintage do. We even learned how to set a table and where to put the knife, the fork, the spoon, the water glass.

Sometimes it was hard to keep a straight face during these freshman etiquette sessions, but we didn't dare laugh. Dean Brazeal made it clear he was serious. Of course, many of us came from farms deep in the country. Most were the first in their families to go to college. They didn't know the social graces. And part of becoming a Morehouse man was to know how to conduct yourself properly. We were to be "well spoken, well dressed, and well behaved," as a later president put it, in addition to being well educated.

Morehouse then was small enough so that Dean Brazeal and even Mays himself kept track of how individual students were doing. Brazeal knew about students' comings and goings and about their strengths and weaknesses, and he kept in regular touch with parents, not just by phone and letter but in person. When he traveled he would visit students' homes to chat with mothers and fathers about their son's progress. I don't remember whether he ever got down to Blakely, but if he did, there's no doubt he stopped by for a talk with Walter Sr. and Lubirda.

Morehouse expected you not only to study hard and succeed but to be a gentleman. It was an important part of the ethos. Not that polite conduct was what we necessarily experienced outside the college. Atlanta was in some ways a progressive city, at least compared with the rest of the South. But in 1950 Jim Crow laws were in full force. Outside the college there was considerable ugliness. Atlanta had a history of it.

In 1906 a horrendous race riot had ripped through the city. Twenty-five blacks had been killed and many hundreds savagely beaten. Blacks were thrown off city trolleys into the arms of the mobs. Black homes and businesses were smashed, including the barbershop on Peachtree Street owned by Alonzo Herndon, who was just then in the process of starting up the Atlanta Life Insurance Company, where my father was later to work as an agent. Herndon had closed his shop early, but the barbershop across the street hadn't and the barbers there were murdered. A black section south of downtown, where Atlanta University and Clark College were located at the time, was the center of a gun battle between police and blacks who had armed themselves to defend their neighborhood.

Nine years later the second coming of the Ku Klux Klan was launched at Stone Mountain, ten or twelve miles outside the city. The Klan held rallies there; they'd set a huge cross afire on the summit, which you could see for miles. Atlanta was the Klan headquarters and the so-called Imperial Wizard, William Joseph Simmons, lived in the city. When I was a student, a gigantic bas-relief of Confederate heroes Robert E. Lee, Stonewall Jackson, and Jefferson Davis had been partially carved into the mountain face. Work was resumed on this piece of monumental art in 1964, the year the civil rights laws were passed. It was finished in 1972 and is still a southern attraction, though not a pleasant one for blacks. As far as race relations went, Atlanta was a very mixed bag.

One flashpoint was the city's segregated trolleys and buses. My first experience of Jim Crow buses was in Savannah, where Walter and I had gone to stay with my mother's family. Savannah had a public transportation system, and I rode a city bus there for the first time. I must have been about ten years old then. I got on with my grandfather, and while he was putting money in the fare machine I went and sat down in the first empty seat, near the front, in the white section, which I had no idea about. My grandfather quickly grabbed me, pulled me up roughly, and sat me down in the back of the bus. "You're to sit here!" he said. I was confused as to why he had acted that way, as if I had done something wrong.

In Atlanta I took the bus only when there was no alternative. I'd try to get a ride if I could, or walk, or just not go. I had deep and strong feelings of resentment about it. Sometimes the back of the bus would be crowded, while there was plenty of space up front. If a lot of whites got on, blacks were expected to vacate. There was always a hint of fear, too. Things could happen. Things did happen. People were arrested when they shouldn't have been. The law was our enemy.

The buses were a constant source of tension. It was no particular surprise when Rosa Parks was jailed in Montgomery—the incident that set fire to the civil rights movement—the year after I graduated from Morehouse. She wasn't the first African American to refuse to move out of her seat, and that particular arrest wasn't the first upsetting bus experience she had had either.

Trains and railroad stations were segregated too, another source of tension. Atlanta's "colored" waiting room was a dirty, cramped affair; the white room clean and spacious. You could board trains directly from the white waiting room, but from the colored room you'd have to walk around outside. Dr. Rufus Clement, who was president of Atlanta University while I was a student at Morehouse, tried to walk through the white waiting room to avoid going outside in the rain, a crime for which the white cop on duty there threatened to shoot him. Clement wasn't trying to sit in the white room, just walk through it.

Mays tells this story in his autobiography, *Born to Rebel*. When Mays was dean at Morehouse, before his presidency, he himself was almost killed by a mob of white passengers who objected to his occupying a Pullman berth on a trip from Atlanta to Saint Louis. Worse was what happened to Hugh Gloster, an English professor at Morehouse a few years before I arrived there. Gloster later became dean at Hampton Institute, then succeeded Mays as president of Morehouse. It was Gloster who in 1971 launched the idea for a medical school at the college and asked me to head it. We were friends and colleagues in that endeavor for years. Here he is describing what happened to him on a train from Atlanta to Memphis, shortly after he joined the Morehouse faculty:

"When the train reached Amory, Mississippi, a large number of Negroes, mostly small town and farming people . . . boarded the train and took up all the seats allotted to them, leaving many standing. They were afraid to go into another section, because this would mean sitting in front of the conductor and the baggage man who were occupying the third section. . . . This meant that one-third of the coach was jammed with Negro passengers while two-thirds was not in use, except where the conductor and baggage man were holding forth. The conductor got up, took up tickets from the last passengers to get on, then went back and took his seat, leaving Negroes standing, some of them women and children, rather than give up any of the unoccupied part of the coach. . . . When he got up again a few minutes later . . . I said, 'Conductor, these people are not taking seats because they do not want to sit in front of you and the other gentleman.' The conductor said, 'You have a seat, don't you? That's what's wrong now. Too many niggers trying to run the train.' I told him, 'I am not a nigger, and I'm not trying to run the train. I was simply trying to make a suggestion for the comfort of the other passengers.' The conductor did not reply. . . . I knew I was in trouble. I could see him talking to the baggage man, and I knew they were planning something for me. I told the man sitting next to me that if anything happened to me he should get in touch with Dr. Benjamin E. Mays, president of Morehouse College in Atlanta.

"When the train stopped at Tupelo the conductor went into the station and either called or had somebody call the police. Three, maybe five minutes later, the police boarded the train, came into the coach, and demanded, 'Where's the nigger who's trying to run the train?' . . . I was snatched out of my seat, kicked down the aisle . . . and thrown off the train onto the station platform. Then they started beating me. I tried to cover my face and head as best I could. They beat me for what was probably only a few minutes but which seemed like hours and then they took me off to jail. At the jail they looked into my billfold, found I was a teacher at Morehouse College and that I had a brother who was a doctor at Tuskegee Institute. After that, they didn't beat me any more, but by that time I was in pretty bad shape. Although I had tried to protect my head and face, I was badly mauled; and I had suffered the most excruciating agony when one of the brutish policemen had put all of his two hundred and fifty pounds into a hard kick into my groin. Even now, after many years, I can still feel the pain of that kick, and I still have aches and twinges in that part of my body."

Gloster was rescued from jail by two lawyers who came down from Memphis. I worked closely with him for fifteen years while he was Morehouse's president, presiding over a mixed white and black faculty and board of trustees with whom he worked harmoniously. In all that time I never heard or sensed a trace of anti-white feeling on his part. He had white friends, colleagues, and supporters, but this was in his background too, and it stayed with him, just as memories of terror and humiliation stayed with Mays himself.

Yet these men and others like them were able to relegate or at least compartmentalize their feelings and dedicate themselves to doing their best for their institutions, which meant working with whites, understanding whites, and finding friendship with whites too. They were the models we were exposed to, not just in terms of education, but in terms of how a person could stay healthy psychologically in a conflicted and in many ways poisonous world.

When I was at Morehouse, the civil rights movement was percolating, but it hadn't yet boiled over. Rosa Parks was arrested the year after I graduated. Little Rock's Central High was integrated two years after that. The lunch counter sit-ins started in 1960; the Freedom Rides came a year later. In my time the atmosphere wasn't quite ready for those kinds of public confrontations. It was considered a daring, dangerous thing to do when a white Morehouse professor from New York, Ethel Werfel, used to take students riding around downtown Atlanta in her convertible with the top down.

But the atmosphere for confrontation was definitely charging up. Mays wasn't one to lead demonstrations; he wasn't that kind of activist. But he told us that we should not be patronizing segregated establishments more than absolutely necessary. And he himself, in his fierce pride, began sitting in the white waiting room at the train station whenever he traveled, which was often. That was the talk of the black community, and maybe of the white too. His stature and recognition were such that no one dared touch him. Others might be threatened or beaten or arrested, but if Mays had been abused in any way, the city would have erupted, something nobody wanted. He spoke constantly too about the dignity of man, the evils of segregation, how this was a system we needed to get rid of, how segregation hurt everyone. It hurt the oppressed and it hurt the oppressor. The energies that are used to keep a system like that in place, he said, are energies that could be turned to productive uses. It robs both the black and the white man of the best uses of their talents.

Mays was a sought-after speaker in both black and white forums around the country, and everywhere he went that was his message. At Morehouse we heard it from him, from the faculty, and from other chapel speakers such as "Daddy" King (Martin Luther King's father) and John Wesley Dobbs (Maynard Jackson's grandfather), a civic leader who had founded the Atlanta Negro Voters League.

We, Morehouse's students, should be working to overturn this system. Segregation had to be rolled back; people had to get out to vote; black officials had to be elected. Our job in particular was to go out and make our mark in the world, earning a place and becoming influential ourselves. That was our role in the struggle. That's what we were supposed to do.

Martin Luther King Sr. was the head of Ebenezer Baptist Church, a person of great moral stature who had earned respect even in parts of the white community. Dobbs was a major political force in the city. He and attorney Warren Cochran controlled the black vote; his support was decisive in getting William Hartsfield elected mayor in 1949 and for several elections after that. After Hartsfield black voters mobilized behind Ivan Allen, who defeated the ax handle–wielding segregationist Lester Maddox. Both Hartsfield and Allen worked closely with black community leaders. For twenty-eight back-to-back years they gave Atlanta a strong progressive government that revolutionized the city's race relations.

People like Mays and Gloster had gone through hell with whites, but there were also whites who advocated and worked for equality. Ivan Allen testified in Washington in favor of the civil rights laws, the single southern elected official to do so. In 1968, when Martin Luther King Jr. was assassinated, Atlanta was the only city of its size that didn't have a riot, because Mayor Allen worked with black leaders and the police to manage the dismay and rage that were sending blacks into the streets elsewhere.

Allen's behind-the-scenes ally was a white Atlantan who had been supporting activities in the black community for years. This was Robert Woodruff, the head of the Coca Cola Company and one of the era's great philanthropists. The story was that Woodruff called Allen and said, "Mr. Mayor, we cannot have a riot in Martin Luther King's home. Whatever you need, if you don't have it in your budget, I'm good for it."

Immensely wealthy, Woodruff was Atlanta's leading businessman and a giant influence in the city. Given the times, he didn't publicly display his efforts to help blacks, but people knew anyway. During graduation ceremonies at Booker T. Washington High School, the principal always announced that there were gifts and prizes from an "anonymous donor." A ripple of laughter would accompany that announcement. Everyone knew the anonymous donor was Bob Woodruff. One of Woodruff's sayings was "There's no limit to what a man can accomplish if he doesn't care who gets the credit for it."

Woodruff helped Mays and Morehouse. So did Margaret Mitchell, who wrote *Gone with the Wind*. Mitchell also did her giving quietly, and she and Mays became friends. Even during the bleak rule of Jim Crow things like that were going on, not generally known to the public. Mays said he could never sing "Dixie," but he certainly could sing Atlanta.

My own contact with whites was mixed. In the first place, I didn't have much. I hadn't had any white friends in Blakely, and race relations there were rough. I didn't have any white friends in Atlanta either, and living in a segregated place meant that racial tension was part of the atmosphere. It made you wary and suspicious.

But my experience at Morehouse was different. There were a couple of white students in our class. We also had a fair amount of interaction with white students at Emory University, discussion groups that met alternately at the two schools. With the Emory students we talked about religion and politics and, of course, the racial situation. The tone of these discussions was almost always positive. Segregation, most of the white students thought, was an unfortunate legacy of slavery, due to be scrapped, which could probably be done best through the registration of black voters.

Also, the Morehouse faculty was integrated. My German and social science professors were white and so were others. The white professors treated the students with the same sort of teacher-student decency as the black professors did, as well as the same kind of rigor. Race relations outside the college might have been fraught, while inside they were far better. But what we were mostly concerned about was our studies. Academically, Morehouse was a strenuous place. Just how strenuous was made clear in my first economics class with Professor E. B. Williams.

Like Dean Brazeal, Williams had a doctorate from Columbia. After our mid-term he announced the results to the class. "One student," he said, looking at me, "got eighty-nine out of ninety questions correct. Good . . . but not perfect. So, of course, not an A." In the first semester of my comparative anatomy class with Professor Samuel Nabrit I got a C. I hadn't been paying enough attention, but still I was surprised and embarrassed (I did get it up to an A in the second semester). Many years later I went back to Atlanta for a black fraternal organization gathering and found myself sitting at a table with Nabrit. I was a professor at Boston University by then, and he had gone on to a storied career as a leading marine biologist, university president, and member of the Atomic Energy Commission. John F. Kennedy had appointed him ambassador to Niger. "You know," I told him, "you were the only person who gave me a C when I was at Morehouse." "Not true, young man," he said. "I didn't give you a C. You *earned* a C."

In my freshman year one of my dorm mates was from Nigeria. Babatunde Olatunji had come to Morehouse on an International Rotary scholarship, and when he first arrived, he had no friends and no familiarity with the culture. As a result he spent a lot of time by himself in his room, playing his drums, not softly. His incessant drumming wasn't conducive to studying, which is what most of us were trying hard to do. I'd yell at him, "Tunji, stop that noise. Nobody can study." Others were at least as aggravated. Sometimes this went on far into the night. But it was hard getting the man to stop, or even just to tone it down.

During the summer break after our freshman year, Olatunji went up to New York, and when he came back for the start of the new semester, he had an RCA recording contract. He later went on to become world famous, one of the fore-most jazz and African drummers of his generation. He played with John Coltrane, Cannonball Adderly, Stevie Wonder, and many others and started an African cultural center in Harlem. I'm not sure any of us who were yelling at him to shut it off would have predicted such a meteoric career for him.

Olatunji and I were friends, and we ran against each other for class president, an election I won by a few votes. Some of our classmates thought that because it was so close, we should vote again. I agreed, to my regret—this was my first lesson in politics. A couple of other candidates who had received small numbers of votes threw their support to Tunji, and the next thing I knew, he was class president and I wasn't, which I thought was kind of a dirty trick. He should have just said, "Congratulations, you've won." At least that was what I was telling myself after the fact. That election frayed our friendship a bit, but we did stay in touch after graduation and even saw each other on occasion.

Morehouse put an emphasis on its graduates building professional lives for themselves, and every year we had career seminars to help us figure out how best to do that. People from business life and from graduate and professional schools around the country came to talk to us. They opened up a world of possibilities that we might not otherwise have thought about. In my junior year a fellow from the NAACP came down to talk about careers in medicine. The NAACP, he said, was working with students and schools all over the country. We shouldn't think that we were restricted to applying to Howard and Meharry, the two traditionally black medical schools. The big white schools looked like they were becoming more receptive to black applicants. My adviser, James Birnie, was telling me the same thing. Howard and Meharry are fine places, he said. But they weren't the only possibilities. I should be applying to other schools too. There was no reason to limit myself. I could go anywhere.

I don't know if I actually believed I could go anywhere, even though I was doing well academically. When I graduated I was salutatorian, second in the class, same as I had been in high school. But southern medical schools were off-limits. In 1954 almost all of them were still white only, and that was about a third of the medical schools in the country. I had lived in Georgia my entire life, but there was no way for me to attend medical school in my home state. Northern schools didn't have the same official color bar, but very few of them ever accepted African American students either. On the other hand, Birnie had done his graduate work at Syracuse, Mays at Chicago, Brazeal and Williams at Columbia, Nabrit at Brown. It was certainly worth a shot. So I applied to Howard and Meharry but also to Michigan, Boston University, and Columbia.

The first one I heard back from was Boston University. They had received and reviewed my application and wanted me to make an appointment for an interview with a BU graduate physician who was practicing in Atlanta—a white physician. I made the appointment and went downtown to see the BU doctor, thinking that this was going to be a kind of screening interview. If I did well enough here, they'd probably invite me up to Boston for a real interview at the medical school.

The doctor I saw was not noticeably excited about the prospect of my attending Boston University. He asked why I wanted to be a doctor, why I thought I could be a doctor, what I thought I'd be doing as a doctor—perfunctory questions. It didn't seem to me that he was taking this interview very seriously. I left his office thinking that if this was representative of Boston University, there wasn't much chance that I'd be going there. I still hoped that maybe they'd invite me for a real interview. But I hadn't made a dazzling impression in this one, so I expected that the next thing I'd get from them would probably be a letter of rejection.

Two weeks later a letter arrived from BU. I tried to contain my nervousness; it was most likely a rejection letter, but who knew. Maybe they were asking me to come up after all. I opened it and read, "Dear Mr. Louis Sullivan, we are pleased to inform you that you have been accepted as a student in the entering Boston University School of Medicine class of September, 1954."

I was overwhelmed. I barely knew what to do. Birnie, I thought. I have to tell Dr. Birnie. Birnie lived in faculty housing on campus. Clutching the letter, I raced to his apartment and banged on the door. It was a hot spring afternoon; by the time I got there, I was covered in sweat. Birnie opened the door, bare chested and in his undershorts, which was a bit of a shock. He was a rather proper individual, and I had obviously surprised him. He may even have been having an afternoon drink or two. Everyone knew he liked his whiskey. "Dr. Birnie," I said. "Look! I've been accepted!" He grabbed my hand and pumped it. "Congratulations, Lou! Congratulations! That's just great."

I'm not sure how his other advisees told him their news. Nineteen of us were premed out of a graduating class of fifty-seven, and eighteen were admitted to medical schools—the nineteenth got into dental school. Many of us were his advisees. But I was probably the only one to see Professor Birnie in his undershorts.

My guess is that Birnie was beaming with pride at our performance. This was the first time some number of Morehouse premeds would be going to schools other than Meharry and Howard. I was off to Boston, William Jackson was going to Illinois, Perry Henderson to Case Western, Henry Foster to Arkansas. I was so happy with my acceptance that I accepted BU right back. I eventually was accepted at my other schools too, but by the time I heard from them, I had already sent in my deposit and was trying to prepare myself emotionally for the city of Boston, a great medical center, a great center of learning, the place where the American

Revolution had started, the epicenter of abolitionism. I was going to have a completely new kind of experience there.

I was about to launch myself into a white universe. How would I be accepted by the natives of that universe? And how would I stack up against my fellow students, almost all of whom were bound to be white? They had probably, I thought, gone to places like Harvard and Yale and Dartmouth. I was excited to go, but I also wondered how this was all going to work out.

CHAPTER 3

Medical Student

For many years Boston had a bad reputation among African Americans. But that wasn't true when I arrived for medical school in 1954. That was before the busing battles of the mid-1960s and 1970s, when the city was attempting to integrate the school system, and angry protests and near riots erupted. A city council member named Louise Day Hicks fanned the flames, organizing an antibusing movement called ROAR—Restore Our Alienated Rights. She almost got herself elected mayor, and Boston got tagged as a racist city.

Boston's sports teams furthered the perception. The Boston Red Sox were the last major league baseball team to integrate. They brought in their first black player in 1959, twelve years after Jackie Robinson broke the color bar. The basketball champion Celtics fielded a predominantly white starting team for years, well after the rest of the league had turned mostly black. Their great star, Bill Russell, regularly blasted the city's fans and sportswriters as racist.

But all that developed after I got there. When I arrived, African Americans considered Boston a good place. The city's history was a big part of that. The all-black Fifty-Fourth Infantry Regiment that fought in the Civil War came from Boston (the one that later was highlighted in the movie *Glory*). Frederick Douglass moved to the Boston area shortly after he escaped slavery; he began his antislavery work there. The great abolitionist William Garrison was from there and published his newspaper, the *Liberator*, in Boston. The city was the hotbed of the American Revolution; Crispus Attucks, a free black, was one of the first to die for it. At least from a historical point of view, Boston had an excellent reputation.

I soaked the city up. I walked the Freedom Trail and visited the museums. I went to see Harvard, with the statue of John Harvard sitting in the famous Harvard Yard. There were no "colored" public water fountains in Boston, no segregated waiting rooms, no riding in the back of the bus, none of the wariness and constant assault on your dignity that were part of living in segregated Atlanta. Boston was liberating. I felt as if a heavy weight had been lifted from my shoulders.

On the other hand, I had no idea what to expect from people at the medical school. From an all-black environment I was going into an all-white one. And I was going to be the integrator. How was I going to be treated by those white people? Maybe I'd be studiously ignored. Maybe I'd be the object of hostility or condescension. I didn't know.

But whatever fears I might have had along those lines evaporated almost as soon as I showed up for orientation. I was the only black student in my class of seventy-six, which I more or less had expected. There were two more of us in the school, one a senior, one a junior: three out of about three hundred students. But my reception couldn't have been friendlier, by the professors as well as the students. My antennae were up, but I didn't catch a single hint that I didn't belong. It was remarkable. Being a minority of one in my class might have been intimidating, but it turned out to be the opposite.

But I was still nervous. Just as I thought, my classmates had in fact done their undergraduate work at places like Harvard, Amherst, Williams, Columbia, Middlebury—mostly Ivy League and New England schools. I had absolutely no idea if I would be able to measure up to that kind of competition.

"Where did you go to school?" they asked me.

"Morehouse College."

"Sorry, where?"

"Morehouse."

"Oh, Morehead. Sure, I've heard of that."

"No, not Morehead. More-House."

"I'm sorry. Where?"

So I was apprehensive. I didn't want to embarrass myself by screwing up. All through Morehouse, and high school before that, our teachers were constantly giving us lectures, expecting us to be the leaders of the future. I didn't want to let them down. I was representing them, and I was the only black person in the class, so I was representing my race too. What if I failed? And it wasn't just that my classmates had gone to those prestigious schools—it was also medical school itself. Everyone talked about how hard it was going to be.

So I wasn't the only one who was nervous. Everyone was excited to be there, but you go into medical school with a certain amount of apprehension no matter where you're from. After a while you find out that if you're well prepared it's not an overwhelming intellectual challenge, but the amount of information you have to absorb is mind boggling. You're under water practically from day one.

So at first I was in information overload crisis, but so were all my classmates. We were all in this together. Then there was anatomy lab, where we were introduced to our cadavers. Another common challenge. We walked into the lab in silence, eyeing all the tables, each table with a dead body covered by a white shroud. It seemed eerie, foreboding. There were four of us assigned to a table. Hesitantly, my teammates and I peeled the shroud back from our cadaver. The body was lying on its stomach, a male. He was immense, six feet four or six feet five. We turned him over. His thick mustache made him look like Joseph Stalin, so his nickname instantly became Joe. I touched his chest. It was ice cold. I thought I felt icicles under his skin. Then I realized they must have just taken him out of the freezer.

Of course I had plenty of experience with dead people at the funeral home. But that was much more intimate. Back in Blakely we knew many of the departed, and even if we didn't know them personally, we knew who they were, who their families were. The four of us around the table stared at Joe. Nobody knew what to do. It felt strange and awkward staring at this dead person we were going to be taking apart tissue, muscle, and nerve by tissue, muscle, and nerve. We had all known what we were getting into, but after seeing this ice-cold giant, I think each of us felt a little shell-shocked.

But we were in the same boat. The gross anatomy lab binds you to your teammates. You're all working together, dissecting, cutting away skin and fat, isolating nerves and muscles. You depend on one another. And if we found something that was an anomaly—and about 10 percent of any particular body is—we'd announce it to the lab, and everybody would come to take a look. Somebody would announce something from another group, and we'd go see the different way the iliac artery ran in some other cadaver. So we had our immediate foursome, but we were connected to everybody else too. In the beginning all this cadaver work was a bit traumatic, but within a couple of months, one of us might be dissecting a body part and the others would be sitting around watching and eating lunch, something absolutely unimaginable at first.

My anatomy mates included Pat McLellan and Glenna McDonough, two of the seven women in our class. We were bragging about the fact that next to the Women's Medical College in Philadelphia (now Drexel University College of Medicine), we had the highest number of women of any medical school in the country. We were especially proud of that because BU Med started out in 1868 as the New England Female Medical College. It became coed sometime after the turn of the century and affiliated with BU. So we felt that we were upholding the tradition of the school's origins, even though seven out of seventy-six wasn't that great, considering that in earlier years 100 percent of the students were women. In medical schools in the fifties women weren't quite as scarce as African Americans, but there weren't many of them either.

Pat and Glenna were very bright. We worked together all the time around the cadaver, and we had formed an easy relationship. Pat and I even had a bit of chemistry together, so I asked her if she'd like to go out to dinner some night. She said, "Sure," so off we went one weekend night to a restaurant in Chinatown. We were seated in a small room with only a few tables. And one diner at another table said, "Waiter, would you find us another table please." They moved out. Of course at that time mixed couples were rare. And with my experience in the South, this guy's behavior was no surprise to me at all. That was a first, a date with a white girl. I could just imagine what would have happened had I tried that back in Atlanta. Pat and I never became boyfriend/girlfriend. But she was someone I'd go to a movie or to some outing with on occasion. People would look, but mostly it was just curiosity, not rage and threats of violence.

I also found plenty of other friends in the class. Barry Manuel, who later became a surgeon, then a dean at BU, was one of the first people I got to know well. He was from Boston, and during our first week he invited me to his house for dinner. His mother served matzo ball soup, something I had never heard of.

Not only had I never heard of matzo ball soup, I had never, to my knowledge, met any Jewish people before. The matzo balls were an object of conversation, along with chicken soup—soul food for Jews, Barry said. As we were talking about

Jewish soul food and black soul food, Jewish this or that and black this or that, it dawned on me that here were people who had their own specific life experience apart from the white mainstream. You couldn't just lump all white people together.

So, on the personal side, everything seemed to be working out. Then something else happened. About three weeks into the semester we had an anatomy exam, and I got an A. I did as well as anybody and better than most. What a relief that was. It told me I could compete. I wasn't going to be an embarrassment. I could actually feel myself relaxing.

Arriving in Boston, race was right up in the front of my mind. But six months later I was hardly even thinking about it. I knew for sure that I had been accepted. Looking back, it's hard to believe that there wasn't a single person at BU Med who might have had some reservations or even hostility, but if there was, I never saw it. The tone of the class, and of the school, was that that was not acceptable. For both my professors and classmates I was Lou Sullivan, not "That Black Guy." The following year my classmates even elected me class president.

Outside the school I began to have another life too, out in the black community. At Morehouse my fraternity was Alpha Phi Alpha. As soon as I was settled in at school I looked up the local chapter and went to meet the brothers, one of whom was Ed Brooke. Brooke was already a politician, though it would still be a number of years before he was elected senator, the first African American in the Senate since Reconstruction.

My cousin Evadne Priester had gone out with Brooke for a while. They had broken up but were still friends, and she had told me to look him up. "I'm Evadne's cousin," I said, introducing myself. "Evadne," Brooke said. "What a beautiful woman." Which she was. Evadne was beauty queen beautiful. "God, was she gorgeous," Brooke said.

The Alphas showed me around Boston and introduced me to people, including to my first date other than Pat McLellan. Annette Ganges and I went out to the Boston Symphony, a nice musical evening, a nice person, but by the end it was clear to both of us that if we never saw each other again that would be just fine. I was bored stiff and it was pretty obvious that she was too. Then about two weeks later Annette called. "There's an event coming up, Lou," she said. I waited for her to describe it, scrambling to figure something to say to get out of whatever she was going to propose. Whatever it was, I was going to have an anatomy exam the next day.

Instead she said, "I have a friend who's new in town, and I think the two of you might hit it off. I'd like to introduce you. Maybe you'd like to take her." Annette was living in the Franklin Square House, a woman's dormitory near the medical school, and the friend, a new student at Northeastern University, was one of Annette's dorm mates. Annette's friend, Ginger Williamson, had just come to Boston from Pittsfield, a small city in western Massachusetts. I rapidly recalculated. "Sure," I said. "I'd be happy to meet her." So we set it up, a blind date.

The next Saturday one of the Alpha brothers and I double-dated to a fraternity social in his car, a two-door model. We picked up his date, then drove to the Franklin Square House, where Ginger was waiting. In those distant pre-Internet, pre-Facebook days you took a real chance with a blind date. You never knew what she or he might be like, or look like. But Ginger Williamson was an extremely attractive sight. Really beautiful, I thought. And very soft spoken and amiable when I helped her into the backseat of my friend's car and got in next to her.

When we arrived at the party I got out first, pushing the front seat back as you have to in a two-door car, which makes stepping out a little awkward. When I was out I held out my hand to help Ginger, but she stumbled and half fell toward me. I caught her in my arms. To this day, fifty-plus years later, she insists that was a complete accident, which I still don't believe.

Our next date was almost our last. I arrived at the Franklin Square dorm at the appointed time, but there was no Ginger. She was out, one of her dorm mates said, but she'd be back very soon. Ten minutes later, no Ginger. Fifteen minutes later, still no Ginger. After twenty minutes I got up to leave, extremely annoyed. We had hit it off so well, I thought. And now she was standing me up like this? What in the world was this about? Anyway, that, apparently, was that. But just as I was leaving Ginger rushed in through the door dressed in tennis whites. She had been playing. She had lost track of time. She was so sorry. Couldn't I please stay and wait for her? I stayed.

After that we started dating regularly. Ginger told me that before she left Pittsfield her mother had sat her down and given her strict instructions about being careful in Boston. The big wicked city was full of temptations; it would be easy to go wrong there. Ginger should watch out for various things, especially the boys in Boston.

When Ginger thought her mother was finished, she got up.

"Wait," her mother said. "One more thing. When you go down to Boston, whatever you do, *do not* get mixed up with any of those southern boys. *No southern boys*!" It seemed that much earlier in her life Ginger's mother had had some kind of unfortunate experience with a young man from Birmingham. She still believed that boys from the South were all rotten to the core.

My first two years at medical school I had a cafeteria job at nearby Mass. Memorial Hospital busing trays and tables, which I squeezed in during lunch and dinner. It didn't bring in much, and Ginger had very little extra money, but it didn't seem to matter. We studied together. We took long walks, especially along the Charles River Esplanade, which we loved. I had sung in the Morehouse Glee Club, and also the club's quartet, and if no one was around I'd sing to her while we walked. She didn't seem too embarrassed, so sometimes I'd sing her all the parts on one of the glee club arrangements, tenor and bass.

After a few months we were pretty much inseparable. I knew how serious it was when Ginger invited me to Springfield for a weekend to see her family, which in addition to her mother and stepfather included three brothers and a sister and what seemed like a small army of cousins, uncles, and aunts, all of them looking me over, some not so subtly. Ginger's brother Frankie told her, "He's a little square, isn't he? But I guess he'll probably do."

With that provisional acceptance from the family, that spring Ginger and I got engaged. We weren't in a hurry to get married. We were both studying hard, and we didn't have the resources for it, but by that time we were sure we wanted to make our futures together.

———

As good a science preparation as I had gotten at Morehouse, when I went to Boston I was astonishingly ignorant of the world of medicine. I hardly knew anything about the various specialties, let alone subspecialties. At one point one of my classmates said he was planning to be an internist. "An intern?" I said. "Everyone's an intern."

"No," he said. "Not an intern, an internist. You know, internal medicine."

I didn't know. My idea of being a physician was Dr. Griffin. My plan had always been to become a doctor like he was and go back to Georgia to help take care of people, more or less the way he did. The man was a hero to the black rural community and to me too. He had been my role model since I was five.

But at BU I began learning that medicine offered more possibilities than being a general practitioner. My anatomy professor, Elizabeth Moyer, liked my work in her class and took me under her wing. Halfway through the course she sat me down and asked about my career plans. "I want to be a family physician," I told her. "I'm going to go back to Georgia and practice."

That might have surprised her. I don't think many of her students had equivalent kinds of futures in mind. "Oh, no, no, no," she said. "You're really too talented to do something like that. You should be thinking about how you can make the best use of your potential." It hadn't occurred to me that there might be a better use of my potential, and I'm not sure she meant it like that. But I was flattered and intrigued that she might be taking an interest in my career, something she continued to do as I moved forward.

Another professor who made an impression was Franz Ingelfinger, who was chief of gastroenterology and had made such significant advances in esophageal and gastrointestinal medicine that he was known as the "father of gastroenterology." Ingelfinger had been born in Germany, and he had a precise, scholarly, Germanic way about him. But he was also a big practical joker.

Ingelfinger taught the second-year course on clinical medicine, an introduction to the subject that covered the various functions of the human body: how the body maintains blood pressure, how the skin reacts to sunlight, how the gastrointestinal system works, and so on. In one lecture on the GI system, for example, he discussed gastric secretions: the importance of gastric juice; its pH, volume, and enzymes, and the gastric glycoprotein that's used in the absorption of vitamin B_{12}.

Each lecture in this course was followed by a laboratory in which students worked in groups of four to explore the new material. One of the four would serve as the subject for whatever lab exercise was at hand; either someone would volunteer or we'd rotate. The lecture prior to the lesson on gastric secretions had been on the blood, and I had been the lab subject, which meant that my lab mates had taken turns stabbing me with needles in their amateurish attempts to draw blood. In this particular lab we were to get a sample of gastric juice, measure it, observe its characteristics, and write up our findings.

Near the end of his lecture Ingelfinger explained how we would get the gastric juice. As he was speaking he took a nasal gastric tube that had been sitting on the lectern. Still talking, he began to insert this tube into his nose, without missing a beat. As we watched, mesmerized, he fed the tube all the way down into his stomach until just the end was sticking out of his nose. Lecturing away as if nothing special was going on, he then took a syringe, attached it to the tube, and aspirated a sample of gastric juice. He held it up for us. "See," he said. "This is how you get your sample. Nothing to it."

It looked so easy. The whole procedure hadn't interrupted a single syllable. In the lab there was a rush of volunteers. The next lab would likely be something a lot more painful or difficult. But as we began, the room was suddenly filled with sounds of retching, gagging, and choking. Running a nasal gastric tube wasn't easy. It wasn't simple. It triggered unpleasant peristaltic reactions. And, of course, none of us had ever done it before. A light bulb went off in all our minds almost at once. Ingelfinger, the father of gastroenterology, had obviously intubated himself a thousand times. He could have done it in his sleep. We had been had.

The man was a jokester. In another lecture he talked about what to look for in the examination of the urine: volume, color, clarity, odor—what each of those characteristics might mean medically. Also the taste—what did it taste like? A diabetic's urine might be sweet. As he was talking he dipped his finger in the urine sample and tasted it. "No, this sample isn't sweet; it's slightly bitter. It's not from a diabetic." And so in the lab exercise we examined our urine, tasting it, of course. Repulsive. Then we wrote up our results: the pH, the turbidity, . . . the taste.

In the next lecture Ingelfinger went over the elements of physical diagnosis: auscultation, palpation, percussion, close observation—the basic tools. "In terms of observation," he asked, "how many of you observed during the previous lecture that I put my index finger in the urine sample, but I put my middle finger in my mouth?" "Aaaw." A chorus of groans arose from the class. "Jesus!" "Dammit!" Various other exclamations. Ingelfinger! But that lesson on observation stayed with me the rest of my life as a physician: the absolute necessity of precise observation.

Ingelfinger later became the highly influential editor of the *New England Journal of Medicine*, where he established what was known as the Ingelfinger Rule. He mandated that any paper submitted to the *New England Journal* could not have been published or publicized in any form in the lay press or elsewhere prior to submission. That discouraged medical scientists from going public with findings that had not first been subjected to rigorous peer review. The Ingelfinger Rule decreased the likelihood that unsubstantiated discoveries would become part of the public understanding of health issues, and it raised the reputation of the *New England Journal* and the other medical journals that followed suit.

But the professor I admired most was Chester Keefer, BU's chief of medicine, a world-renowned infectious disease expert and a gifted diagnostician. During the war he had been the "Penicillin Czar," the designated judge of domestic use for the severely limited supplies of the still incompletely proven miracle antibiotic. Keefer was charismatic, not to say theatrical. A smallish, wiry man, his eyes gleamed out from behind his glasses. He exuded energy and purpose. His very presence seemed to demand complete attention.

Keefer had a photographic memory and an encyclopedic mind. He seemed to know everything about everything. He could dredge up the most arcane facts, often related in some surprising way to the subjects we'd be discussing. All our professors were extremely knowledgeable in their fields, but their understanding of nonmedical issues might have been limited. Keefer's range of knowledge was extraordinary; it intimidated people. That's what I wanted to be like, not necessarily intimidating, but I wanted to know as much as possible. I wanted to constantly expand my knowledge base. That was my goal, and Keefer was my model. If I could know half of what he knows, I thought, I'd be satisfied.

Every Monday morning Keefer would conduct chairman's rounds. At nine o'clock precisely the elevator doors would open and he would strut out, all business. The chief resident would be waiting, along with the head nurse, the other residents, the nursing staff, and the students, an entire entourage. The chief resident would greet him. "Dr. Keefer, good morning. We'll take you to the patient we're presenting."

If you were a student and the chosen patient was one you had been assigned, you'd be told about the presentation the preceding Thursday. After that you were excused from everything else so you'd have four days—Thursday, Friday, Saturday, and Sunday—to prepare the presentation, which included everything you could possibly learn about your patient's condition.

In the patient's room Keefer would stand at the head of the bed on the right-hand side. You, the student, would be opposite him on the left. Then the others would arrange themselves in strict order of hierarchy. Once everyone was in, you—the student—would begin, trying hard to keep your nerves from short-circuiting your brain. The last thing you wanted to happen would be for Keefer to interrupt you and start asking questions. You never knew where that might lead, but wherever it was there was a good chance that no matter how hard you had prepared for this, it wasn't enough. If Keefer felt the patient had not been adequately diagnosed and treated he would let you know in a way you would definitely remember. It was terrible to have that happen.

The Keefer story everyone told had happened the year before I started participating in his rounds. A patient had been selected who had prostate cancer. The presenting student described the prostate on digital rectal examination. He said the gland was "about the size and consistency of an English walnut." Keefer, the

Renaissance man, said, "English walnut? What do you know about the English walnut?" whereupon the student proceeded to describe the genus, species, nutritional value, number of pounds produced, domestic consumption, export figures, economic value to England, and a list of other facts. The student had decided to use the English walnut as an example and, correctly anticipating that Keefer would ask him about it, had spent his four days off combing encyclopedias and agricultural reference books for information. "Well," said Keefer, after a moment of silent reflection. "That's quite a dissertation on such an esoteric subject. Let's move on." And that was it.

With Keefer (as that student understood too well) you absolutely had to know what you were talking about. Chester Keefer was a character as well as a great teacher. He was a pervasive influence at the medical school generally and a powerful influence on me personally.

By the end of our second year we had been introduced to all the major specialties. At first I thought that I wanted to be a surgeon. I was fairly adept with my hands, and surgery was where the drama was. But during my surgical clerkship my idealized vision of what a surgeon's life was like suffered some erosion. In the operating room there could be flashes of excitement and high tension, but a great deal of the work seemed more or less mechanical. Surgeons were highly skilled, but taking out gallbladders or kidneys or fixing fractures didn't seem to present the problem-solving challenges that internal medicine did.

At the same time, my attraction to bench science was growing. Back at Morehouse I had loved the microscope work I did in Jim Birnie's biology lab, where we had examined amoebae, paramecia, and other one-celled organisms. Now, during my second year at BU, I had an assistantship as a researcher in a physiology lab. I enjoyed the lab work a great deal, and the paper I helped write about the effect of estrogens on food intake and weight gain was published in the *Proceedings of the National Academy of Sciences*, which was exciting by itself.

Two years later, when I was a senior, I did a three-month elective with Dr. Charles Emerson, a hematologist. The lab work there was fascinating—looking at cells; making and staining blood smears; identifying red cells, white cells, and platelets; analyzing the counts; and finding the problems. Hematology was a combination of bench science and taking care of patients with leukemia, anemia, platelet irregularities, hemophilia, and other blood disorders. I loved the clinical work, and the challenge of trying to solve blood mysteries was fascinating. I didn't exactly have a eureka moment when I decided to go into hematology instead of surgery, but by the time I graduated I had evolved into it.

By that time too, I was well settled into marriage. Ginger and I had gotten married during my second year in front of a justice of the peace in a little town outside of Pittsfield. Her mother was there, as were a few of Ginger's friends and mine. It was a simple, informal affair. My parents had wanted to come, but I had dissuaded them, telling them we'd come down soon to visit, which would give us a little time to spend together rather than the hurry we were in now, in the middle of the semester with no free time at all.

Afterward, Ginger and I had gone down to Blakely a couple of times to visit during breaks, and my parents fell in love with her, as I knew they would. They finally came up to see us in Boston when I graduated in June 1958. The commencement was a proud moment for my mother and father. They were there with an old friend from Blakely who had settled years before in Randolph, outside of Boston, and with Ginger, holding our first baby, Paul, who had been born the previous year.

After the ceremony my father took me aside to tell me something. "Louie," he said, "I want you to know that you've fulfilled my dream. I always wanted to be a doctor myself." I was startled. My father had never so much as hinted at such a thing before. In fact, I always felt he was a little closer to Walter, his first son, whom he had been training to go into the business. But being a doctor was apparently what he had been planning way back when he had gone to Claflin College for two years, before life's necessities sent him down another path.

———

As I started looking for internships during my final year I was pretty sure I could get a place at Boston University's Massachusetts Memorial Hospital. But I had done my student clinical work there and at Boston City Hospital, and I really wanted to experience someplace new. So I applied to Massachusetts General Hospital, Cornell's New York Hospital, Columbia Presbyterian, Rush Hospital in Chicago, and several others.

At Mass General I applied for a surgical internship along with my classmate Mort Buckley. Mort had graduated second in our class and I had been third. No BU medical student had ever been accepted at Mass General, but our new dean, Lamar Soutter, had come from there, so one of us, we thought, might have a chance, even though by this time I was leaning heavily toward hematology. I knew Soutter had talked to the school about me and that they were interested. I was sure he was pushing Mort as well.

At the other hospitals I applied for internships in internal medicine. Cornell New York was another program that had never taken anyone from BU. It had also never accepted any African Americans, and Jews were discouraged as well. It had the reputation of being an extremely WASPy place. I wasn't focused on breaking any color bars, but I was applying to Columbia and NYU, so I thought I might as well apply there too, even though I was pretty sure I was wasting my time.

My interview at Cornell was with Marvin Sleisinger, the chief of gastroenterology. He was engaging, and I thought we had a good talk. It seemed like he might be interested. Then at the end of our interview he asked what my schedule was for the rest of the day.

"Well," I said, "I have an interview at Presbyterian this afternoon."

"If you don't mind," he said, "I'd like to see if I can get you an appointment to see our chairman of medicine."

That meant only one thing: I had passed the screen. But I hadn't been expecting to see the chairman of medicine. I had no idea who he was. Forty-five minutes later Dr. Sleisinger took me to see the chairman, Dr. Hugh Luckey. By then I was thinking, hey, maybe there's a possibility I might get into this place. I was excited. We opened the door to Dr. Luckey's office, and a haze of cigarette smoke streamed out. Luckey himself arose from behind his desk, where a cigarette was smoldering in an ashtray. His large florid face was set on a bull neck on top of a barrel-like body. He stuck out a beefy hand and said, in a deep southern drawl, "Ha son, nahs to meet you."

When I heard that my heart fell. I thought, oh my goodness—a southerner. Why are they doing this to me? But by the end of our talk I was thinking differently. "Lou," Dr. Luckey said, "I really am pleased to meet you. You know, with the intern-matching program, we're not supposed to comment to applicants about what our level of interest might be. But let me just say, I hope you're interested in us."

When matching day arrived, the list came up. Mort Buckley had been accepted for surgery at Mass General. Lou Sullivan was going to Cornell Medical Center in internal medicine. Dean Soutter was more than a little surprised. "Mr. Sullivan," he said, "please, if you could come back to my office." As his door closed he said, "What happened? They accepted you at Mass General but you're going to New York Hospital?" Soutter (with whom I became good friends later on) was chagrined. He was going to be the proud dean with his graduates filling two of the highly selective surgical slots at Mass General. I had to confess. I had decided against surgery, and when it came to sending in our internship choices, I had axed Mass General.

Two weeks into my internship at Cornell's New York Hospital I was getting along fine. New York was a private hospital, but it had a public ward where the interns and residents were really in charge, along with an attending physician who oversaw the whole floor. I was assigned there, and with all the responsibility it was a great learning experience.

But one day the head nurse came up and said, "Dr. Luckey would like to see you in his office." Wonder what this is all about? I thought. Everything had been going all right. Could this be something about me being African American? I was still conscious that I was the first black person there.

Luckey, in his southern drawl, said, "Sit down."

I waited for the shoe to drop.

"How you doing?" he said.

"Fine."

"You learning anything?"

"Oh, yes. Yes."

"Got any problems?"

"No, no."

"Anybody bothering you?"

"Uh, no."

He saw I was on edge. "Lou," he said, "let me just tell you something. You know, I'm from Tennessee. I came to New York twelve years ago to be chief of medicine at the Cornell service at Bellevue. For the last four years I've been chairman here. People in New York believe that all southerners think alike. I'll tell you, they don't. You know that you're our first black intern. I want you to know that I intend for you to have a good experience here. I want you to learn a lot and do well. And I want you to know, if anybody gives you any problems of any kind, you come directly to me." Luckey was as good as his word, although I had only one incident during my two years of internship and residency.

One busy Sunday I was working on the hospital's private ward. By and large house officers don't enjoy working on a private service. The patients there are really the private doctor's patients, and the hospital staff physicians, in particular the interns and residents, mainly end up doing the scut work.

Typically, three or four admissions a day would keep us tied up, but that Sunday I had had seven. I had been running all day. Toward the end of my shift I got a call from a nurse who said, "Dr. Fortner has a patient who's been admitted, and you're up for the rotation." It was my turn again. Dead tired, I went down to see the patient. I got on the floor, and while I was still in the hallway I heard loud, boisterous complaints coming from this patient's room. He sounded drunk. When I knocked and walked in, the patient, an older white man, looked up from his bed with an expression of surprise, then anger. "You get out of here!" he yelled. "Don't you dare touch me!"

"I don't think I want to touch you," I said, and left. I went to the phone and called Luckey. "Dr. Luckey, I'm calling about a patient of Dr. Fortner's. I think he's been drinking. I don't know anything about him. He refuses to let me examine him. I thought I'd let you know."

Now, Dr. Fortner had a large Park Avenue practice called Passports International. In addition to his American patients he had developed a clientele of wealthy and often high-profile foreigners. One of his patients I saw was the queen mother of Nepal. Another of Fortner's was Rafael Trujillo, the Dominican dictator, though I didn't treat him personally. Trujillo had taken over the entire end of one wing, with his guards posted. Fortner admitted a lot of patients to the hospital. He brought in very considerable revenue.

Handling one of Dr. Fortner's clients with anything other than kid gloves was a risky business. But twenty minutes after I called Dr. Luckey, the obstreperous, racist patient was being wheeled out of the front door. Luckey wasn't going to put up with that kind of behavior, whether it meant taking on someone like the heavy-hitting Dr. Fortner or not.

<hr>

During my stay at Cornell a fellowship in hematology unexpectedly opened up. The person who was supposed to fill it couldn't come for some reason, so I was able to take his place. If I needed any confirmation that hematology was what I wanted, the several months I spent in that fellowship provided it. Afterward I saw my path clearly. I applied for a one-year pathology fellowship at Massachusetts General Hospital and also for a two-year hematology fellowship at Harvard's Thorndike Laboratory unit at Boston City Hospital.

I'd do Mass General first, I thought. Pathology focuses on laboratory medicine, looking into disease processes through the interpretation of lab results. That would give me a solid background for hematology research, and Mass General's pathology program was one of the best in the country. It specialized in analyzing difficult and unusual cases, which were written up weekly in a special section of the *New England Journal of Medicine*. Then I'd go to the Thorndike, a well-known stronghold in hematology training. The Thorndike Laboratory boasted a Nobel prizewinner, George Minot, who had discovered the cure for pernicious anemia. His successor there as chief was William Castle, who was doing his own revolutionary research. Many people thought that Castle had deserved to share in Minot's Nobel. My immediate future, at least, looked like it was set. I could hardly wait to get started.

CHAPTER 4

The Kamikaze School of Medicine

Through medical school Ginger and I had lived in housing we found through Boston University's lists. We never had problems finding a decent living situation, and when we came back to Boston in 1960 so I could take up my Mass General fellowship I wasn't expecting anything different.

But problems cropped up. I'd read rental advertisements in the paper and call up. "I'm Dr. Louis Sullivan. My wife and I are looking for an apartment. Can we arrange to see the one you're renting?"

"Sure," they'd say. "Come over."

We'd get to the address a short time later and ring the bell, but nobody would answer. They'd seen us out the window. Sometimes we could see them peeking out, then ducking away. Or the husband would answer and it would be, "Oh, I'm so sorry. I didn't know my wife had just rented the place ten minutes before you called."

No one would actually say, "We don't rent to blacks." That would have gotten me angry, but at least it would have been honest. At least they would be telling me up front where they were coming from. It was more frustrating seeing them duck behind the curtains or husbands saying their wife had just rented the place. But that's what it was in Boston.

Of course, we did finally find a place. And in Boston the name Sullivan could come in handy. When I finished my fellowship at Mass General and had moved over to Boston City Hospital, we were living on Alpine Street in Cambridge, the one black family on the block. A registered letter had come. We had gotten a notice: "Please make arrangements to pick the item up at the post office." I called from the hospital the next day. "This is Dr. Sullivan. I'm at Boston City Hospital. It's very difficult for me to get away. Would it be at all possible to have the letter delivered to me here?"

"No, no," said the voice on the other end. "We can't do that. What did you say your name is?"

"Dr. Louis Sullivan."

"Oh, well, maybe we can arrange that, doc. O'Shaugnessy can deliver. It's good to know that one of our boys made it."

But I was finding that being black in the North could lead to awkward, unpleasant situations. Nothing like that had occurred while I was in medical school, but that had been a bubble of sorts. There I was cushioned by the support of my friends, classmates, and teachers. The apartments Ginger and I rented we found on the university's no doubt vetted lists. Living as independent adults on our own we were more vulnerable.

A year after I began my hematology position at Boston City, I was looking for a way for us to spend the summer vacation months. On the hospital bulletin board were ads posted by people looking for doctors to do various things. One was for a physician to serve as a summer camp doctor at Camp Wavus on Damariscotta Lake in Maine. The doctor would be provided with a cabin and a monthly salary. If the doctor had camp-aged children, they could enroll at reduced rates.

I called up. "I'm Dr. Louis Sullivan. I saw the ad. I'd be interested."

We talked. I told them about my background. They said, "Gee, you sound like just the person we're looking for. We'll send you a letter of engagement, and we'll look for you."

There was one thing I failed to tell them. This was the summer of 1962. We drove up from Boston to Maine and found the camp. We got out of the car, myself; our son, Paul, who was six then; and Ginger with our new baby, Shanta. The director was standing at the door of the office watching. He looked worried.

"Hi, I'm Dr. Sullivan."

"Oh. You're Dr. Sullivan? Uh, please come on in."

We went in—he went into a back room. He came back out a couple of minutes later with his wife. They were the owners. "Doctor, I'm afraid there's been a terrible mistake. I'm not prejudiced, but, you know, we can't tell how our campers and their families would react. And our life savings are invested in this camp. We're sorry for the inconvenience this is causing . . . we'll pay you the $2000, but we think it would be best if we not engage you."

After our apartment difficulties in Cambridge, I wasn't totally surprised. My expectation by then was that you never knew what might happen. I'd hope that it wouldn't, but if it did it wasn't exactly a shock. I was not going to tell this camp owner on the phone, "By the way, I'm black. Does that matter?"

I said, "Look, we signed an agreement. I'm here to perform my side of it. My credentials are as good as everyone else's. I'm ready to start."

They went into the back room again and came out with a third person, Uncle Zeke. The owners were in their fifties; Uncle Zeke was maybe ten years older. He had been around a long time as one of the staffers. He was the wise old man of the camp. I think Uncle Zeke calmed them down.

"Doctor," he said, "let's try and see if we can't make this work." So we went ahead with it. Paul was about a year younger than they usually took their campers. But they agreed to put him in with the youngest group. This was what we had in mind. Paul would have a camp experience, and Ginger and I would have what amounted to a vacation. As a camp doc there might possibly be an emergency or two, but mainly I would be treating cuts, scrapes, poison ivy, and allergies. It wouldn't be a heavy caseload.

After the initial encounter we settled in and ended up having a great summer. We even became good friends with the owners. We went back to the camp for several reunions, and Paul had such a good time that when he grew up and had children of his own, he sent them there. That was the kind of thing any black person might have experienced. We were lucky that it turned out well, but you never quite knew what you would run into.

When I finished my pathology year at Mass General, I headed over to the famous Thorndike Laboratory, part of the Harvard service at Boston City Hospital, for what would really be the start of my professional career. Hematology is a subspecialty of internal medicine, and the field has its own distinct areas of concentration. Some hematologists are red blood cell specialists, some white cell specialists; some are focused on coagulation, others on blood banking.

The Thorndike was known for its research on red cell hematology, which was my primary interest. Red cells were exciting. I loved to study them under the microscope. Depending on the health of the patient or the nature of disease the cells would assume various sizes, shapes, and colors. They could be disk shaped or flat or aberrant and irregular, as they were in sickle cell anemia. They changed shape and color. They had a life span; they were born and died. They were dynamic. Beyond that, patients with serious, even fatal illnesses could make truly dramatic recoveries. They might come into the hospital at death's door, lethargic, confused, laboring to breathe, almost comatose, and with the right treatment two or three days later they would be up and about as if nothing had ever happened. And the Thorndike was where many of the groundbreaking therapeutic discoveries had been made.

The lab had achieved international prominence initially through the work of George Minot, who had shared the Nobel Prize in 1934. Minot was working on pernicious anemia, a disease that led to a variety of degenerative symptoms and was invariably fatal. It was thought to be a kind of leukemia. Once a diagnosis was made, a patient might have a life expectancy of four or five months.

Through his examination of red blood smears Minot began to think that the disease had something to do with bone marrow, the body tissue that produces blood cells, and he suspected that the culprit might be related to diet. He then read about some experiments in which a medical scientist at Rochester, George Whipple, had restored dogs suffering from blood loss by feeding them large amounts of liver.

Wondering if something similar might be effective in humans, Minot began feeding pernicious anemia patients a half pound of raw liver a day or its equivalent in liver juice. His dying patients, at least those who could stomach the diet, improved almost magically. He had discovered a revolutionary cure. The therapy was odious, but patients were told, "This is it, or you're going to die."

William Castle, the Thorndike's current chief, had worked with Minot in the 1920s and 1930s. Some other researchers had shown that anemia patients lacked gastric juice, so Castle had the idea that if he mixed gastric juice with whatever it was in liver that cured pernicious anemia, that combination might be curative as well. In addition, he hypothesized that whatever the effective substance was in liver, it might also be present in beef.

Castle's experiments along these lines were death defying. Every morning, having eaten nothing since the night before, he fed himself two-thirds of a pound of raw hamburger. He'd let that sit in his stomach for an hour, then he'd stick his finger down his throat and regurgitate (his papers referred to this as "pharyngeal stimulation"). Then he'd put the mixture through a fine sieve and introduce the resulting fluid into the stomachs of unsuspecting anemia patients through a nasal gastric tube. His experiments showed conclusively that patients who didn't respond to either raw beef or gastric juice alone did respond to the combination. He deduced from this that there was an "extrinsic" (outside-the-body) element in the beef and an "intrinsic" (produced-in-the-body) element in the gastric juice and that the two needed to interact to achieve a therapeutic effect.

Years later the extrinsic factor was identified as vitamin B_{12}. The intrinsic factor is a glycoprotein manufactured by cells in the stomach lining that binds with the B_{12} and transports it to the site in the small intestine designed to absorb it. Minot, the Nobel laureate, had fed such massive quantities of liver to his patients that the high volume of B_{12} forced its absorption by the intestine through osmosis, which was why the gastric juice combination hadn't been needed.

With our more stringent patient-consent requirements today, Castle's methods probably couldn't be duplicated, but it's interesting to think about. He was a unique character. For years he slept in the room next to the Thorndike's kitchen. It was unclear why he did that. By all accounts he was happily married. But then again, he was going through that morning eating-and-regurgitating routine, which might have been less than welcome in his household.

Castle was also famous for his inveterate tinkering. He owned a Model T Ford he enjoyed driving around that needed constant mechanical attention. But it wasn't just the car. He kept a set of tools in his office, which he used to fix things up around the building. I'm not sure when the Thorndike Laboratory building was built, but it was fairly ancient, and its systems would break down from time to time, the heating system in particular. When that happened Castle would take out his toolbox and get to work on the radiators or the heating plant. At one point when the old elevator stopped working, he got into his coveralls and was on his hands and knees fixing something in the door when a visitor arrived. "Say, buddy," the visitor asked, "can you tell me where Dr. Castle's office is?"

"Sure," said the repairman. "Upstairs to the right, at the end of the hall."

When the visitor arrived, Castle's secretary said that he was tied up for the moment, but he'd be available shortly. Ten minutes later the repairman walked into Castle's office with his toolbox, and a few minutes after that the secretary said, "Dr. Castle will see you now." One day my own supervisor, Victor Herbert, was in the laboratory when Castle walked in. The Thorndike had big soapstone sinks in the bathrooms and the labs, and while Castle and Herbert were talking, Castle turned to the sink, unzipped his fly, and began urinating into it, with no letup in his discussion. When he saw Herbert's expression, he said, "It's okay. When you're the chief of the unit you can do things like this." He was an eccentric man.

The fact that Castle inflicted his raw beef and gastric juice experiments on himself led us, his fellows, to call the Thorndike "The Kamikaze School of Medicine." It was a nickname that stuck. Castle wasn't the only Thorndike professor who qualified as a kamikaze. My supervisor was another. Victor became famous later, not only for his many hundreds of influential papers but as the country's most outspoken critic of quack medicine and remedies. He detested the health food industry's claims for unproven supplements, including unneeded vitamins, believing they did more harm than good. Perhaps his greatest contribution had to do with understanding the metabolic function of folic acid and the anemia caused by its deficiency. In his human experiments in that area he, like Castle, subjected himself to experiments in a way few others would ever think of doing. As his research fellow, I helped him do it.

Folic acid had been identified in the early 1950s. A deficiency of the substance caused a slowdown in the production of red blood cells, an anemia that looked very much like the pernicious anemia caused by the lack of vitamin B_{12}. At the Thorndike, Herbert was studying the minimum daily requirement for folic acid. He wanted to determine what level of deficiency would induce anemia.

To do that he became his own guinea pig. For months he put himself on a diet free of folic acid, subsisting on rice, potatoes, thrice-boiled chicken, marshmallows, and jelly. As Victor's body depleted its stored supply of folic acid, his marrow decreased its production. His red blood cells, living out their normal 120-day life cycle, died off and were not replenished. Over time, as the volume of red cells diminished, the oxygen these cells supply to the tissues did also. Victor began to develop the anemia symptoms he was looking for: fatigue, shortness of breath, and confusion.

The gross symptoms, though, developed only gradually. Meanwhile, we were looking for the changes in his blood that indicated how the anemia was progressing on a cellular level. As the blood volume decreased, large red blood cells proliferated. White cells became unusually segmented. To trace the course of these changes, we took regular samples of Victor's peripheral blood and also of his bone marrow.

Drawing blood is an easy procedure that causes minimal pain; it's basically the prick of a needle. Taking bone marrow samples is another story. Victor would take bone marrow samples on himself every week. I was the one who performed the marrow extractions. There are several ways to get bone marrow from a person. The most common and easiest is to do it from the sternum. For this procedure you need a sharp, heavy gauge trocar that contains a metal stylus to give it rigidity. Anatomically, the sternum, or breastbone, has an outer and inner table of bone and in between is the bone marrow. You insert the trocar into the space, then you remove the stylus, attach a syringe, and aspirate the marrow.

Puncturing the bone isn't the most painful part. Before the procedure you inject Novocain, which anesthetizes the skin and the fibrous covering of the bone, where most of pain nerves are. That part is uncomfortable, but it's tolerable. The major source of pain is the vacuum you create when you aspirate the bone marrow. The two or three tenths of a milliliter of bone marrow you aspirate is gelid, which is why you need a large gauge trocar. Sucking out the marrow, you create a sudden vacuum that pulls the inner lining of the bone off its moorings. That's the painful part.

The whole procedure takes five seconds or so. Doctors tell patients, "You'll feel pressure when the needle goes in, but you're well anesthetized." They can take that. Then, once it's in you tell them, "Okay, now you're going to feel this, but it will be over in a few seconds." Then you aspirate. Some patients scream. Victor didn't. He knew it was coming, and he was used to it, to the extent a person could get used to it. Also, he had a very cute technician who held his hand tightly, so that was a distraction. And, of course, it was his research; he was motivated and excited about doing this study. In the papers we wrote we determined the minimum daily requirement of folic acid and related metabolic functions concerning B_{12} and iron. "Rarely if ever," say the editors of *Hematology, Landmark Papers of the Twentieth Century*, "has an experiment with an experimental population of one yielded so much data of such importance." Victor gave me the option of participating as a subject, but I respectfully declined. Doing the bone marrow extraction was traumatic enough.

Victor was a controversial character. "There are two kinds of people in the world," I told him at one point. "People who see a fight and run the other way, and people who see a fight and jump into it. You're in the latter category." Victor was very smart but also somewhat insecure. He had had a tough upbringing. His parents had died when he was young, and he had lived in various orphanages, which I think had an impact on him. He came to Harvard's Thorndike from Mount Sinai in New York. He had been a star protégé there, and his chief had arranged for him to go for seasoning to the Thorndike, which, under Castle and Minot before him, was clinical investigation's holy of holies.

So there Victor was, at Harvard, and his competitive instinct was sharpened to a razor's edge. He wasn't afraid of fights, and he didn't care whom he took on, actually the bigger the target the better. He took on Linus Pauling, for example, the Nobel Prize–winning chemist who was a great advocate of vitamin C. Victor decried Pauling's loud cheerleading for vitamin C supplements. His criticism was scathing, merciless. According to Victor, Pauling had been duped and had become the public voice for a fraud. Pauling answered that in his opinion Victor was the one who was a fraud. According to Pauling, Victor wasn't even an actual scientist; he was nothing more than a blowhard dilettante.

I don't know that Victor was right in all his many criticisms of supplements, but in the end he seems to have been quite correct about Pauling's beloved vitamin C, at least insofar as its effects on the common cold go. Victor was, to say the least, a lively addition to life at the Thorndike.

I didn't escape the Thorndike's kamikaze ethos myself. In addition to the bone marrow, the liver and spleen are also involved in manufacturing blood cells. In patients with pernicious anemia, the body is struggling to produce more red blood cells, but the deficiency doesn't allow it. One consequence is that the liver and spleen both enlarge. The question was, is there something in the normal spleen that would boost red blood cell production?

To test that theory we needed spleen. In Worcester, thirty miles west of Boston, we found a slaughterhouse that would sell us fresh beef spleen. Bringing it back to the lab, I'd cut it up, homogenize it in a Waring blender, and add a little Tabasco and horseradish sauce to make it more palatable. Then I'd drink it; it was like a thick milkshake, a spleen milkshake. After a designated period I'd take a blood sample to see if my blood volume had increased. For a month I consumed a pound of raw beef spleen daily. It was not pleasant, but it was far preferable to getting my bone marrow extracted. At the Thorndike, if you needed a normal subject, and you were normal, you were the subject.

One of the most significant studies I was involved in while I was there had to do with the effect of alcohol on the formation of blood cells. We wanted to determine if drinking affected hematocrit levels, that is, the volume of red blood cells as a percentage of the total circulating blood. Because red blood cells transport oxygen into and carbon dioxide away from the body's tissues, it was important to know to what extent, if any, alcohol impaired the ability to sustain normal functioning of tissues and organs.

The National Institutes of Health approved our grant request for this study, but the finance office at Boston City Hospital was harder to convince. We had designated a substantial amount of money for the purchase of alcohol, which looked suspiciously as if we might actually be buying it for our personal consumption. So we had to rework the grant application to show that this wasn't some kind of alcoholic doctors' boondoggle. Once the approval went through, we needed a regular supplier, because we'd be buying a significant amount and we didn't want to have to keep running out to the corner liquor store. We also needed a secure place in the hospital to store our supplies. It turned out that the Thorndike's deputy director, Maxwell Finland, had an active relationship with Ideal Liquor, seven or eight blocks from us, so they became our vendor. At the hospital we were given a locked storage closet, so we felt confident we could secure our stock, a confidence that did not prove altogether warranted.

Next, we needed patients who would be our subjects. Since Boston City Hospital cared for the poor and indigent, alcoholics weren't hard to come by. These heavy drinkers often hardly ate; they just drank all the time. Since they didn't eat, or if they did, their diets were terrible, they were often suffering from folic acid deficiency and anemia. The first patient we studied was someone I'll call Tina Tarply. Tina was maybe fifty-eight or sixty years old; she wasn't sure. She had come into the hospital with severe anemia. When we approached her about the study, she was happy to volunteer. Initially we let her consume whatever amount of alcohol she wanted, but we also fed her a healthy diet. Her normal alcohol intake turned out to be about a pint a day; eighty-six-proof Imperial Whiskey was her favorite. So that became our standard dose, a pint of eighty-six proof per twelve-hour period. With a free bed, free food, and free whiskey, Tina was happy as a clam.

Tina had my telephone number, as did the nurses, in case something untoward happened. One Sunday Tina called, extremely upset, complaining loudly that a nurse was drinking her medicine. The hospital was a twenty-minute drive from my home, and when I got there, I couldn't find the nurse who was assigned to the study. Finally I located her in a back room, snoring away. The place reeked of Imperial Whiskey. Tina was right—the nurse was drinking her meds.

Much later I was able to see the humor of it, but at the time I was really ticked off. The nurse was disrupting everything. She had protocol responsibilities, monitoring Tina's pulse, temperature, and other vital signs, which she was obviously doing in an impaired state. Second, if she was drinking the alcohol, that meant she was making up our measured dose by adding water to Tina's whiskey. She was interfering with the accuracy of our study.

After Tina had gotten comfortable with her surroundings, we withdrew the alcohol but made sure she was eating normally. After three or four days her blood count started to improve. The question was, was this because she was now eating, and so she was getting sufficient folic acid and other nutrients? Or was it because she was not drinking? In other words, was alcohol itself causing the anemia?

Tina was our first case. We learned quite a bit from her, and we were able to replicate our findings with other anemic patients. We first put them on Victor Herbert's thrice-boiled, folic acid–free diet, and we saw that their anemias did not improve, even though they were getting no alcohol. Then we gave them folic acid, and they would improve. Then we started them on alcohol. For our second patient we used pure ethanol rather than commercial whiskey to make sure the active substance was actually in the alcohol and not in something introduced by the distilling process.

These patients would be reasonably intoxicated by the afternoon. We tried, mostly successfully, to make sure that they wouldn't become combative—the metabolic ward had other patients as well. We learned that the alcohol would knock their new red blood cell production down to zero. So, alcohol itself clearly did suppress the formation of red blood cells. When we tried halving the alcohol intake we found that the blood count did decrease, though not as robustly as with a full pint. So the amount was important. One or two glasses of wine wouldn't do much, especially in people who were eating normally. But many heavy drinkers drink far more than even a full pint of whisky.

We carried out this investigation in accord with the ethical standards of the time, though it could hardly be done today. It was an important study, and it gained widespread attention. Subsequently, other investigators demonstrated the same syndrome in platelets—blood cells that play a central role in coagulation. All blood cells, in fact, react similarly to alcohol. So what we showed, ourselves and those who did the subsequent work, was that alcohol is toxic to blood marrow. We knew that alcohol damaged the liver, but this was the first time it was shown that it affected the blood system.

We published our study in the prestigious *Journal of Clinical Investigation*, and I was invited to present the paper at the annual research meeting of the American

Society for Clinical Investigation in Atlantic City. My presentation was given an optimal spot, late in the morning on the second day of the meeting, which meant that the planners were giving it a high priority. That was extremely gratifying, a confirmation that we had done something of significance.

This was a giant meeting, with perhaps four thousand leading researchers and clinicians gathering in the Atlantic City Convention Center. By the second day everyone had arrived, and by the fourth spot on the morning's program the hall was standing room only. Up on the podium I scanned the sea of faces in front of me. I had never been involved in anything remotely like this. I continued doing biomedical research for many years after my stint at the Thorndike, but that study, and that presentation, remained one of the high points.

During my fellowship at the Thorndike I worked with Victor, Bill Castle, and others on research involving vitamin B_{12}, anemias, alcohol's relation to blood production, and many other elements of nutrition and the workings of marrow and blood cells. The laboratory was a great learning environment, full of creative people doing important work, not just in hematology but in cardiology and gastroenterology. But with my two-year tenure coming to an end, I was looking forward to my next step. I was being recruited by the Duke University School of Medicine, for what looked like an extremely interesting and worthwhile position.

The chief of medicine at Duke was Eugene Stead, a renowned cardiovascular scientist and clinician who had built the Duke medical service into one of the strongest in the country. He and my chief, Bill Castle, were colleagues and friends, and Castle had recommended me for an opening as head of the medical service at Lincoln Hospital, a community hospital in Durham, not far from Duke's medical school.

Lincoln was a black hospital in what was still the segregated South. Two African American physicians there had approached Stead about the possibility of affiliating Lincoln with Duke, and Stead responded positively. The affiliation would bring Duke residents and students to rotate through the hospital. It would put Lincoln into the Duke orbit, enhance its level of care, and provide teaching and eventually research there, which would elevate the hospital. It would also begin the business of integrating the Duke medical center, one of Stead's goals.

Stead had offered me the position, and I had accepted. This was going to be a big step. Becoming chief of a hospital medical service would be a major change from the research positions I had been in, a challenge I was looking forward to. I would also be going back to the South, which I had left a decade earlier. It was the spring of 1963. A few months earlier Martin Luther King had confronted Bull Connor in Birmingham. National Guard troops had moved George Wallace out of the schoolhouse door. Affiliating black Lincoln Hospital with the still lily-white Duke medical school would mean getting to play a role in the vast changes that were beginning to crack the old racial system into pieces. Ginger and I were all set to go to Durham.

One day I was in Castle's office discussing some research we were doing, and while we were talking, Castle's secretary buzzed him. Eugene Stead was on the line from Duke. I got up to leave, but Castle motioned me to stay, so I sat there listening to Castle's side of the call.

"Hello, Gene," Castle said. "Good to talk with you. What? Oh no!" Castle's long face turned dark. "You're kidding! I can't believe this. This is just too bad. No, don't worry about that. I'll take care of things on this end. But this is terrible." I was thinking, what in the world are they talking about? It was obviously something extremely distressful.

Then Castle turned to me. "Lou, everything is fine. We're going to take care of things, so I don't want you to worry. That was Gene Stead. The chancellor of the university just vetoed your appointment. Stead is beside himself, but there's nothing to do about it. But don't worry—we're going to see that you get an appointment here at the Harvard faculty."

It turned out that Stead had insisted that my new head-of-hospital position at Lincoln would include faculty status at Duke. I would, in fact, be Duke's first African American professor. "That meant you'd be eligible for faculty housing," Castle told me. "That's why the chancellor refused to sign off on the appointment. They couldn't accept having a black family in faculty housing."

This was completely out of the blue. I hadn't thought about faculty housing, or any housing at all yet. I didn't even know they had faculty housing. I had been looking forward to Duke. Stead, like Castle, was an icon. He was an innovator, ahead of his time. He had initiated the physician's assistant field—against a lot of resistance from physicians, who felt threatened. He was a famous clinician and teacher; he had a tough, tough reputation. He had decided on this step, and now he was being stymied. He was furious and embarrassed.

I was surprised and disappointed, but I can't say that I was furious. I might have even been relieved to a degree. It was clear that Stead was way out in front of his university. They were not ready. I was also going to get to spend another year at the Thorndike, with a faculty appointment this time. I loved the research I was doing there, and I loved living in Boston, whatever the city's underground ripple of racism.

In fact, Boston's racial situation was complex. Our housing difficulty sent one message, but almost everything else that touched our lives sent another. We were friendly with all our neighbors, mostly young married couples with children, like ourselves. My relationship with my colleagues was as warm as ever. Ginger and I had joined Christ Church in Cambridge, which had a mixed congregation and a history of social activism. We truly felt part of the Boston community.

That summer, not long after Duke voided my appointment, civil rights leaders called for a huge march on Washington. All the major black leaders were going to attend and speak: Martin Luther King, A. Phillip Randolph of the sleeping car porters union, Roy Wilkins of the NAACP, John Lewis of the Student Non-Violent Coordinating Committee, and Whitney Young of the Urban League, among many others. I had never met any of them. As the civil rights movement was ramping up, I had been in medical school, then a resident, then a research fellow, completely immersed in my work. But I had followed all the developments and events closely, as had Ginger. And when the march was announced, we knew we had to go.

Thinking that others in our church might want to go as well, I and one or two others arranged to charter a bus. But when we announced what we were planning, so many in the congregation clamored to go that we ended up not with one bus but with twenty-seven—a giant convoy that snaked its way out of Cambridge onto the Massachusetts Turnpike late on the night before the march. The air of excitement as we got rolling was like nothing I had ever experienced. People were clapping and singing "We Shall Overcome" and other movement songs for hours, until even the most fervent finally dropped off to sleep.

We left at nine thirty on the night of August 27. At five the next morning I opened my eyes to see that we were crossing the high Memorial Bridge over the Delaware River. As we rolled into Delaware, suddenly crowds of people out on the roadside were cheering and waving us on, people with placards and flowers and flags. It was an amazing sight. We had no idea how they had known that the buses were coming, but there they were, not just for us, of course, but for the growing volume of traffic heading toward Washington.

We arrived in the capital at eight or eight thirty in the morning. Everyone was getting off, but there was a paraplegic person on the bus whom I didn't know, though I had noticed him when people helped him on. As the riders piled off in high spirits, he just sat there.

"Aren't you getting off?" I asked.

"No, I'm not," he said. "I just wanted to be here for this. I don't want to be a bother to anyone."

"Like hell," I said. "You're not going to come all the way down here to sit in the bus. Let's get your wheelchair, and we'll push you over." Ginger and I helped him into his wheelchair and started pushing him through the tremendous crowds. We had had no idea how many people were going to be in Washington; I don't think anyone did. The place was thronged. But because we had the wheelchair, the crowds parted to let us through, right up to the front, only fifteen or twenty yards away from the speakers' stand. There were Wilkins and Bayard Rustin and James Farmer. There were Walter Reuther, the UAW president, and A. Phillip Randolph. And sitting up there with them was Martin Luther King Jr.

King was the great hero, the acknowledged leader of the movement, famous for what he and his Southern Christian Leadership Conference had done in Montgomery and Birmingham and so many other places. This was the first time I had ever seen him, though he too had gone to Morehouse and then to graduate school at Boston University. His father had spoken to us in the Morehouse Chapel many times, but even his eloquence didn't match the power of his son's words on that day in Washington.

John Lewis gave a fiery speech about going into the streets. James Farmer and others moved the crowd with their appeals to the conscience of the nation and to the ideals that defined America yet were so far from the American reality. But when it was King's turn, and when he put aside his prepared speech to speak from his heart, and when he began that rolling thunder of "I Have a Dream," his spirit seemed to take possession of those hundreds of thousands of people listening on the mall, and of Ginger and me along with them.

CHAPTER 5

Professor

After the fiasco with Duke, Bill Castle arranged a one-year Harvard faculty appointment for me, as he had said he would. At the same time he assured me that I'd find many opportunities around the country and that he'd work to make sure good things happened. Also, the Thorndike being what it was, professors from medical schools visited frequently, some of them looking to recruit.

One of these was Dr. Harold Jeghers, chairman of the department of medicine at Seton Hall University. Jeghers had previously been chief of the Boston University service at Boston City Hospital. He and Castle knew each other well, and he had an ongoing relationship with the Thorndike. When Seton Hall established a medical school in the mid-1950s, Jeghers had gone down to help develop its programs. In 1963, on one of his return trips, Castle introduced me to him. He was still building his departments, Jeghers told me, including hematology. Might I be interested in joining him?

Seton Hall University was in South Orange, New Jersey, but the medical school was located at the Jersey City Medical Center, twenty or so miles away. The center was huge, a vast complex overlooking New York harbor. The original buildings went back many years, but much of the construction had been done in the 1930s with WPA funds. It was commonly understood that the new buildings had been a reward to Jersey City's famous, or infamous, Boss Frank Hague, who had delivered the Hudson County vote to Franklin Roosevelt in 1932, giving FDR the state of New Jersey in the presidential election. Roosevelt had personally dedicated the giant new buildings on their completion, fulsomely thanking Hague for his vision and devoted service.

Whatever its origins, the medical center was impressive. As a major clinical institution it had welcomed Seton Hall's new medical school, which brought in the teaching and research activities the center had previously lacked. When I visited, the school was still fairly new—its first class had graduated only three years earlier. I could feel the enthusiasm and entrepreneurial spirit of the faculty and researchers. They seemed excited to be where they were. Ginger and I looked at the area and found that South Orange, where the university was located, had attractive homes and excellent schools. We liked what we saw there. So I accepted Jeghers's offer and started at Seton Hall as an assistant professor in July 1964.

When I arrived, Jeghers's hematology staff consisted of one part-time physician who, in addition to his faculty appointment, carried on a private practice, which meant that I was the department's first full-time professor as well as the only researcher. I was truly getting in here on the ground floor, which was exciting by itself. In addition, I was bringing with me sufficient funding to establish my own laboratory. The previous year I had been awarded two research grants from the National Institutes of Health, including a five-year research career-development award given to "young investigators of promise." This provided enough money for salary, equipment, and technician assistants. I was pleased and flattered to have gotten this award. It meant that I didn't have to worry about my own living or laboratory expenses, besides the prestige that came with it. I was starting off at Seton Hall on a high note.

Jeghers had also informed me that the school was in the process of making a transition. Seton Hall University had launched the medical school, but it was finding that an institution of this kind was extremely expensive as well as being difficult to run. The university had concluded that the medical school was a stretch for its resources and had petitioned the state of New Jersey to take it over, which the state had now agreed to do.

That seemed to me another positive. I would be going to an institution that would be financially supported by the state, which would give it great financial stability. Other faculty were also enthusiastic about the prospect. We were all eagerly anticipating the takeover and speculating optimistically about the benefits it might bring.

But as the months went by little seemed to be happening. The state was slow in appointing trustees, the first step in the formal takeover. The idea was that once the board was completed they would convene and officially transfer the school to the state. A chairman had been appointed, George Smith, CEO of Merck Pharmaceuticals, but progress on filling out the board was glacial. People began to wonder what was going on.

A year into my tenure, the transition was still stuck. I had my laboratory up and running and my research on anemias and related areas was gathering steam. But I was getting concerned. Then suddenly, at the end of 1965, a front-page article in the *New York Times* announced that the medical school would be moving from Jersey City to a new home, though there was no indication where that new home might be.

I tried to reach Dr. Jeghers, but I couldn't get through. His line was constantly busy; I was sure the entire medical faculty was calling him. It took two days before I was able to get in touch, though information was circulating from those who had managed to reach him. Why were we moving? people asked. The Jersey City Medical Center was immense; there was plenty of room. Why were we leaving there? Where would we go? When would we go? What would it mean for the school? But Jeghers had no answers. It was obvious that he was as surprised as we were. It was anything but reassuring.

When school resumed in early January we demanded a meeting with the chairman of the board, George Smith. The medical school had now been officially transferred, so he was formally in charge. Again things seemed to move in slow motion, which raised the already high anxiety level. It was another two months before a meeting was scheduled. In early March the faculty finally had a chance to hear Smith's explanations. In front of 120 or 130 anxious doctors and scientists the chairman stood up and delivered a three-minute pep talk. He was proud to be heading the school, he said. We were going to make this the finest medical school, not just in the country, but in the world. Nobody should have the slightest doubt about that. He was as enthusiastic about the prospects as he knew we all were. Now, were there any questions? Almost every hand in the room shot up. Smith looked surprised.

"Question. If we're moving from Jersey City, where are we going to?"

"I'll have to get back to you on that," he said.

"When are we going?"

"We're making those arrangements now."

"Why are we going?"

"I can't describe that briefly."

"Why are we learning about it like this? We're the faculty. Do you think this is the proper way to treat your faculty?"

After the fourth or fifth question, Smith said, "Look, fellows, I told you we're going to take care of things. Everything is going to be just fine. You leave these questions for me and the board to work out. We'll take care of them. You go back to your labs, do your research and teaching. Like I said, everything's going to be fine."

You could feel a chill descend on the room. People were angry and frustrated. They were frightened. They, we, had committed ourselves to this place, and now what? Where were we going to teach? Where were we going to see our patients and do our research? More to the point, it didn't seem as if the chairman or the board of trustees had a clue about how to run a medical school. Were they competent to do it? On the way out people were talking. "I'm sending my CV out." "I'm getting out of here."

I didn't feel quite the same way. Ginger and I were comfortably settled in South Orange. Paul was doing well in school. I had just gotten my lab working the way I wanted it to. The last thing on my agenda was to uproot ourselves and start searching around for something new. I didn't like what was going on, but I wasn't overly worried either. This was rough and unsettling; they were handling it badly, to say the least. But I had no doubt that eventually it would all be worked out. Others might be leaving, but I was far from ready to start looking for another job. At the same time, though, word about the problems had gotten out, and I began receiving calls. Rush Medical College in Chicago called, wanting to know if I might be interested, as did the Medical College of Wisconsin. "Thanks," I said. "But I'm not moving."

Others were though. An exodus of sorts had started. The chief of cardiology announced that he was leaving for Mississippi. The head of rheumatology said he was accepting a position at Jefferson. The head of infectious diseases was going to Georgetown. About a month after the meeting with Smith, news circulated that the school would be moving to the public hospital in Newark, Martland Medical Center, another place that had not had an academic affiliation. But it wasn't clear where my laboratory would be. It seemed there wasn't space at Martland for all the offices and facilities. I wasn't happy about having my research disrupted with some move that was less than well organized. Equally unsettling were the rumors that we were going to Martland as a political payoff to the mayor of Newark. That had the ring of truth to it. There hadn't been any obvious reason to move from Jersey City. The facilities there were commodious; Martland was far less so. My discomfort was growing as I waited to find out what they were going to do about my situation.

In April I was told that the school had found space for me, not in Newark but in the VA Hospital in East Orange. That would be a disadvantage; I wouldn't be near the medical school. On the other hand, East Orange was right next to South Orange. The commute would be a few minutes. Also, the VA had its own funds, so that was a source I'd likely be able to tap into to support my research.

Despite my concerns, I was ready to view the move positively. Then I was taken out to the VA hospital to look at the space they were allocating for me. I'm not sure what I expected, maybe an unused lab that I'd need to refurbish and equip. But when we got there I was shown an abandoned kitchen crammed with old furniture and assorted junk. I looked at that, went back to my office, and sent out my resume. Then I began making calls.

I got back to Rush and to the Medical College of Wisconsin, the schools that had contacted me previously. I also called Bud Emerson, Boston University's chief of hematology, who had been one of my medical school professors. All three places offered me jobs. At that point I probably would have had other opportunities as well. I was bringing my own money with me—the NIH grant—which was a large incentive. I had been at the Thorndike and had Bill Castle's support. Not least, by then medical schools were looking hard for black faculty. As an African American I was, maybe for the first time, a sought-after commodity. It was quite a change from what had happened at Duke only three years earlier.

I chose Boston University. My old professor and role model, Chester Keefer, was now dean of the medical school. Franz Ingelfinger was still chief of gastroenterology. BU's medicine department enjoyed an excellent reputation, and I had great respect for Emerson, the hematology chief. Bob Wilkins, another of my professors, was the new head of medicine; he had won the Lasker Prize a few years previously for his work on hypertension. Going to Boston University was like a homecoming. I felt as if I had dodged a bullet. I had landed safe and sound after an unsettling journey. Ginger and I were also very fond of Boston. In Chicago or Milwaukee we would have had to get to know a new community. Boston we already knew well. Ginger's family was in Massachusetts as well. Going back to Boston was pretty much a no-brainer.

———————

Not long after I moved to Boston we decided to establish a BU hematology service at Boston City Hospital. BU had a medical unit at Boston City, as did Harvard and Tufts, but the BU service didn't include hematology, one of the smaller specialties. The Harvard and Tufts hematology units were actually sufficient to handle the hospital's patient load, but I thought it was important for our students to be able to see hematology patients, especially the anemia cases, which were fairly rare at Mass. Memorial, Boston University's other teaching hospital. My own ongoing research on blood and nutrition also depended on having access to patients. Mass. Memorial was a private hospital; few patients showed up there with nutritional anemias, as opposed to the clientele at Boston City. So I pushed hard for the unit and got backing from Franz Ingelfinger, head of the Boston University service at the hospital, as well from Bud Emerson, my immediate chief.

Once we had decided to establish a service, I needed to find space for my laboratory. Ingelfinger was supportive, but nothing was immediately available. "We'll keep looking," he told me. "Don't worry, we'll find something soon." But I knew the hospital and its culture. Boston City was not a well-organized place. Finding a lab for me might take months. So I started looking around myself, walking the hospital's corridors and peeking into rooms. I finally found a room that was empty and looked about the right size. I didn't ask whose it was or if I could have permission to use it. I simply moved in, set up my equipment, and hired my technicians. Before long I was up and running.

Some months after I did that an official-looking person from the hospital administration came by. "Our roster shows this room as empty," he said. "What are you doing here?"

"Oh," I said. "This is my research laboratory. If you have any questions, please check with Dr. Ingelfinger." And that was the last I heard about it. So I had my lab, but the situation at Boston City was in flux too. Not like Seton Hall but still a bit uncertain. Harvard, Tufts, and Boston University were all running services at the hospital, which meant duplication in many areas, along with extra costs and the competition and bickering that often go on in those kinds of situations. As a result, the hospital was trying to get the three schools to combine their services. But they weren't having much luck with that.

When it was clear that the schools were not going to agree with one another, the hospital asked each of them to submit a proposal to run all the services. The selected school would stay at Boston City Hospital, and the others would be asked to find different homes. I set up my laboratory and offices in 1966. A year later Boston University's bid was chosen. Harvard and Tufts left, the Thorndike moving to Beth Israel Hospital, Tufts to the New England Medical Center. The hematology heads of each of these services, myself, Bill Moloney at Tufts, and Jim Jandl at Harvard (Castle was now retiring), maintained good working relationships. But the BU service was now the only one at the hospital.

I was now teaching at the medical school in the same clinical medicine course Franz Ingelfinger had taught when I was a student. I was seeing patients, conducting the hematology rotations, and continuing my research. Then, in 1970 an opportunity came to broaden our scope. In the run-up to the Richard Nixon–Hubert Humphrey presidential election of 1968, Nixon's polling among African Americans was dismally low. In the course of trying to figure a way to lift his standing, Nixon and his staff hit on the idea of promising to launch a national sickle cell anemia program. Sickle cell disease is a condition in which red blood cells assume abnormal shapes and show other problematic characteristics. The disease occurs throughout the Mediterranean basin—in North Africa, Italy, Turkey, and other places—but it is primarily a problem in people of African descent. Some 10 percent of African Americans either carry the sickle cell trait, most often without exhibiting symptoms, or suffer with the full-blown anemia. So, Nixon's thinking went, the promise of a campaign against the disease should garner support from the black community.

Whether it did or not I don't know, but Nixon did prevail over Humphrey, and he had made the promise, so something had to be done. The problem was, nobody knew what a sickle cell anemia program was. To figure that out, the National Institutes of Health convened a committee of doctors, social workers, and others to think it through and set the parameters for a national program. I was invited to serve on the committee.

The plan we came up with included research, screening, treatment, and education. Most people didn't know much about the disease. They didn't know whether or not they carried the trait. They didn't know what the chances were for children to have the disease if one parent or both carried the trait. They didn't know about the available treatments or the research that was underway. A national program, we thought, should address the spectrum of needs. We recommended that ten centers should be established around the country to provide comprehensive services: screening, counseling, research, treatment, and public education.

When our plan was funded I lost no time in applying to create one of those centers at Boston City Hospital. Although the Harvard and Tufts hematology departments would soon be leaving the hospital, I thought it important to include them in the proposal. A mutual effort would bring additional resources to bear and would further the working relationships I wanted to maintain with my colleagues at those schools. When our application was approved, Jane Desforges at Tufts became our first director, with Harvard's David Nathan and myself as associate directors. In 1973 we rotated and I became director for several years.

Most if not all of the sickle cell clinical work fell to us at Boston City Hospital. We held a sickle cell clinic every week, where we would typically treat ten to fifteen patients. Some of these were adults, but at that time many patients did not live much past their childhood. Sickle cell disease is an anemia that affects the ability of red blood cells to transport oxygen to tissues and organs. What happens is that the sickling phenomenon causes the cells, normally disk shaped, smooth, and flexible, to assume angular or crescent shapes, and the cells' hemoglobin to crystallize. The rigid, jagged cells twist up on one another and can block smaller blood vessels and capillaries, restricting the transfer of oxygen to tissues and building up carbon dioxide waste.

Sickle cell is a truly terrible disease in which children often die from cardiovascular or other organ failure or suffer strokes when blockages happen in the brain. Even in milder cases patients often experience painful episodes caused by occlusions that could be severe and last for hours or days. Some of our patients came in frequently with these crises. Others we might see once or twice a year. Occasionally the disruption of normal red cell functions was so drastic that the bone marrow itself shut down production in what is known as an aplastic crisis.

Harvard's David Nathan, who later became head of the Dana Farber Cancer Center, conducted the bulk of our center's sickle cell research, though to this day no cure has been found. Our unit treated patients with painkillers, IV fluids to help support circulation, or sometimes transfusions that would dilute the sickled cells with normal cells.

When sickle hemoglobin was identified in 1959, our understanding of the disease improved dramatically. Hemoglobin is the protein within the red blood cell that carries oxygen from the lungs to the body's tissues, and it is the crystallization of this protein that causes the cells to distort and harden (Max Perutz and John

Kendrew of Cambridge University won the 1962 Nobel Prize for that discovery). With our center and others, wide-scale screening became possible, along with counseling and more available treatment that over time helped to extend the lives of sickle cell patients so that today people with the disease often live into their forties and fifties.

My position as chief of hematology at Boston City Hospital made me somewhat more visible than I might have been otherwise, and at one point I was contacted by the Charles Drew medical school in Los Angeles. They were looking for a chairman of their medicine department and would like to offer me the position. Would I consider?

Charles Drew had been founded as a postgraduate medical school at the Martin Luther King Hospital in Los Angeles. Drew was not a medical school in the traditional sense, but an institution that developed residency programs in surgery, internal medicine, obstetrics, gynecology, and other fields, the idea being to increase the number of black doctors in the Watts area of Los Angeles, which was essentially a medical desert.

I was interested. Drew, like Seton Hall, was a new venture. It had been established as part of an effort to build a health care infrastructure for the poor, largely black, and woefully underserved neighborhoods in southeastern Los Angeles. When I visited I found myself drawn to what they were trying to do. "They want me to come out again," I told Ginger. "They'd like you to come too."

But Ginger was less attracted. "I'm not going out there," she said.

"Why not? We're not obligating ourselves to anything."

"I am just not going!" she said, in a tone that meant "Don't bother me anymore. That's it."

We had been married then for more than ten years, but this was the first I learned that Ginger was deathly afraid of earthquakes. She was not under any circumstances going to go live in an earthquake zone. A few years later a big quake did strike Los Angeles. Highways ruptured and buildings collapsed, including a VA hospital. Thousands of people were injured and almost a hundred were killed. It was a major disaster. We watched the news reports on television. "Look at that," said Ginger. "See?"

———

Not long after the Drew offer Ginger and I were having dinner with Bud Emerson and his wife Annette at their home. This was a special event, the first time we were invited to my chief's home. We were in the middle of dinner when our son Paul telephoned. The rector of Christ Church had called our house. Martin Luther King had been assassinated. The church was holding a prayer service later that evening.

The four of us stared at one another, numbed. "What an unspeakable tragedy," said Bud.

Ginger looked at me. "We have to go," she said.

We left the Emersons and drove to Christ Church. People were pouring in, and by nine or nine thirty the sanctuary was packed. The church knew King. He had given his first speech against the Vietnam War at Christ Church. Members of the church had filled that huge convoy of buses for the March on Washington, where we had heard King's monumental "I Have a Dream" speech.

Christ Church itself had been actively involved in civil rights efforts for years, and those efforts had a history. Earlier on there had been some conflict in the congregation about how far to back the civil rights movement. Some of the old-line Yankees thought that things were moving too fast, that some prominent people in the movement were troublemakers and rabble rousers. Many of the younger members thought differently.

The congregation at Christ Church was integrated, but there were only ten or so black families. We were, though, an active group. In response to the ferment in the congregation we had formed Blacks in Christ Church to support civil rights activities, and we had succeeded in bringing the church along with us. Even the more conservative old-timers came around. And now the whole congregation was there to mourn for King. People read passages from books, essays, and poems; they prayed. They stood up to voice their grief and their hopes. It was a profoundly moving time. The entire congregation was wrapped in sorrow.

Five days later I flew to Atlanta for King's funeral. Ginger wanted badly to come, but with three young children at home (our third child, Halsted, had been born a year earlier), it just wasn't possible. I didn't go to Ebenezer Baptist Church, where King's father was pastor and where the official funeral was held. The sanctuary there was small and packed with mourners, including many of the powerful and famous. Instead, the Morehouse College family gathered on the school's quadrangle to remember its most revered son, which is where I found myself, along with thousands of others. Alumni had come from all over the country. Students from Morehouse were there together with those from the adjacent Clark College, Spelman, Morris Brown, and Atlanta University. Outsiders filled out the crowd that overflowed the quadrangle, listening as Benjamin Mays delivered the eulogy.

Mays was no longer president then. He had retired the year before and was serving as chairman of the Atlanta public school system board of directors. Hugh Gloster had succeeded him, but Gloster had made way for Mays, who had been King's intellectual and spiritual father, which was how so many of us felt about him.

Mays stood on the steps of Harkness Hall, opposite where his memorial now stands. This was, he told us, "like eulogizing my deceased son, so close and so precious was he to me." "It was my desire," he said, "that if I predeceased Dr. King, he would pay tribute to me on my final day. It was his wish that if he predeceased me, I would deliver the homily at his funeral. Fate has decreed that I eulogize him. I wish it might have been otherwise." Mays closed by evoking King's unfinished work. King's life, he said, would forever serve as an inspiration. (The full text can be found in Mays's book *Disturbed about Man.*)

King's death turned my thoughts away from the work that ordinarily preoccupied me—as I believe it did for many others throughout the country. I began thinking about Boston University, where I had been a student and was now a professor. When I entered the medical school in 1954, I was the only black student in my class, one of three in the school. Now, fourteen years later we had seven. I had been so busy that I really hadn't paid much attention to that. If anything, Boston University had always been proud that it was accepting black students at all when so few other schools were. But seven out of three hundred plus was negligible. Seven out of three hundred plus was a legacy right out of segregation.

At most medical schools black students were rarer than hen's teeth. Outside of Howard and Meharry, in 1968 there were 133 African American medical students in the entire country. I remembered that when I was a resident at New York Hospital, one day I had looked across the ward and seen another African American about my age wearing a white coat and a stethoscope. Curious, I walked over to say hello. The young doctor looked up at me and said, "What in the world are you doing here?" Neither of us had ever had another black person in our peer group. That other young man, a medical student as it turned out, was Alvin Poussaint, who later became an internationally known psychiatrist and long-term professor and associate dean at Harvard Medical School.

I had not had any black fellow medical students during the whole of my training. Nor had I ever had a black professor. At Harvard Medical School there was one African American faculty member, Harold Amos, a surpassingly creative microbiologist who looked on all the black medical and science graduate students in Boston as his personal responsibility and would have been available if I had had any problems. For those few of us at Harvard, Tufts, and Boston University medical schools Amos was a comforting presence, whether or not we ever had occasion to go to him. But he was it, the single one in the great medical city of Boston.

I never spent any time lamenting the fact that we were so few; it seemed, somehow, normal. But given the innate talent pool in America's black community it was in reality unimaginably far from normal. When I had presented my research on alcohol and blood cell production at the 1964 American Society for Clinical Investigation convention in Atlantic City I had looked out from the podium on a sea of biomedical scientists almost four thousand strong—and there was not a single black face among them. Nor as a research scientist and professor at Boston University had I ever had a black colleague until a year or two before King's assassination, when Edgar Smith was appointed in the biochemistry department. Several years after Edgar came on, we were joined by David French, a pediatric surgeon recruited from Howard. But at the time of King's murder there were just Edgar and myself.

I found myself thinking then—not only about the injustice of all this but of the shameful, destructive, and self-destructive waste of talent it represented. Our parents had gotten Walter and me out of Blakely as fast as they could, but I knew youngsters back there, our contemporaries, who were in every way as capable as we were. Given their circumstances and the bigoted, closed-off world they lived in, they had never had a chance. I remembered the story of Jacob's Drugstore on West Hunter Street in Atlanta, at whose lunch counter a black soda jerk had come up with the formula for what was to become Coca Cola. That may possibly have been an urban legend, though most Atlantans were convinced of its truth. But Hamilton Naki, who worked with heart surgeon Christiaan Barnard, was no urban legend, no more than was Vivien Thomas, Alfred Blalock's associate at Johns Hopkins.

Naki was a black South African with a sixth-grade education who during the apartheid period worked in the animal laboratory at the University of Cape Town Department of Medicine. Starting out as a groundskeeper, then an animal caretaker, he learned to administer anesthesia and then proved to be remarkably adept at animal surgery, most especially in experiments involving organ transplant research. Working with Dr. Christiaan Barnard, Naki helped develop the techniques that allowed Barnard to perform the world's first human heart transplant. He was, said the world-famous Barnard, "one of the great researchers of all time in the field of heart transplants." "Technically, he is a better surgeon than I am."

Hamilton Naki's name is not known in the United States. As a black man in South Africa, he was never allowed to actively assist with operations on white patients, but he developed procedures that made the most advanced techniques possible, and he taught a generation of white South African students and doctors.

Vivien Thomas's name is known. The TV movie *Partners of the Heart* and his autobiography of the same title told the story of his partnership with Johns Hopkins's chief of surgery Alfred Blalock, first as his lab technician—with the job title "janitor"—then as Blalock's lab chief, and later as chief of all of Hopkins's surgical laboratories. Together with Blalock, Thomas identified the cause of shock and developed methods for treating it, saving thousands of soldiers' lives in World War II. In 1944 he and Blalock originated the so-called blue baby operation, which made Blalock and pediatric cardiologist Helen Taussig famous. The *Journal of the American Heart Association* article that reported this revolutionary operation made no mention of Thomas, though his participation had been equal to Blalock's in every way.

Thomas was a consummate surgeon himself, and he trained many Hopkins surgery residents who went on to major leadership roles, including Denton Cooley, who performed the first artificial heart implantation. "There wasn't a false move, not a wasted motion when he operated," Cooley said. "Even if you'd never seen surgery before, you could do it because Vivien made it seem so simple." Thomas, the grandson of a Louisiana slave, had never had a chance to go to college.

Back in 1910, when Abraham Flexner completed his national study on medical education standards and curricula, Johns Hopkins became the model for American medical schools. Yet when Vivien Thomas walked its hallways in his white coat, people stopped to stare. Hopkins, like the city of Baltimore, was segregated. No one at the hospital had ever seen a black person on the hospital staff who wasn't either a janitor or some other service person. That was in the forties, in what was still a southern city. Now it was 1968 in Boston, but if you walked the halls of Boston's medical schools and hospitals you would hardly find more black doctors, students, or medical scientists than you would have found in Baltimore back then.

There wasn't much I could do about a world that choked off opportunities for young African Americans. But by then I was a full-time, long-standing member of the BU medical community. I had studied at the medical school, taught there, treated patients at BU's hospital, and run a BU service. I was BU family. I couldn't do much outside the school, but I could certainly speak to the school as an insider. I could at the least try to make some changes in what had become my own home place.

With that in mind I went to talk to Frank Ebaugh, our dean. Ebaugh was a hematologist who had come to BU from Dartmouth. We had known each other for quite a while from various hematology symposia and conferences. "We should be doing better than this," I told him. "It's just not right."

"Lou," he said. "I agree. We should be doing something. What do you have in mind?"

I did have something in mind. Before I went to Ebaugh I had put my head together with Edgar Smith, my one fellow African American on the faculty. Then Edgar and I had talked with three other professors, Richard Morrow, a psychiatrist; Carl Franzblau, a biochemist; and Ephraim Friedman, an ophthalmologist. Together we had come up with a plan. Almost immediately a group of about twelve faculty formed around us to flesh out the idea.

"We want to have a recruitment weekend," I told Ebaugh. "We'd like to bring students from black colleges up here to Boston, show them the school, and encourage them to apply. We'd like to show them who we are and make it clear that they'd be welcome here."

Ebaugh didn't even blink an eye. He was all for it. "That's a great idea," he said. "But we don't have any money. If you could raise some money—and I'll help you with that—we'll do it. "

With Ebaugh's enthusiasm and the energy of our faculty group it didn't take long before we had gathered $40,000 in donations from Boston businesses and foundations. Our plan was to bring twenty-four top candidates to Boston from traditionally black colleges, one from each college. Not only did we want to recruit them, we wanted them to go back to their schools with the news that Boston University was open to qualified black students. We wanted to spread our wings as far as we could.

We all felt very strongly about doing this. What King's death said to us, so powerfully, was that we had to get involved. All of us wanted to carry on his work as best we could. King's life, Mays had said, should be an inspiration, and I don't think it's too much to say that we felt inspired. Edgar Smith had been heavily involved in various efforts to bring more black high school and college students into science, but the rest of us had more or less been spectators before. Now we weren't just looking any longer—we were doing something we could do in a place where we had the influence to do it.

Having been at Morehouse College, I had a pretty good idea of the schools we wanted to include in our search—twenty-four of them, though at this point I can't recall exactly how we came up with that number. We included Florida A&M, Xavier, North Carolina, Talladega, North Carolina A&T, Hampton, Tuskegee, Tougaloo, Fisk, and others. My colleagues hadn't heard of half of these places; of course, most of them hadn't heard of Morehouse either. We put together letters to the deans of students in the institutions we had selected and sent them out. We'd be holding our open house over the Thanksgiving weekend, to give ourselves and the students plenty of time to get to know one another. Soon we had acceptances from each of the invited schools.

Everyone on our committee, and I think most everyone on the faculty, was excited by the prospect of hosting these students. People felt as if we were doing something important, something that would help address a crying historical injustice. But as we geared up for it one of our group said, "Wait a minute. What if all these students are qualified and want to come?"

"Oh my God," somebody else said, which was what we were all suddenly thinking. The medical school took seventy-six students per class. If we recruited all twenty-four, that would be a third of the class. Coming from where they came from, most of these students were bound to need scholarships. But BU didn't have anywhere near those kind of resources. We needed some way around that, and quickly.

What we needed to do, we decided, was to open up the recruitment drive to other medical schools and change the event to something more inclusive—make it a New England event rather than a BU event. That meant getting the other New England medical schools on board. Before the King assassination that probably would have been a quixotic notion. But in the wake of King's death everyone was doing a good deal of soul searching. Some of the other medical schools, in fact, were already thinking about their own lack of black students and how they might remedy that. At Harvard a faculty committee had gotten together under the leadership of chief of psychiatry Leon Eisenberg, and we quickly coordinated with them and with counterparts elsewhere. In the end only Yale declined to participate—they were really more aligned with the New York area schools than those in New England. The University of Connecticut did not join in either, since they were restricted by state law to accepting students from Connecticut. But that still left us with Harvard, Tufts, the University of Vermont, Dartmouth, and Brown, in addition to ourselves.

A side note of interest regarding Harvard is that their faculty debated long and hard about increasing the number of black students. No one, apparently, objected to the idea in the abstract, but the Eisenberg committee recommended accepting fifteen black students a year rather than the traditional two or three, and that caused some consternation. In the end the feuding faculty reached a compromise. Harvard would take fifteen, but the school would also raise the number of overall acceptances by fifteen. At BU there was no such discussion. Dean Ebaugh and the BU faculty went along with our proposal without a single dissenting voice.

That long Thanksgiving weekend turned out to be even better than we hoped. Each school that participated had a number of rooms where they interviewed students, and every student during the course of the weekend "visited" each school. They met faculty from each place and got to understand something about each school's programs and strengths. "I think that the students might have been a little hesitant at first," remembered Edgar Smith. "They were quite forthright in their questions. They mainly wanted to know if we were serious. But when they saw Lou and myself and learned that we had both graduated from historically black colleges, they understood that we were very serious. Then they met the BU faculty and the BU students who were involved, and they saw that everyone was supportive."

We wanted every student who had the interest and ability to get an offer, and in the end all of them did. The following fall the only participating school that didn't have additional black students was the University of Vermont. The black students, of course, were all from the South, and apparently Burlington, Vermont, closely resembled their image of the North Pole. So Vermont was disappointed, most especially Larry McCrory, an African American physiologist who had represented the university in Boston and had been extremely excited about the recruiting prospects. But everyone else, I think, was highly pleased with the results.

———

That was an extraordinary time. Martin Luther King had focused everyone's attention on the profound racial injustice that for so long had sapped the country's strength and poisoned its ideals. His death galvanized people into action, we at the medical school along with so many others in their own spheres of life. It inspired us. In some way, it transformed who we were.

But even with that, and with all the excitement that carried us along, my own long-term goals did not change. In 1968 I was thirty-five years old. I was getting great satisfaction from research and teaching and caring for patients. I was running a hematology unit for a major medical school. I was embarked, looking forward to advancing through the academic ranks and gearing up, I hoped, to someday become chairman of a department of medicine. That was my goal. I thought that would be the crown of my career. My direction was set, and I wasn't expecting any major distractions or surprises along the way.

CHAPTER 6

An Offer

Four years later I almost achieved that goal. I got a call one day from Dr. Marion Mann, who introduced himself as the dean of the Howard University medical school. Howard was looking for a new chairman of medicine. My name had been brought to his attention. Might I be interested in exploring the possibility?

I knew about Howard in general. I had applied to medical school there, though I had never visited, so I hadn't seen the school close up. But Howard had a history. Its hospital, originally established to care for black patients, went back to 1862, prior to emancipation. At one time or another its faculty included legendary black physicians: Alexander Augusta, who served in the Union Army as a surgeon, the first African American to do so; Charles Drew, renowned for his work on blood banking and transfusion; and Montague Cobb, who was still chairman of the anatomy department. Cobb was a distinguished anatomist and physical anthropologist who had authored many books and articles and had led the fight to integrate America's hospitals.

When I went down to Washington, Mann and I hit it off immediately. He was knowledgeable and approachable. He was obviously a good administrator, and he had good personal skills. I was impressed. He was someone I thought I could work well with. I met other faculty too, including Cobb, with whom I got to spend twenty-five or thirty minutes. The more I saw, the more I liked.

I visited Howard twice more, and I finally told Mann that I was quite interested. The salary offer was fine. The school itself even received a special federal subsidy, so it seemed on firm financial grounds. The final thing for me would be to talk to the president, James Cheek, to get his thoughts about the medical school. What was his vision for it?

I needed to meet Cheek, not just to introduce myself, which was important by itself, but also to discuss where I wanted to take the school and to judge the level of support I might have. Medicine is typically the lead department in any medical school; this is still true, but it was even truer then. Medicine is the largest clinical department. It's the basis for the bulk of instruction and patient care. So the chief of medicine ordinarily plays a pivotal role.

I knew that if I took the Howard position I'd want to shake things up. I saw Howard as a solid institution, but a place that was somewhat lethargic, not at the cutting edge in terms of teaching or research, certainly not considered one of the leading medical schools. But I also saw it as a place that had the potential to develop into that kind of leading institution. To get there, though, would mean setting standards of performance. Some faculty would be able to meet new expectations, others would not. I'd be making changes; inevitably I'd be getting push back. If I were backed by the dean and the president I could be effective. If not, I'd most likely be a short-term chairman.

I had raised these issues with Marion Mann, and he was supportive. "I agree," he said, "there's lots of room for improvement. That's exactly what I want." He said he'd arrange for me to meet with the president.

I went back to Boston and waited. And waited. Six weeks went by. I called Marion. "Is there a problem?"

"Oh no," he said. "Sometimes these things just take time."

Another month passed. Still no call. At some point I concluded that this just wasn't for me. Whatever the president was doing, the medical school clearly wasn't high on his priority list. If this is his response while they're trying to recruit me, I thought, imagine what it will be once I've signed up. I wouldn't have access. I wouldn't know if I'd have support. It would be like stepping off into the unknown.

So I withdrew myself as a candidate. I was sure it was the right decision. By now I was a full professor. There was a good chance that somewhere down the line another chairmanship opportunity would come along.

Later that year I got a call from Joe Gayles, a professor of chemistry at Morehouse College. Morehouse, he said, was considering establishing a medical school. They were in the process of putting together an advisory committee of Morehouse alumni in academic medicine to help determine whether such a thing was feasible. They had received a grant for it. A number of other Morehouse alumni were already on the committee. It would be an honor if I might join them. Would I?

That was intriguing. My instant reaction, though, was skepticism. How could a small liberal arts college like Morehouse ever hope to establish a medical school? It sounded like a fantasy. On the other hand, they were asking me, so there was no way I was going to decline. Being a Morehouse alumnus was like being a proud member of a club. The school was a binding force. Maybe the idea didn't make sense up front; I certainly had a host of questions. But if they needed advice about something like this, I would obviously do my best to contribute.

This was an interesting development. As far as black four-year medical schools went, Howard and Meharry were it. They had both been established in the nineteenth century and there had been nothing since. I didn't know offhand the exact statistics on the number of practicing black doctors or the ratio of black doctors to the African American population as a whole, but I did know that the numbers were dismal. I had seen that up close back when I was a child in Blakely, and it hadn't changed all that much since. That's what had motivated me to become a doctor in the first place.

I knew that between them Howard and Meharry graduated more than two hundred MDs a year. Since 1968 more blacks were being admitted to mainline medical schools, including in the South now, but the overall numbers were still abysmal. As far as academic medicine went—African Americans teaching and doing research in medical schools, outside of the Howard and Meharry faculties—I could practically count them on my two hands.

There was a crying need for more African Americans in medicine. Another black medical school would be extremely welcome. But could that possibly be the right thing for Morehouse? Medical schools were expensive, complicated businesses. Medical faculty salaries are higher than other faculty salaries; laboratories are larger and require a different level of funding. At many universities medical schools take up half the budget, so there were always tensions between those schools and other parts of their universities. The idea of a small college like

Morehouse having either the money or the sophistication to establish a successful medical institution sounded unrealistic at best. Benjamin Mays had been a terrific fund-raiser—his nickname at the school had been "Buck Benny." But when he became president, the college had practically been bankrupt. He had put it on a solvent footing, but the school was always strapped for cash. The new president, Hugh Gloster, was also a first-rate money man. But you would have to be an unbridled optimist to think that Morehouse might have the resources to undertake a medical school.

I had seen something about how that worked with much larger institutions than Morehouse. Seton Hall hadn't been able to sustain its medical school back when I was on faculty there, which had precipitated such terrible problems with the state of New Jersey. Before that, when I was a student, BU's medical school had been looking for a different university home. There had been a lot of unhappiness between the medical school and the university, and the medical school dean, James Faulkner, had explored affiliating the school with other institutions. He had approached MIT, Princeton, and Mount Sinai Hospital in New York, among others, but one after another had declined. Some of these potential partners had significant resources, but they weren't interested. Medical schools were highly troublesome affairs.

On the other hand, Morehouse had gotten a grant to do a feasibility study. They were clearly serious, which meant they had already put substantial thought into the idea. And for this advisory committee they had drawn together alumni who had significant experience in academic medicine. David Satcher was on it, an MD, PhD from Case Western who was director of the hypertension service at the Martin Luther King Hospital in Los Angeles (later in his life Satcher was to become surgeon general). Henry Foster, the dean of Meharry, was on it, along with Ezra Davidson, who had been my roommate at Morehouse—Ezra was chairman of ob/gyn at Drew—and Perry Henderson, vice-chair of ob/gyn at the University of Wisconsin. Whatever my skepticism, accomplished people were involved, and the idea of a new black medical school was important for a whole variety of reasons.

When I went down to Atlanta for the first committee meeting, Joe Gayles laid out the history of the concept for us. The idea for a medical school, he said, wasn't actually new at all. The story went back six years to a study done by the Georgia Department of Public Health, which looked at the state's ongoing need for physicians. Georgia, they found, ranked thirty-eighth among the fifty states in physicians per capita. Worse, while African Americans constituted 28 percent of the state's population, only 2 percent of Georgia's doctors were black. There was 1 white doctor for every 795 whites in the state. For Georgia's blacks the number was 1 for every 13,810.

Many parts of the state had no doctors at all. It was no wonder that Georgia's health statistics were deplorable. The incidence of stroke, cancer, heart attack, and diabetes was far higher than the national norms. In almost every category of illness Georgia fared poorly. Moreover, the doctor shortage was, if anything, on a downward trajectory. Every year Georgia's youngsters were going out of state for their medical training—there were far too few places in Georgia's two medical schools, Emory and the Medical College of Georgia—which meant students were much less likely to end up returning home to practice. As a result, the Public Health Commission recommended raising the number of training opportunities within the state. They also recommended that the increase in medical school slots should address the extreme shortage of black physicians. That was part of the background for Morehouse's efforts, Gayles told us; that was what had precipitated events.

The Public Health Commission had been cochaired by Rhodes Haverty, the head of the Georgia chapter of the American Medical Association, and Louis Brown, the head of the state National Medical Association, the AMA's black counterpart. Brown was an internist in Atlanta. The report had convinced him that Georgia desperately needed a black medical school. And the most logical institution to foster that school was Atlanta University.

Atlanta University was the graduate school for the black colleges that were clustered in Atlanta's West End. It had initially been an undergraduate college itself, but back in 1929 a consortium of black colleges had been formed, with Atlanta becoming an exclusively graduate and professional school. My mother had gotten her master's in education at Atlanta when she brought Walter and me to school in the city. As far as Louis Brown was concerned, there absolutely needed to be a black medical school, and Atlanta University needed to be its home.

With that goal firmly fixed in his mind, Brown had presented the idea to Thomas Jarrett, Atlanta University's president. But Jarrett, a former English professor, wasn't taken by the idea. At the regular meeting of the consortium's presidents, they too were unenthusiastic. None of them had had any experience with medical schools, but they all knew that they were huge, costly undertakings, and the idea that Atlanta University could afford such a thing sounded absurd on its surface.

But Louis Brown had an evangelist's zeal for this project. He pressed Jarrett. The shortage of black physicians was acute all around the country, but in Georgia especially. And all we had were Howard and Meharry. What other black school in the country had the academic base that could serve to develop a medical school? None! Atlanta University had to consider it.

Tom Jarrett thought the idea was irrational; he believed such a thing might destroy the university. But he was under pressure from Brown and from other black physicians, and Brown was the Georgia NMA president. So he buckled. He received a grant from the Josiah Macy Foundation to do a feasibility study. He brought in John A. D. Cooper, the president of the Association of American Medical Colleges, to chair the study and matched him with Howard Kenney, deputy chief medical officer of the Veterans Administration, as vice-chair; Cooper was white, Kenney black. He sought advice from major medical schools, including Stanford, Dartmouth, and Emory, and he commissioned a team of outside consultants to conduct the research.

When the process was completed, the consultants and the outside medical schools all agreed that despite the need, Atlanta University simply did not have the resources to pursue the idea. They were concerned about the academic strength of the university, the financial picture, and the administrative leadership. They noted the lack of enthusiasm. They recommended against it, to Jarrett's great relief, no doubt. It was even rumored that he had rigged the committee to draw that conclusion.

The feasibility study report was presented to the Atlanta University trustees in April 1971. The presidents of Spelman and Morehouse were at the meeting as well; the original consortium merger had guaranteed them seats at the table. After discussion a vote was taken. The trustees found the report convincing. They voted unanimously against moving ahead with the idea.

After the vote, Hugh Gloster stood up, walked to the front of the room, and said, "Now that you've voted, let me ask if the trustees would have any objection if Morehouse looked into this question ourselves. We've followed the issue closely, and we have an interest here."

The Atlanta University trustees sat there, nonplussed. They had just heard all the reasons Atlanta University shouldn't involve itself. And now Morehouse wanted to? Bill Bennett, an official of the National Institutes of Health's Bureau of Health Manpower, was also in the room. The bureau was responsible for advising on the creation of new medical schools, and Bennett, an African American, had taken a personal interest in this discussion. As he said later, he was relieved by the report's conclusion and the trustees' vote. He didn't believe Atlanta University was in a position to develop a medical school either. When Gloster stood up and said what he said, Bennett thought, this man must be nuts. Whatever the trustees might have thought, none of them said a word. If Gloster wanted to pursue this, it was Gloster's business. Maybe they couldn't believe it, but they had no objections.

That was the recent history of the medical school idea, and the origin of Morehouse's efforts. But the idea had a deeper history too. Morehouse and other black colleges had been founded during Reconstruction, often by white benefactors. Morehouse had been started by northern Baptists; its first three presidents were white. John Hope was the fourth president, the first African American.

Hope was the one who in 1929 had championed the idea that Atlanta's black schools should form a consortium. But earlier he had proposed that the five colleges—Morehouse, Spelman, Morris Brown, Clark, and Atlanta—should merge into one institution. Given the aggregate resources, Hope believed they could form one strong university rather than five struggling colleges, a university incorporating undergraduate and graduate programs and professional schools, including a school of medicine.

Despite his failure to get the schools to agree to a merger, in the 1920s Hope recruited Dr. Marque Jackson, a Morehouse graduate who had gone to the Chicago Medical School and was practicing in Chicago. He asked Jackson to work toward developing a medical school. Jackson did, but then in 1929 the Depression hit and Hope told Jackson that they'd have to put the idea on hold for a while; they would come back to it later. But in 1933 with the Depression deepening, Hope died, and with his death the idea was shelved. Now Hugh Gloster, Hope's successor forty years on, was reviving it.

Tom Jarrett's blue ribbon committee had said the idea wasn't feasible for Atlanta University. And if it was impossible for the university, what business did a small liberal arts college have with it? But Gloster had his reasons. In the first place, Morehouse was extremely successful with its premed program. In terms of sending black students to medical school, Morehouse ranked number one in the nation. One reason for this was the strength of its science departments. Morehouse boasted people such as Henry McBay in chemistry, Claude Dansby in mathematics, and Sam Nabrit, my old comparative anatomy professor who was a leading marine biologist.

Beyond that, Morehouse had an ambitious, energetic institutional culture. Benjamin Mays had been a visionary, inspiring leader. You could hardly exaggerate the imprint he had left. We could do anything, he told us. The tragedy of life was not failing to reach our goals; it was not having goals to reach. That was an attitude that stamped itself on the students and carried over to the institution. Morehouse had an outsized vision of its role and its capabilities, so marked that others on occasion might have even felt there was a touch of arrogance to it. But that was its ethos, and Hugh Gloster shared in that ethos fully. He was himself an energetic man, brimming over with ideas and optimism. He felt in his heart that this was something Morehouse could do.

As I got to know Gloster over the years, it seemed to me that there were other elements too behind his decision to strike out toward such a distant shore. Gloster had come in after Mays, the man who embodied the institution. And though Gloster was highly competent, he inevitably found himself working in Mays's shadow. Gloster chafed at that. I think he saw it as a challenge. He was at his core an intensely competitive individual. A robust fund-raiser, he had improved the campus with new buildings and facilities. People said, and he heard them, that Mays built men and Gloster built buildings. I think he took that as derogatory, the idea that Mays was able to shape character (Martin Luther King was his student), while he himself could only put bricks and mortar together. I think he saw Mays's legacy as something he needed to break free of. And here was a project, the creation of a medical school, that Atlanta University and a high-level committee considered unattainable. I think that fed into his willingness to take this task on. It was a challenge that engaged his ambitious, competitive nature—and one that was driven by the very real, even urgent need to produce more black doctors for a desperately underserved people.

There was another element in Gloster's background too, that very few people knew about. I myself only learned about it from his wife, Yvonne, many, many years later. Gloster had a much-older brother who had fought in World War I and had been wounded. This brother had not gotten the treatment he needed, assumedly because he was black. Later the brother had become a doctor himself at the va hospital in Tuskegee, which was located very near the Tuskegee Institute. "Hugh talked a lot about his brother's experience," Yvonne Gloster told me. "I think something about his brother having been a physician became part of Hugh. And when the idea of a medical school came up, I think he had feelings about when his brother was hurt and the kind of care he should have received but didn't. I believe all of that played a part in his willingness to go into it."

Wherever his motivation came from, Gloster had taken the idea to heart, and he had been preparing his campaign quietly but carefully. He had discussed it with a small group of his faculty, people he thought would be responsive. He had found an especially close ally in Calvin Brown, a local doctor who was vice-chairman of the Morehouse board. Gloster was reading the tea leaves too. He understood Tom Jarrett's antipathy toward the idea, and he might well have anticipated the outcome of the feasibility study and the Atlanta University trustees' vote. He had also been talking with Bill Bennett, the Bureau of Health Manpower official who was so taken aback when Gloster announced Morehouse's intentions and asked for the Atlanta trustees' go-ahead. Bennett had openly shared his thoughts about a medical school, although at the time he had no idea that Gloster was planning to pursue this himself.

Gloster had even raised money to do his own feasibility study, and once he was launched he submitted a grant request to the NIH Bureau of Health Manpower for $800,000 in planning money. The committee I was part of wasn't really exploratory in the sense that I initially assumed. When we came aboard there was already great enthusiasm within the Morehouse leadership. We were there to act as a kind of double check, academic medicine people who might identify obstacles others hadn't seen and who could lay down guidelines for how a medical school actually functioned and what sort of resources would have to be brought to bear. How would faculty need to be developed, both clinical and research faculty? What kind of hospital affiliation would be needed? What role would research play? Where would scholarship money come from? What size student body would make the most sense? What kind of administrative organization should there be? These were the sorts of questions we took up over the course of almost a year.

I had known some of the people on our committee before. The others I got to know through our work together. But whether we had known one another previously or not, we were all Morehouse men. Getting our group of alums together served a purpose beyond providing expertise. However enthusiastic Gloster and a core of his faculty and trustees were, the idea still generated a lot of skepticism. The thought of Morehouse College undertaking a medical school just seemed at first glance so off the charts. Gloster knew that if he was going to get the support he needed, he had to win over the alumni. And if we, alumni with deep experience in academic medicine, supported the project, that would not just weigh heavily with unconvinced trustees and faculty but would also address the credibility concerns that alumni in general were going to have. Having us endorse the idea meant other alums were likely to get on board with it. It would get people fired up for fund-raising and recruiting.

During the course of that year, I found my initial skepticism diminishing and my enthusiasm growing. The deeper our committee went into it, the more a confluence of factors seemed to be favoring the project. Rhodes Haverty, who had cochaired the state manpower study, was solidly behind the Morehouse endeavor. Haverty, the dean of allied health at Georgia State University, was widely connected and widely influential. As chairman of Georgia's AMA chapter, he was in a sense the spokesperson for the state's white physicians. His counterpart at the African American NMA, Louis Brown, was the original cheerleader for a black medical school. The AMA had historically prohibited black doctors from joining and had thrown up barriers to their professional lives. And here the state's white and black docs were working together for this.

Along the same lines Arthur Richardson, the dean of Emory's School of Medicine, was throwing his weight behind the idea. Emory was still practically all white, but in these postsegregation, post–Martin Luther King times, Richardson and his colleagues saw an opportunity—and felt a sense of obligation—to help build black medical capability. In the Atlanta health care world, nothing was more essential than Emory's cooperation. NIH's Bill Bennett was fully invested too. He had worried over the Atlanta University idea, but Gloster had completely won him over, and he had become a central cog in the planning. It was Bennett who had brought in the $800,000 start-up grant.

Then again, an NIH Bureau of Health Manpower report had projected a major shortfall of doctors and recommended that schools should increase their capacity. In the 1960s many new schools had come on line. Federal dollars were still available. The environment was still conducive. I was beginning to feel that this was a unique opportunity. New schools were springing up, and here we had the chance to carve out space for a new predominantly black school, the first in a century—at Morehouse, my alma mater, which was giving me a special sense of excitement and pride. The longer we worked, the more personally committed I was to getting the Morehouse medical idea off the ground. I was feeling something like what Gloster must have been feeling, and probably the rest of the committee as well. Morehouse being Morehouse, why couldn't we accomplish this?

By the late spring of 1974, with the whole committee on board, Joe Gayles told us the time had come to think about whom we might try to recruit as the first dean. Would we please, he asked, think through that question and engage our networks in the process? "Send us the names of the prospects you believe might fit that role," he said. "Give us a list."

There weren't many blacks in academic medicine, and I knew most of them. I went through my list, doing my best to assess their strengths and weaknesses. I finally came up with eleven people I thought were capable of undertaking a challenge like this, and I forwarded their names to Gayles.

Two weeks later he called me. "Lou, we very much appreciate your sending your list down. But, frankly, we were disappointed to find that it wasn't complete."

"What are you talking about?" I said. "Who do you think I've left out?"

We talked for a bit before I picked up what he was hinting at. "Wait a minute," I said. "You're not talking about me, I hope. I'm not interested. I'm not a candidate."

"Well, Lou. We were at least hoping you would be on the list. But I understand. If you're not interested, you're not interested. Anyway, we were wondering if— not as a candidate but simply as a consultant—would you be willing to come and talk to our committee? We're going to be meeting in New York, so it won't mean coming all the way to Atlanta. Before we go any further, we'd like your personal assessment of whether we should actually move forward. We've still got questions about that, and about what the school should look like if we do go ahead with it."

"Okay, Joe," I said. "I'm certainly willing to talk. But let's be extremely clear. I am not a candidate. I'm a hematologist. I'm happy with that, and I'm not going to change it. But I'll be pleased to come down and go over things with you." I meant that. I was doing what I considered important work, with my research, my students, my patients. I couldn't have been happier with the way my career was going. I felt I had really hit my stride. I should have noticed I was stepping on a banana peel.

It was mid-September 1974 when I went down to New York for this meeting. Ginger and I drove down on the Merritt Parkway, the early fall foliage already touched with color. I was going to have lunch with the Morehouse committee; Ginger would go off to visit friends. The meeting was at twelve, a luncheon meeting in a private room at the New York Hilton. How long could it take, I thought, probably an hour and a half, two at the most. We arranged for Ginger to come back and pick me up at two thirty. Then we'd drive back through the beautiful New England countryside.

It was a small committee, only eight people. Joe Gayles had been the point man for much of the planning. He greeted me and I shook hands with Hugh Gloster; Pierre Galletti, vice president for biology and medicine at Brown; Arthur Richardson, dean of the Emory School of Medicine; Bill Bennett of the NIH; Ed Mazique, a physician from Washington, D.C., who was on Morehouse's board; Calvin Brown, vice-chairman of the board; and Alfonso Overstreet, the board's alumni representative. I had met Gloster briefly before, and I knew Joe and Bill Bennett from my work on the advisory committee, but the others were new faces to me.

We talked. They asked questions about the obstacles they felt would be ahead and about the ideas that had been floated to deal with the challenges and shape the school. Some of the ideas made great sense; we had been discussing many of these issues on our academic alumni committee. Others I thought were unworkable, and we discussed why. I was pleased I had been asked to explore these matters, and I didn't hold anything back. I was in favor of this project, but I still had reservations, and I welcomed the chance to get these out on the table. They asked what qualities I thought they should be looking for in someone to head the school. I answered that it should be someone capable of fund-raising, managing the interface between the college and the medical school, handling accreditation, building a faculty, and providing a vision for the school's future.

We were still lost in these discussions when the phone rang. Ginger was on. It was two thirty; she was ready to pick me up. I didn't know where the time had gone. "This is taking a little longer than I expected," I told her. "Could you come back in an hour?"

Three thirty came. The phone rang.

"Give me another thirty minutes," I said.

Just before four it seemed we were about ready to wrap it up. We had been sitting there for four hours. At the end Gloster took the floor, the president of the college. "Brother Sullivan," he said (the alumni were always addressed as "brother"). "Brother Sullivan, first I want to thank you for coming down. This has been an extremely helpful, clarifying discussion. Now, I know you came down here as a consultant, not as a candidate. And I can't speak for the committee, but I do want to tell you that in my mind, you are just the person we're looking for. I know you didn't come as a candidate, but I would ask if you might think about this while you drive back to Boston. I believe you could give us exactly the leadership we need to start us off on the right track. I'm sure you'll do us the favor of giving it your most serious consideration."

Ginger and I drove back up the Merritt Parkway in silence. I loved the New England fall colors, so much more vivid than in southern Georgia, where it's mostly pines, and in northern Georgia, where the deciduous leaves turn shades of brown before they fall off. It was a fascinating botanical phenomenon, and every autumn Ginger and I enjoyed taking foliage tours.

Ginger didn't ask, but the expectation was building. I was going to have to say something.

"Well," she said, finally. "Aren't you going to tell me what happened?"

"Do you think," I said, "that you could consider the possibility of living in Atlanta?"

She looked at me. "I knew it," she said. "I just knew it."

<hr/>

Gloster had asked me if I would consider it, and I asked Ginger if she would. We talked it over. It would mean uprooting the children; it would mean uprooting ourselves. Ginger was a native New Englander. I was at least an honorary one. We went skiing in Vermont. We visited Tanglewood for the Boston Symphony's summer concerts. We took our vacations on Martha's Vineyard. I had learned to sail and went out on the Charles River and along the Boston coastline as often as I could. I had left Georgia behind twenty years ago.

If I did this I would be exchanging my life as a clinician and researcher for one as an administrator. Was that something I really wanted to do? Hematology was poised to make significant advances, driven by new technologies that allowed for automated analyses of blood cells. I was making serious progress in basic research on nutritional anemias and on understanding blood marrow as a dynamic organ, and I wasn't getting tired of the work. On the contrary, it was more and more interesting. I had NIH grants. I was training hematology fellows. Why would I want to leave all that for something I'd had no real experience of and didn't even know if I could do?

I had serious conversations with a number of people whose judgment I trusted. Their advice varied. "Are you crazy?" said one of my BU colleagues. "Why would you do something like this?"

"Lou," said another. "This is a high-risk venture. It could easily go flop. You've got a great career path. You don't want to spoil it."

I talked at length with Pierre Galletti, who had been head of physiology at Emory, then had helped found Brown's school of medicine. He was a world leader in bioengineering as well as a distinguished figure in medical education. He had been in that meeting in New York, which I realized after the fact had been arranged more so that the committee could get a good look at me than for anything else. Pierre's advice was measured; he had been a groundbreaking researcher who had gone into administration and medical education, so he had seen the issue from both sides. I'd be taking a risk, he said, no doubt about that. But in his experience it was a risk worth taking. This was an exceptional opportunity.

I went to see Lamar Soutter, the founding dean of the University of Massachusetts Medical School in Worcester. Lamar had been my dean when I graduated from BU. "Of course nobody can tell you what to do," he said, "but I think you ought to take it." Then came a bit of advice about the travails of dean-ship. "If you do decide to go, get used to the fact that people are going to try to steal your faculty. The only thing worse is if they *don't* try to steal them." He saw more humor in that than I did, though I appreciated it better later on.

Herb Mescon was chief of dermatology at BU, a good friend. He seemed to have intuited what direction I was leaning toward. "It's a bad idea," he said. "But you may have already decided to do it. But if you do, don't resign. Take a leave of absence for a couple of years. Don't cut your ties." That didn't sound exactly right. If I did do it I didn't think it should be on a contingency basis. If I did do it, I'd go all in.

I thought about it. As chief of hematology at Boston City Hospital, I found that in spite of my desire to devote myself to research and teaching, I was spend-ing almost 25 percent of my time in administration: overseeing the blood-bank budget, hiring technicians, improving the on-call schedule, attending committee meetings, and so on, run of the mill, less than thrilling activities. I began thinking, you know, if you're going to have to be in administration anyway, you might as well be in something exciting. Developing policy, shaping an institution, leading an institution—that would be exciting. That would be a worthwhile challenge.

I made as honest an assessment as I was capable of. The research I was doing was important. But it wasn't going to get the Nobel Prize. A lot of other people in the field, very good people, were doing similar work. If I dropped out, I wasn't going to be missed in any significant way. But starting a medical school was major. If I could succeed at that, I'd be making a contribution far beyond the contribution I might make as a hematologist pushing vitamin B_{12} across cell membranes.

Not least, Morehouse was my alma mater. I couldn't imagine I'd want to make this 180-degree turn in my life for some other school. And Atlanta was really the black mecca in terms of leadership, in terms of business, politics, civil rights activities, and education. I loved Boston, but Atlanta exerted a strong pull.

If I came in as dean there would be a unique concentration of circumstances around me. I knew the city; I had been born there and had spent many of my growing-up years there. I was more or less a native son. I had graduated Morehouse twenty years before, but some of the same faculty were still at the school, my old teachers. They would be emotionally invested in my doing well. There were those among the trustees and alumni who still weren't sure of the wisdom of this idea, but as a graduate myself I'd be at a major advantage in bringing them around.

Most important of all, if I could make this work I'd be making as major a contribution as I was capable of to improving the health and lives of African Americans. I had started my own medical training thinking that I would come back to Georgia and practice among people who needed medical care so badly and did not have it, exactly as my childhood idol Dr. Griffin did. Along the way I had gotten sidetracked, seduced by the attractions of science and teaching and a specialized knowledge of healing. In a sense this was my second chance, an opportunity to fulfill that young person's aspiration, but now on a vastly larger scale. Morehouse School of Medicine, if it was successful, would be training whole cohorts of doctors, many of whom would apply themselves to just the kind of practice that I had envisioned. If the school was successful it would be doing that not just for a generation, but for a hundred years, or two hundred, or more.

I thought, maybe this is grandiose thinking. Maybe I'm just believing my own ads. One thing was for sure, if I did do it I wouldn't be able to turn back. Once I was out of science for a couple of years, it would be almost impossible to get back in. The field would have left me behind. But this was something I wanted to try. I'd enjoy the challenge of it. Knowing myself, I'd be completely driven to make it work. But could I actually do it? Did I know medical education well enough? Did I have the leadership skills to recruit a faculty and mold an institution? I appreciated Hugh Gloster's confidence. I wasn't quite as sure myself, but how could I turn down the chance to find out?

CHAPTER 7

Founding Dean

"Dr. Sullivan, welcome to Atlanta." The man holding out his hand was Boisfueillet Jones, head of the Woodruff Foundation, named for Bob Woodruff, the Coca Cola magnate who had endowed it. Hugh Gloster was introducing me to Atlanta's business and philanthropical world, and this was our first stop. Woodruff was the largest foundation in the Southeast.

The Woodruff Foundation did all its giving in Georgia and nearby states. Other local foundations were around, but Woodruff set the tone. Gloster had emphasized the absolute necessity of getting them on board. "If you don't get support from Woodruff," he had told me, "you're dead in the water. They're the leader. You go to the Campbell Foundation, the first thing they ask is, what has Woodruff given you? If you say, 'We haven't heard from them yet' or 'They're not funding us now,' you'll hear, 'Well, let us know when they do give to you. Come back then and we'll talk.'"

Woodruff gave to Morehouse College and the other Atlanta University Center schools. Health issues were a major concern of theirs. There was every reason to be optimistic that they'd be generous with a new medical school. It was September 1975, and I was just starting as dean. Funding was at the top of my agenda.

This was my first time talking with a potential donor, and I wasn't comfortable. I had never really been in this situation before. It was awkward. I hoped I wasn't showing it, but inside I was feeling embarrassed. Boisfueillet Jones was an old-school, white southern gentleman, and here I was getting my courage up to beg money from him.

But my embarrassment, as it turned out, wasn't necessary. "Welcome to Atlanta," Jones said. "We're glad to have you here. I really wish you well in the development of this new school. But I have to tell you in all candor that you cannot look to us for support. We have one medical school that we're committed to funding"—he was talking about Emory; Bob Woodruff was an alumnus and munificent supporter. "We're supporting one medical school, and that's extremely expensive. We just don't have the resources for another one. I hate to disappoint you, but I think the best thing I can do is be honest with you."

So, nothing from Woodruff. We had $800,000 in planning and start-up funds from NIH, a bare-bones amount. Penn State was just now opening its own medical school; a friend of mine had been named founding dean. The Hershey Foundation had given them an initial grant of $30 million. Eight hundred thousand was not going to take us very far.

I was concerned. Funding was lifeblood, and I knew I had to learn how to do it effectively. Hugh Gloster was more than concerned. The medical school was his baby, important to him beyond measure. And despite all the preliminary discussions about cost, when it came down to it, he just wasn't prepared. He was extremely nervous, even frightened, about finances. I had already had my own experience with him on this score. I had agreed to come on in the fall of 1974, but it had taken us the better part of a year to negotiate a contract. As a professor at BU I had been making $45,000 a year. He had offered me $40,000. "That's the top salary at the college," he said. "I can't go above that."

"This isn't a college," I told him. "It's a medical school." It had gone dead against his nature to come around to the $43,000 we eventually agreed on. The encounter with Woodruff was disconcerting. Then there was the meeting with the Atlanta University trustees. This was a special meeting of the trustees' executive committee, called to discuss whether Morehouse even had the right to launch a medical school. Gloster filled me in on the background. "They're going to question whether we're in violation of the affiliation bylaws of the University Center," he said. "Back in 1929 when the schools formed the consortium, Morehouse and the others agreed that Atlanta University would become the graduate institution, which includes professional schools. Grace Hamilton thinks the medical school puts us in violation. She'd like to close us down before we get started."

Grace Hamilton was vice-chairman of the Atlanta University trustees. She was also a state legislator and a stalwart on the board of Atlanta's big Grady Hospital. Hamilton was a pioneering black woman in Georgia, a real powerhouse. I hadn't been in Georgia for twenty years, though, and I had never heard of her. It was also the first I had heard that we might be in violation of the affiliation bylaws. One of my BU colleagues had said, "Lou, this is a high-risk venture." Maybe I hadn't given that warning enough credence.

As Gloster explained it, the context for this challenge was highly personal. He and Grace Hamilton had a history. Not only that, Hamilton had a history with Morehouse College itself that went back long before Gloster's time. All too obviously I was about to plunge headfirst toward the dangerous shoals of events and relationships that hadn't anything to do with me but were going to impact me and what I needed to do regardless. Forewarned is forearmed, but I hadn't been forewarned.

"It goes back to 1929," Gloster said. "When John Hope pushed for the schools here to form a consortium, many of the Atlanta University alumni got upset. Hope wanted to close down Atlanta as a college and make it into a graduate institution for the other schools, which is what happened. Many of the Atlanta alumni believed he had taken their school away from them. Angry doesn't begin to describe how they felt. And Hope, of course, was Morehouse's president. So, Morehouse had destroyed Atlanta, if you wanted to look at it that way. That was a lasting resentment. For some of them it still is, including Grace. She's one of those 'old Atlanta' alumnae. She doesn't have good feelings towards Morehouse."

There was more. Hamilton's husband had been the longtime registrar at Morehouse. I remembered him well from the time I was a student, "Cookie" Hamilton, though I couldn't recall his real first name. He was a fixture. Gloster had succeeded Mays as president in 1967, thirteen years after I graduated. As he explained it, by then Cookie Hamilton had become feeble, a fragile old man who just was not functioning any longer. Gloster had tried to get him to retire, but he had refused. Eventually Gloster had to terminate him. After that, not only did Grace Hamilton hold a grudge against Morehouse, now she had a grudge against Gloster too. The medical school was Gloster's project. She was against him, and she was against it. Hence this emergency trustees meeting.

I found this history fascinating, and more than a little incestuous: Grace Hamilton harboring a long-term grudge while her husband was an administrator at the school she felt had injured her. I knew what John Hope had done back in 1929. He had a vision that went beyond his leadership at Morehouse, and he had the stature and determination to make his vision a reality—even if he hadn't succeeded in getting the other presidents to buy into his original idea of merging all the schools into one. I also knew that when the schools did affiliate into a consortium, Atlanta University's president had resigned in anger—he had opposed the concept—and Hope had taken over as president of Atlanta as well as Morehouse. For two years he had worn both hats. Then he recruited Samuel Archer to succeed him as president of Morehouse, so he could concentrate on building Atlanta as a graduate institution, which hadn't gone over well with the Morehouse alumni. They felt as if Atlanta University had taken their president from them. I knew that—it was part of Morehouse historical lore. But I hadn't thought much, or at all, about how Atlanta's loyal alumni must have felt, which apparently some still did, forty-five years later.

Gloster took me with him to the trustees meeting, together with Thomas Kilgore, chairman of his board of trustees. Grace Hamilton was there, not smiling—nor were any of the others sitting around the big table. There was no way of missing the tension. The chairman called the meeting to order. "The question we are posing today," he said to Gloster, "is, what is Morehouse College's intention in announcing the development of this medical education program? This is in clear violation of the affiliation bylaws."

Gloster was not the man to go into a meeting like this unprepared. "The Morehouse medical program is not in violation," he said. He had a copy of the articles of affiliation with him. "Morehouse only undertook this project after the Atlanta University trustees decided it wasn't feasible and that they had no intention of going forward. I asked you that question in 1971, four years ago, and on the basis of that answer, from your trustees, we proceeded. In addition, Morehouse College does not intend to permanently operate a medical school. Our immediate goal is to launch a medical education program, but in time it will become an independent school.

"We can't say yet how this will eventually look. There are several options. One is that the medical school will become wholly independent and have no formal ties to Morehouse or to the Atlanta University Center. Another is that the medical school might become a separate institution within the Atlanta University Center.

Third, it could affiliate with Atlanta University as a professional school of the university. Those are all possibilities. But our first task is to develop a viable medical education program. That is what we are doing now, and Dean Sullivan is leading this effort. But again, we have undertaken these efforts with the full permission of this board, which I am sure you will find recorded in your minutes."

That couldn't have been unexpected. I didn't know exactly, but I was pretty sure that many if not most of the trustees sitting around the table had been on the board when the university voted no to the project. Not only that, but Tom Jarrett, who had been against the medical school project from the beginning, was still Atlanta's president. He was sitting right there. They all knew. The only conclusion to draw was that Grace Hamilton had pushed hard for this meeting, and she was not a person anyone wanted to get on the wrong side of. So they had called the meeting and put the question on the table.

"That's right," said one trustee after Gloster had made his presentation. "Dr. Gloster's account is accurate. Atlanta University took a pass. The trustees were asked to vote on the medical school idea, and we took a pass."

"Yes," said the chairman. "Thank you. Is there further discussion?"

There was, almost all of it from Grace Hamilton. Her questions were sharp and persistent. The trustees' vote in 1971 was not formal. Regardless of the sense of that meeting, Morehouse was still in violation. But no one followed up on her line of argument, and when that petered out the chairman said, "All right. The executive committee will take the results of this inquiry under advisement and present the question to the full board." He looked at Gloster. "Thank you, President Gloster," he said. "You will hear from the board shortly." Several days later we did hear. The trustees' answer was ambiguous. We were not in violation of the articles of affiliation, they concluded. We could move ahead, but the university reserved its right to operate a medical program if they wished.

"The only thing that's important," Gloster told me, "is that we're not in violation. They have no interest in a medical school." And in fact that was the last either of us ever heard about a desire on Atlanta University's part to exercise any kind of oversight. All this was a bit unsettling, Woodruff's response, then this trustees meeting. But I also understood that maybe I shouldn't be surprised by such things. The fact was that I was simply not educated yet about the lay of the land here. I could hardly expect to show up after two decades in New England and suddenly find everyone in sight bending over backward to make things as easy for me as possible.

But these two incidents weren't my only surprises. Another was Calvin Brown, the vice-chairman of Gloster's board. He had been enthusiastic about the medical school idea from the beginning; he was one of Gloster's original kitchen cabinet of coconspirators. In addition, he and Gloster were close, card-playing friends. I considered Calvin a friend as well. He had graduated Morehouse two years before me and we were in the same fraternity. We knew each other fairly well, going back to high school. He was one of the people I was looking to for advice and support.

For some reason, though, Calvin seemed lukewarm when I talked to him about the school, more than a little distant. It seemed strange, but I interpreted it as his desire to give me frank, unvarnished advice. It wasn't till later that I learned that Calvin had thought that Gloster would come to him to lead the school. It was a disappointment that Gloster hadn't, especially in regard of the warm friendship they shared. In a way, I thought, not going to Calvin was an indication of Gloster's hard-nosed seriousness about making the medical school a success. Calvin was a good doctor with a successful family practice, but he had never been in academic medicine. I was sure Gloster knew he would be hurting Calvin's feelings in passing him by, but he understood that whomever he chose, it needed to be someone with experience on the academic side.

The fact was, though, that I had very little time to mull over my lack of understanding of the personal or institutional histories, as important as they could be. The task in front of us was immense. Before we could bring in our first class of students, we needed to be provisionally accredited by the LCME, the Liaison Committee on Medical Education, and the LCME's requirements were extensive and challenging.

The LCME was the agency that evaluated and made accreditation decisions about all U.S. and Canadian medical schools. For newly established programs, the LCME would examine the proposed curriculum, the faculty credentials, the adequacy of the facilities, the strength of the administration, and the financial soundness, as well as the mission the school set for itself and the viability of its plans to realize its mission. All these and other institutional requisites had to pass muster before the agency would accredit, and accreditation was necessary before we could accept students. Ordinarily provisional accreditation could take four or five years. We needed to get that accomplished as quickly as possible; our shoestring start-up funding was not going to allow us much leeway.

The first order of business was to set up our offices. We were part of Morehouse College, technically "the medical education program" of the college, but

Morehouse didn't have much if anything in the way of extra space. Joe Gayles had solved that before I arrived by bringing in two extrawide trailers and setting them down on the quadrangle between classroom buildings. It didn't look pretty, but it was a start.

As soon as I was settled in I got to work recruiting. I needed faculty, administrators, staff. As part of the college, the medical program operated under the jurisdiction of Morehouse's trustees, but I needed my own board of overseers who could advise me on medical matters and provide support and contacts. To head this board I went to Edgar Smith, my old colleague and friend who had worked with me when we invited those twenty-four black students up to Boston in 1968. Ephraim Friedman also joined, another good friend from BU who had worked on that project with us. Eph had been dean at BU but had recently taken over as head of Albert Einstein in New York.

I also approached Georgia's two senators, Sam Nunn and Herman Talmadge. Their board affiliation would give us political clout and credibility in and beyond Georgia. Both agreed to come on. Nunn was one of the Senate's top defense experts. For a southern senator he was relatively progressive when it came to social and especially racial issues, but Talmadge was a different story.

Talmadge's father, Eugene Talmadge, had been one of the old South's most notorious racist politicians. As a three-term governor of Georgia he had fought hard to "keep blacks in their place," as he put it. Herman had followed in his father's footsteps. In 1964 he and other southern senators boycotted the Democratic National Convention in protest over Lyndon Johnson signing the civil rights laws. But once the racial barriers to voting came down, Talmadge changed his tune. When that happened he and other Georgia politicians needed to establish their credentials with the black electorate. Supporting the Morehouse medical program gave Talmadge an opportunity. Who couldn't agree with the idea of improving health care and increasing the number of primary doctors? So he joined our board along with Nunn. I thought more than once that our medical school was coming along at just the right time. An unprecedented shift in race relations was going on that worked to our benefit in a hundred ways. There could hardly have been a more visible sign of it than Georgia's two white senators sitting on our board.

The first faculty member to sign on was Jim Story, a biologist from Northwestern University medical school. Joe Gayles had found Story. Joe had organized a lot of the planning work for Gloster; among other things, he had taken the lead in recruiting me. Now he was out looking for potential faculty, along with another Morehouse professor, Tom Norris, and Alice Green, who headed Morehouse's development office. Jim Story, out at Northwestern, looked to them like a good possibility. Story was a Morehouse alum with a strong loyalty to the school, someone who had made good in the world of academics and science. He had gotten his doctorate at Indiana and had worked for Abbott Laboratories before joining the Northwestern faculty.

Story was a likely candidate, and the pool of potential black faculty wasn't huge. Not that I wanted an all-black faculty, even if that had been possible. Morehouse School of Medicine was going to be a predominantly black institution. Its central mission was to provide primary care physicians for underserved rural and inner-city areas, which meant mainly black areas. But I needed white faculty as well as black. I wanted balance; I wanted integration; I wanted the best people I could get. Personally I couldn't care less what color they were. What had I done myself my entire professional life but work with white colleagues? But at the same time, having a strong black faculty was fundamental, not least to give our students role models. Once we had the first high-level black faculty member on board, others would be less difficult to recruit. Jim Story was the first one we were going to approach; he was important. Joe Gayles talked to him on the phone, then Joe, Tom Norris, and Alice Green flew out to Chicago to meet him.

"They called me," Jim later recalled. "They called me and invited me to meet them at their hotel. Morehouse was founding a new medical school, and my name had come up. Lou Sullivan had come on as dean. They said, 'If you want to make your mark, if you want to help African Americans better themselves, then you need to be at Morehouse School of Medicine, because that's what we're doing there.' Listening to talk about what Sullivan wanted to do, and how tough the challenge would be—well, I was hooked. When I came home and talked to my wife about my meeting, she said, 'We should go to Atlanta to do that. It's on a much bigger scale, and it will satisfy some of the things you really want to do.' I said, 'Okay then, we're moving to Atlanta.'"

In a way Jim Story was a case study. He was from Saint Louis, the inner city, the first in his family to go to college. Despite the distractions of growing up on the street, he earned good grades and got into Washington University on a scholarship. But he faltered there. He was a singer with a high-tenor voice, and the rock-and-roll group he was part of had made a few local waves. They had even opened a couple of times for Chuck Berry. But trying to go further with his music didn't mesh well with his need to study, and he had almost flunked out. What saved him was transferring to Morehouse.

At Morehouse my old dean, Brailsford Reese Brazeal, looked at Jim's grades from Washington and told him he didn't look like Morehouse material. "If you don't do any better," he said, "you'll be out of here in a minute."

Jim took that to heart and buckled down. His next-door neighbor in the freshman dorm was Dave Satcher, the future surgeon general. Satcher was about as serious a student as you could get. The five or six hundred other undergraduates were a serious group too. Jim had never seen anything like that, a whole community of young black men, most of them studying their tails off and thinking about their future. He had never experienced anything like that, but he quickly found himself adapting. At Morehouse he had discovered a love for science. Morehouse gave him the confidence to grab hold of that and take it forward, first to a master's, then to a doctorate. "Chance," Mays used to say, "favors the prepared mind." Morehouse had prepared Jim's mind, and he was deeply grateful for that.

"I always wanted to be a role model," Jim told me years later. "I always wanted to do what I could to help the younger black folk. I always had this in the back of my mind. I was always aware of the need for African Americans to go as far as they could in education. So when Morehouse called, I knew I had to look at it. I owed everything to Morehouse. So when they came to talk to me, I thought, this doesn't even need to be discussed. I just need to know what to do."

Jim was a biologist, but he was teaching anatomy at Northwestern when Joe Gayles found him. We appointed him as associate professor of anatomy, but he was so personable and so enthusiastic about Morehouse and about giving talented young black kids the best opportunity that I offered to make him dean of admissions and student affairs, which he accepted. Then, since we didn't have students yet, we sent him out to recruit more faculty.

Cyril Moore, our second faculty member, showed up without anybody recruiting him. Cyril just appeared on campus one day in the fall of 1975. He walked in, introduced himself, and said he had heard about the new medical program here and wanted to find out about it. Cyril spoke with a lilt from somewhere in the Caribbean. He said he was a professor of biochemistry at Albert Einstein in New York. He told me he ran summer programs for black students at Einstein. What were we intending to do, and how were we going to do it?

When I looked into Cyril's credentials and record as a researcher and teacher, all I found were positives. His references were uniformly excellent. The man was clearly a bit of an eccentric, a free spirit of sorts (how eccentric I was to find out later). But he was just as clearly a good scientist and someone students loved. I hired him as chairman of biochemistry.

We quickly acquired three more faculty members through the Rockefeller Foundation, more or less by surprise. I had gone to Rockefeller seeking funding. They wouldn't be able to support us, they said. Their funding for medical education in the United States was minimal. But—how would I like to have some faculty?

It turned out that Rockefeller was heavily invested in developing a medical school at Mahidol University in Thailand. Their commitment there included funding three American faculty salaries for five years. Those five-year contracts were now up, but part of Rockefeller's agreement was that they would help these contract professors find places back in the U.S. Would I be interested?

When I looked at their resumes I was impressed. All three were accomplished medical scientists. Rockefeller offered to pay their salaries for two years, which made it all the better. The three were white, but I thought, if they can work in Thailand and be successful, they ought to be able to work at a black American institution and be successful. I hired all of them, and I was right. They all stayed on and played important roles. Together with Jim Story and Cyril Moore, I now had the beginnings of a strong, integrated faculty.

I started work as dean in July 1975. At the National Medical Association meeting that year, the association's executive committee invited me to brief them about Morehouse. I was excited to do that. The executive committee included some of the country's leading black medical figures, and this would give me an opportunity to meet them, tell them what our plans were, and elicit their support. Frank Royal was chairman, by reputation a skilled politician, who also happened to be chairman of Meharry's board.

I was prepared for a serious but warm and friendly meeting. The first black medical school in a century was a major step forward in terms of expanding opportunities for young African Americans and increasing the availability of health care for the badly underserved African American community. But from the start the atmosphere was chilly. The introductions were courteous enough, but it was obvious that the people on the committee were deeply concerned, and not friendly. Most of them were graduates of Howard and Meharry, and they had one thing on their minds: "How do you propose to fund this school?" they asked. "Aren't you going to be taking away the federal dollars Howard and Meharry are getting?" No one was shouting, but I could sense the hostility.

"Morehouse College has a strong academic program and good leadership," I said. "The black physicians in Atlanta and Georgia are very supportive; the white physicians are as well. In regard to federal dollars, our goal is to expand the pool of dollars, not undercut anyone. We'll also be getting funding from the state. Jimmy Carter has voiced support for Morehouse to start a medical school, and we expect that state dollars will be available. Down the line we'll also be looking to the Woodruff Foundation. They're in Atlanta and health care is their number one priority. They're a major funder for Emory, and we have good hopes they'll eventually support us too. No one can overstate the importance of Howard and Meharry, but the need for more black physicians is urgent, and these two schools simply aren't able to meet it. We hope to work with them, with the NMA, and other groups. We need to make a combined effort to address this severe problem in our community."

That was in the summer of 1975. After the meeting I began thinking about some mechanism that actually would give us the ability to work together rather than compete. It took time, but in 1977 we formed the Association of Minority Health Professions Schools—initially Morehouse School of Medicine together with Meharry, the Xavier University School of Pharmacy, and the Tuskegee Veterinary School—to lobby and advocate for African American health initiatives.

The reason Howard didn't join immediately was that they enjoyed a special federal appropriation that had been established in the nineteenth century, which they guarded jealously. They didn't want to do anything that might in any way draw unwanted attention to this annual entitlement. Back then Congress had granted the funding in recognition of Howard's significance in advancing the education of blacks, so in a sense they stood apart. When Carter was elected president it occurred to me that since Georgia now had a friendly ear in the White House, we should see if there might not be some support for a similar federal appropriation for Morehouse.

During Carter's tenure as governor he had encouraged the establishment of a medical school. Health care was high on his list of priorities. He also had close political ties to the black community. Andrew Young and John Lewis had gone to bat for him around the country during his run for president, part of the so-called Peanut Brigade, and African Americans had overwhelmingly voted for him. Carter was close to many of Georgia's black leaders, but there were none he respected more than the two elder statesmen, Benjamin Mays and Martin Luther King Sr. (universally known as "Daddy" King). King and Mays contacted the

White House and said they would like to see the president, and they wanted to bring the dean of the new medical school with them. So a meeting was set.

My very specific goal in this meeting was to see if the administration wouldn't initiate a bill for a federal appropriation similar to Howard's. Our argument was simple. Congress had funded Howard, which enabled it to respond to the urgent need for higher education in the black community. We were now in an identical situation vis-à-vis the urgent need in the country for black physicians. It was to the benefit of all that Congress should support our efforts now as it had Howard's then. The idea that the Morehouse medical program needed and deserved support wasn't new to Carter, and he had asked Bert Lance, his OMB director (another Georgian) to sit in. At the end of our discussion Carter asked Lance to look into it, to see what could be done.

When the White House got back to me a couple of weeks later, the answer was fairly definitive. Lance had talked to key people in Congress. They were aware of the Howard special funding, which had also been extended to Gallaudet University, the institution of higher learning for deaf students. Yes, the congressmen told Lance, they were aware of it, but no, they would not support or sponsor a bill for us. They thought the entitlement was one of the worst mistakes Congress had ever made, and they for sure were not about to do anything like it again.

As time went on I became more successful at raising money. Gloster was extremely helpful with this, introducing me to potential funders and advising me. He himself was an accomplished fund-raiser. He had just completed a successful $20 million campaign, to that point the largest money-raising endeavor in history for a black college.

Alice Green helped a great deal too. Alice was Morehouse College's development person, and at the beginning she played that role for the medical program too. Alice was Gloster's daughter, though both she and her father tried not to publicize that. Gloster was sensitive about possibly being tainted by accusations of nepotism. But the fact was that Alice was an extremely astute, effective individual in her own right. She did the research behind my fund-raising efforts. She knew potential donors' assets, giving history, interests, personal foibles, and friends. She knew how their investments were doing, whether they had come into some money or whether they had tax problems. She prepared me on all these matters. She was my eyes and ears.

Meanwhile, it didn't take too long before I lost the feeling of embarrassment about asking for money. I began looking at it from exactly the opposite point of view. The Morehouse medical education program was an important venture, a historic venture. It was new and exciting; it was making a large contribution not just to the underserved and needy but to the fabric of Georgia's civic and educational life generally, and beyond Georgia as well. I was giving potential donors an opportunity to take part in something extraordinarily worthwhile, to do something that would make a true difference. In reality I was doing them a favor in addition to them doing me a favor. Of course, I never put it that way, but that was how I came to think of it.

I became thick skinned too. You couldn't be discouraged by rejection. Rejections not only happened, they happened 80 percent of the time. If I was lucky, 20 percent of my calls resulted in a donation. But that 20 percent made the entire effort worth it. The essential thing was believing in what you were doing, in the importance of it. The medical school was Hugh Gloster's initiative. But it didn't take long before my own feeling of commitment evolved into something deeper than simple enthusiasm. More and more I was feeling that the school embodied my own most fundamental values and aspirations. Well, I'd say to myself after a turndown by a potential donor, that didn't work out. Let's get right on to the next. In time and with practice, I started bringing in a decent amount of money. After a year or so even the Woodruff Foundation began looking kindly at us.

We were starting from scratch, but the Morehouse name went a long way toward generating support from alumni and others; Gloster had been absolutely right about that. We were lucky in our timing too. From the late 1960s through the 1970s a spirit was taking hold in the black community generally, a spirit that said, be better and we can rise. We *can* do this. I knew we were riding that wave.

We were also now in the immediate post–civil rights era. America was opening itself up to the idea of including blacks in society's mainstream. Part of this was that previously all-white institutions were making efforts to move beyond their exclusionary histories. One of these, to our great benefit, was the Emory University School of Medicine.

Emory's dean, Arthur Richardson, had been behind the Morehouse medical idea from the beginning. Now he came forward with practical support, appointing a liaison to work with us. Jonas Shulman, a professor of community medicine, frequently sat in on my staff meetings, advising us on structural issues and introducing us to others who could provide help. Later on, Charles Hatcher came on as vice president for health affairs at Emory. Hatcher's background helped make him particularly sensitive to our needs. He had done his residency at Johns

Hopkins with the great heart surgeon Alfred Blalock and had worked closely with Vivien Thomas, Blalock's extraordinary African American lab director and partner who had never been able to attend medical school. Beyond that, Hatcher was from Bainbridge, Georgia, forty miles from Blakely, the town where Dr. Griffin had his hospital. He had known Griffin, the one black doctor in a hundred-mile radius. With Hatcher I had a southwest Georgian personal link that enhanced the already-warm institutional ties between ourselves and Emory.

One factor that motivated Emory was that while other major medical schools were making strides toward diversity, they were not. Emory was having a hard time attracting black students, though that was a problem largely of their own making. They wanted A students, student council leaders, promising researchers with impressive extracurricular activities. But African American undergraduates with those kinds of credentials were being swallowed up by Harvard and Stanford and other top tier schools, most often in the North. Emory would admit them, but they would end up somewhere else. As a result, Emory didn't look very good on the diversity front. Their work with us gave them an opportunity to make up for that, to say, we might not be as lucky as we'd like to be in terms of attracting black students, but we're supporting the development of the Morehouse School of Medicine. We're making our contribution that way. And their support was absolutely genuine; it had tremendous practical significance to us.

At the same time, the Association of American Medical Colleges took a strong interest in our development, as did the LCME, the accrediting agency. With their assistance we made steady progress toward our goal. Initially the whole medical school could gather around my conference table. We'd have staff meetings two or three times a week, recruiting faculty, organizing curriculum. We had visits from James Scofield, the LCME's cosecretary, telling us the requirements for accreditation, what we needed: faculty, facilities, administrative procedures, governance, trustees, a financial base, a library. Between 1975 and 1978 we met intensely on these matters, building the school step-by-step.

What I found as we went along was the importance of delegating to people, yet holding them accountable. Hugh Gloster helped me a lot in terms of dealing with personnel—how to set expectations and how to handle it when somebody fell short. And, of course, one of the first lessons I learned was to praise in public, criticize in private. Denigrating people in front of others is the easiest way to destroy your own capital. I also learned to be an example, not just to give orders but to model. I worked and reported my ideas to the group, just as I expected others to do. I'd say, tell me your ideas. We'd have spirited debates, and often somebody else had a better approach than I had. I'd say, fine, let's develop that. Some of this was simple common sense, Management 101. But the end result was a team spirit that renewed my own energy again and again. We were doing something new, something we thought was monumental. It was an exciting time.

On the other hand, it wasn't all smooth sailing. People thought of me as a workaholic. That was a positive for some, but not so much for others, particularly for a few of the local black doctors on my board. I didn't play golf; I didn't have the patience for it. I hardly drank. I didn't play cards. I was just not one of the boys, and that was a problem. They saw me as standoffish, aloof. In my twenty years in the North I had even lost whatever had been southern in my speech, so I didn't even sound like they thought I should have. At one point three or four of them asked to meet with me.

"Lou," one said, "we were wondering. Are you really black?"

I was stunned. "What are you talking about?"

"Well, you don't seem to relate that well to the guys. You don't come to parties; you don't golf."

"Gosh, my focus is devoting my energies to getting the school going."

They understood that well enough, but it wasn't a satisfactory answer. I was from BU, Mass General, and Harvard; I was an elitist almost by definition. Of course I didn't see myself that way. I enjoyed people. I enjoyed inviting friends and colleagues over to the house for the barbecues or dinner parties that Ginger would put on. I didn't even think of myself as a workaholic. I was enjoying what I was doing, so it didn't seem exactly like work. But I was certainly single-minded. I was focused not just on getting a medical school started but on getting a medical school started that had high standards. I was determined to build a school that would measure up on every criterion used to judge medical schools. I wanted Morehouse to be able to compete with any school in the country, and not just compete, to excel.

That was the larger vision I had, and I was determined to accomplish it. I had grown up in a segregated society. What that society was saying to me and to all African Americans was, "You are not good enough! You are inferior, second class, not worthy." I wanted Morehouse School of Medicine to declare emphatically that if we have the resources, we can develop a medical school every bit as good as anyone's. That was my way of rolling back all that denigration and humiliation and saying, this is a lie!

By 1978 we were ready. By then we had hired almost forty faculty, up from twelve the first year. Our departments were staffed and our administrators were in place. We had worked out arrangements with Morehouse College for space, research labs as well as classrooms. We had established a library and recruited Beverly Allen, a first-rate librarian from the University of Illinois. Our finances were far from robust, but they were at least adequate. We had a well-defined mission and a plan for how to move forward. We had, I believed, fulfilled all the requirements for provisional accreditation, the prerequisite for accepting students and accessing federal funds. The LCME agreed, and that March they notified us that that their inspection teams had reported positively on our application and that they were now formally granting us provisional accreditation. In three years of extremely hard work we had gotten over the hump. The Morehouse School of Medicine was finally a living, breathing enterprise.

Jim Story, our dean of student affairs, now began working full-time to exploit the contacts he had been making at traditionally black colleges all over the South. In fact, we had already begun talking with prospective students months earlier, when it was apparent that the accreditation visiting team was going to report back positively to the full LCME. Our plans were to accept twenty-four students in our first class. But we were looking for a special kind of student.

This was a new venture, risky on several counts. Our students would be attending an accredited medical school, but one no one had ever heard of. The name "Morehouse School of Medicine" was not going to enhance their resumes. And being a start-up school suggested that maybe our existence was perhaps still more than a little tenuous. The chances that something bad might happen here were far greater than at some long-established school.

We needed students who wouldn't be afraid of taking those risks. We needed self-starting students with a streak of adventurousness in them. We were building something unusual, and they would be part of it, in on the ground floor; they would be participating in a historic undertaking. We wanted students who would feel that and be motivated by it. Most of all, we wanted students who would commit to the mission we had set for ourselves: to train physicians who would establish practices for the medically underserved and socially disadvantaged.

As it turned out, we didn't have any problem at all recruiting students; the problem was selecting them. Our charter class included fourteen black students, six white students, and four Asian students—fourteen young men and ten young women. We were off to a flying start. I couldn't have been prouder.

We had hardly taken off before it looked like we were heading straight for a crash landing. From the beginning Gloster and I had worked well together. But we had at least one running argument, and it was a constant source of tension between us. When we fought, it was almost always about money.

Gloster was tight, which I understood. Morehouse School of Medicine was part of Morehouse College, and for all Gloster's success raising money, Morehouse's finances had always been and still were limited. But medical schools cost a fortune, and that struck the fear of God into Gloster. He had taken a huge chance with this project. Some of his trustees had thought it was patently insane. "You sure you want to do something like this?" they had asked him. On the one hand, the medical school was going to be his legacy. On the other, the thing could blow up in his face at any minute.

I understood him, but that didn't solve anything. Prudence was one thing; starvation was another. I was driving to build a school, which he wanted as badly as I did. But from his point of view I was always assaulting him with requests he considered outlandish. He was frightened to death that runaway spending was going to put him under.

As a result, he held the purse strings in a steel grip. His business manager, Wiley Perdue (another alumnus), reviewed every dollar we spent. "Look," I'd tell him, "Morehouse College has a great reputation. I want the medical school, which you've fostered, to have that same kind of reputation. And we can't do that without the labs and the teachers. We are not going to have a class A school with class C salaries."

Gloster didn't like to hear that, even if there was no gainsaying the logic. We had vigorous fights, but one thing that saved us was that we were both Morehouse men. Each of us knew that the other had the school's well-being at heart. So we fought, but our fights were family fights. They stayed within bounds.

But my problem wasn't just the money—it was what the money was doing to my relationship with the faculty. I was in the middle, between them and Gloster. They had needs, and it was my business as dean to see those needs were met. I was supposed to protect them and make sure they had the resources to do their jobs. But how could I do that when I wasn't even permitted to hire my own secretaries? It was an impossible situation. I didn't share all this with the faculty. I didn't want to be discouraging. I also didn't want to appear impotent in front of them. The result was that I was feeling embarrassed and frustrated. They were also feeling frustrated, but if I was embarrassed, they were angry.

The incident that ignited this tinderbox had to do with a secretary. Gordon Leitch was one of the three professors being funded by Rockefeller. I had appointed Gordon chairman of the physiology department, a job that really required a dedicated secretary rather than someone from the secretarial pool. Gordon was after me about this, and I was after Gloster. "How do you think I can run a school," I told him, "when you have to personally interview and hire all the secretaries. You're micromanaging. You have to stop it. I need to have some latitude."

In the end Gloster relented, but only on the condition that I interview each secretarial hire myself. So I did. We advertised, I interviewed the candidates for Gordon's secretary, and I hired someone for him. She had been working for about a month when I was called over to Gloster's office. It seemed that the woman I had hired had previously worked at Morehouse, which she had neglected to include on her resume. She had neglected to include it because she had been fired. The reason wasn't clear, but whatever it was had generated a note on her personnel record that read, "This person should never work for Morehouse College again."

Gloster was absolutely livid. He was beside himself. "I gave you this authority! And now, just look at this! This is intolerable! You have to get rid of her!"

So I did, which turned Gordon Leitch livid, which in turn set off all the frustration other faculty had been feeling about the constraints they were working under. They were being held back by the college. I was an instrument of the college. I had to go.

Gordon Leitch precipitated it, but he wasn't alone. Cyril Moore, our biochemistry chairman, was equally aggravated, and he joined in. Cyril didn't need any specific grievance to set him off. Cyril was an idiosyncratic man. Among other things, he simply believed that administrators were always corrupt; they were never to be trusted. He didn't *like* administrators, and he didn't like me as an administrator, which he didn't keep to himself. I didn't enjoy that, but I wasn't that bothered either. The man was a great teacher; the students loved him. As long as he wasn't burning the building down or threatening bodily harm I could put up with it.

But now Cyril joined his unhappiness with Gordon's, which meant I had two extremely disgruntled department chairmen, who were then joined by a number of other frustrated faculty members. Together they sent a letter to Gloster and to Edgar Smith, the chairman of our board of overseers. "We have no confidence in the dean," they wrote. It was Thanksgiving, three months into our first semester, and the faculty was in revolt.

We held the meeting in one of our conference rooms: Gloster, myself, Gordon, Cyril, Beverly Allen, seven or eight other unhappy faculty members, and also several trustees, including Edgar Smith and Eph Friedman, who had flown down from Boston and New York.

I went into the meeting with very conflicted emotions. I understood something about Gloster's position. I was angry at him, but I knew where he was coming from and to a degree I sympathized with him. Presidents of traditionally black colleges often felt they needed to exert strict personal control over their domains, for good reasons. They were heading schools that typically lived very close to the edge, and they had to protect those schools against internal pressures and also against an outside world that was used to thinking of them as inferior and essentially unnecessary. By Gloster's lights, he needed to do everything in his power to protect his college and simultaneously to nourish a bold undertaking that had the potential to sink both him and his legacy. I understood that well enough, not that it lessened my exasperation with him.

At the same time I was upset by what was happening with the faculty, more than upset. It was devastating to think that after all the hard work, after all the excitement and the exhilaration of building the school from nothing and the success marked by our accreditation, that something like this could happen. Did they so little appreciate what we had accomplished? Of course, I couldn't expect them to be sensitive to my problems with Gloster. I had been a faculty member at BU and Boston City Hospital, and I was always fighting for money and space and programs I thought were necessary—and that I often could not get. So I knew what they were feeling. But still, how could they have descended to this?

I hadn't had time to talk much with Edgar and Eph before the meeting, except to get their advice that I shouldn't get caught up in the emotions of the moment, that it wouldn't be productive. That certainly made sense. I didn't want to say anything, period. I felt it wasn't going to be helpful for me to try to rebut the faculty. They had shot their arrow in their letter to Gloster and the board. So this was a discussion among those parties. But how it was going turn out was anybody's guess.

The meeting lasted three hours. The faculty had plenty of time to voice their complaints. They weren't being given the support they needed. It was an untenable situation for them. The medical school shouldn't be run this way. After all the airing and back and forth, Eph Friedman turned to Gloster.

"Well, Mr. President," he said, "you have this issue. The faculty has said to you that they have no confidence in the dean. Do you agree with them? Or do you support the dean?" Gloster was silent. It looked as if he was weighing his answer. "Come on, Mr. President," said Eph. "You need to answer my question. If you support the faculty, we need to fire the dean and get someone new. What is your decision here?"

We waited. I knew Gloster understood we were in this situation because of the chains he had put on me. But I couldn't tell what was going through his mind. Finally he opened his mouth, "No, no," he said. "We have to have Dr. Sullivan."

Eph looked at Gordon Leitch and the other faculty. "We understand your concerns," he said. "We're going to work to improve the situation. But if we're going to have a successful institution, we're going to have to find ways to work together. That's the bottom line here. I do want you to be sure, though, that we have heard you and that we will take steps to address the problems you've voiced."

That mollified them. I was stung, but I knew it was going to be my job to knit this up with them, to show them that I was responsive and to get over this blowup. Gloster and I were going to have to work together too. I knew that despite our quarrels we had great respect for each other and truly enjoyed our collaboration. But this had frayed our relationship. Getting beyond it was going to take some work.

CHAPTER 8

Morehouse School of Medicine

Edgar Smith had advised me not to get involved in any arguments. I shouldn't try to refute what the faculty had to say; I shouldn't react to anything that might be personal or derogatory. I should just listen and allow them to vent their anger and complaints.

That would let them get it off their chests, number one. Number two, I'd be able to hear the whole story and maybe get some additional clarity. Number three, they'd see they were being listened to—at least *I* was listening to them. They'd understand I was doing my best to hear them out, that I wasn't their adversary.

Eph Friedman seconded that. Eph had been dean at BU; now he was dean at Albert Einstein. He was a veteran administrator who had, I was sure, been through his own share of crises. Like Edgar, he wanted me to do what I could to reduce tensions with the faculty rather than inflame them. As far as Gloster went, Eph wanted to bring the problem to a head. That's why he had pressed Gloster to respond.

The underlying cause of this blowup was that Gloster was keeping me on a short leash. That's what had precipitated it. So, the question was, where do we go from here? Was this situation going to stay unchanged? If so, even if we could get beyond this we were just going to be in for more of the same. Or was I going to get his support so that I could be effective as dean? If I wasn't going to get that support, as disturbing as it might be, we ought to get that out on the table right now. If I needed to head back to Boston or somewhere else, I could at least cut my losses. "We need to get to some point of resolution," Eph said, "and not just let this end ambiguously."

When the meeting was over, Eph advised me to wait a couple of days, then meet with Gloster to discuss how things went. "You should go in and express your appreciation for his support. You should also let him know that what's needed is for him to give you the authority to manage. Otherwise, you'll just be facing the same thing over and over."

The couple of days were a kind of cooling-off period, for me as well as Gloster. I thought about that long hesitation of his before he said, "We need Dr. Sullivan." That wasn't exactly a ringing, full-throated vote of confidence. But I also knew he was proud of what was going on with the medical school, even while he was scared to death that maybe he had made the biggest mistake of his life. I had never once felt that he was deliberately trying to undermine me or block me. I respected his intelligence and dedication, and I was grateful to him as well—he had given me this opportunity. I had been working flat out for the past three years to turn this dream into a reality, but he was the one who had made it possible in the first place.

The couple of days off allowed me to let go of my pique and settle into a positive frame of mind. I was sure Gloster was doing his own rethinking. He knew what the problem was. At bottom, his decision at the meeting meant that he was going to have to do something about it. So the chances were good that he would be taking a positive approach too.

Our meeting started out a little uncomfortable and awkward, though it didn't take too long before we both relaxed a bit. Our relationship had always been fundamentally healthy, but we weren't bosom buddies even at the best of times. I was always "Brother Sullivan" or "Brother Dean," and he was "Dr. Gloster." A little formal, I thought, but that was fine, maybe even advantageous in terms of keeping things businesslike.

So we talked. We had a meeting of minds. Over the next two or three months, I got complete responsibility for hiring staff and faculty. I still was careful to report to him, but now I felt positioned to run the program the way I thought it should be run. I understood too that his fretting over salaries was partly due to worries about his own faculty and trustees. Medical school faculty salaries were simply higher than college faculty salaries. But what was he supposed to answer when excellent, long-term undergraduate professors asked how he could approve higher pay for junior medical school people who had just showed up yesterday?

To explain better, and to help protect him, I brought statistics with me on medical school faculty salaries nationally. I showed him that we were bringing people in at the 20th or 30th percentile. Then, after three or four years, if they performed well, we'd raise them to the 50th percentile. That helped him understand how these things worked, and it helped him with his own board. As time went on, and especially as I continued to generate funding, his anxieties scaled back considerably. This revolt situation was water under the bridge. We put it behind us.

After the meeting I also got together with Gordon, Cyril, and the other department chairmen. At the top of my mind was that I wanted to dispel any hint that I thought they had lost and I had won. I told them that I understood their concerns, which I considered legitimate. I was going to work to address them. I told them my door was always open, that they could come to me to discuss anything, that we had a large challenge before us, and if we were going to succeed it had to be on the basis of working together. I wanted them to understand that I saw them as partners in this endeavor.

As we talked they began to see that the decisions that upset them so badly were not decisions I had been making arbitrarily. The reason I was not delivering was that I was not being allowed to deliver. They were frustrated, but so was I. They seemed pleased that I was listening to them and that I was reaching out to them, that I was recognizing them as leaders of the institution and asking for their help. Afterward everybody simply got back to work. It was as though nothing had ever happened.

I did think back on some of my BU friends, though, who had intimated that I should have my head examined for sacrificing a nice, safe, rewarding career in a nice, safe laboratory where things were always more or less under control. Managing actual people was so unpredictable. "You know, Lou," one of them had said, "there's a very good chance they'll drive you nuts." The faculty uprising didn't drive me nuts. I considered it a lesson in leadership, even if I had to learn it the hard way. But some other events that first semester did actually seem crazy.

Many months before our students arrived we arranged with the college for the space we were going to need. We had brought in those double-wide trailers for our administrative offices, and we rented part of Sale Hall, the building just to the right of the trailers. On the second floor of Sale Hall we put faculty offices and conference rooms. Classrooms were on the first floor, along with a women's bathroom. Since Morehouse College was all male, the only previous ladies' room on campus was located in the faculty lounge. In the basement we did extensive renovations to accommodate our gross anatomy lab.

One morning while the renovations were underway, a very agitated Miss Flora Lamar showed up in my office. Miss Lamar was in charge of the student mailroom. Sixty years old or so, she had been at Morehouse for ages. I remembered her well from the time I was a student, though that was before she worked in the mailroom. Back then she was assistant to the hostess, the woman who met with families and hosted them when they visited the campus. Miss Lamar was the sweetest, most accommodating person; the students considered her like a housemother. Seeing Miss Lamar in such an agitated state was a bit unsettling.

"Dean Sullivan," she began, "I am not going to have it!"

"Have what, Miss Lamar? What's the trouble?"

"I just heard there are going to be dead people in the room down the hall from me!"

The student postboxes were in the Sale Hall basement, just down from the anatomy lab.

"Well, Miss Lamar," I explained, "that is going to be our gross anatomy laboratory. But you won't be aware of anything. We're putting state of the art ventilation in there. The students will be very quiet. They won't disturb you at all."

"No, no, no. I cannot have that!" said Miss Lamar.

"Miss Lamar, you don't have a thing to worry about. Dissection is part of the normal instruction for medical students."

"No! Absolutely not! I simply cannot have it!"

Whatever I said, Miss Lamar couldn't have it. "Miss Lamar, it's required that we teach human anatomy. You want the school to succeed, don't you?"

"I am not going to sit still for it," said Miss Lamar. "I won't have it!"

Finally, since she wasn't getting any satisfaction from me, she said, "I am going to see Dr. Gloster right this minute," and she stormed out.

I picked up the phone and called Gloster. "President Gloster, Miss Lamar is on her way over to see you. She's *very* agitated because we're going to have our gross anatomy laboratory down the hall from her. She is clearly not happy with that. She's extremely upset."

"Okay, thanks," said Gloster. "I'll take care of it."

Gloster's experience with Miss Lamar was similar to mine. She wouldn't have it. Finally he made some vague promise to her that he'd do something about it, which of course he didn't. There was nothing *to* do. He thought it would just blow over.

The Georgia medical schools got their cadavers from the state mortuary, located at the Medical College of Georgia in Augusta. Most often those were unclaimed bodies: prisoners who had died, homeless people, others who had no friends or relatives to take them. They were kept in the mortuary a sufficient length of time for any possible relative or acquaintance to claim them, then the medical schools were given permission to use them for dissection.

Shortly before our semester began, Tom Norris, who was now our dean for academic affairs, drove over to Augusta in his pickup truck together with Cyril Moore to get the bodies, six of them—twenty-four students, one cadaver for every four students. Tom and Cyril put the frozen, body-bagged bodies in the truck, drove back to Morehouse, and backed the truck up to the rear entrance of Sale Hall. There they put the bodies on a gurney, one at a time, draping a sheet over them as they wheeled them into the lab, which they apparently thought was more dignified.

But Miss Lamar had seen them, and as they wheeled the first body into the rear basement entrance she fled out the front door and took refuge in the faculty lounge across the quadrangle. Gloster had to hire a substitute postmistress while he arranged to move the student mailroom to another building. Miss Lamar was enthusiastic about the medical school, at least in the abstract. But she had a formidable fear of dead people.

Beverly Allen was no Miss Lamar, though she was at least as insistent a character in her own way. Beverly was our librarian. We had recruited her from the University of Illinois. She had come with first-rate references, and she turned out to be exactly as she had been described, knowledgeable, precise, and dedicated. She was also demanding. She insisted that we accord her faculty status, which I was happy enough to do. She was equally insistent that we meet all her exacting technical standards for the library. There had to be x number of foot candles of light at the desktop, the study space per student had to meet national library requirements, and we had to have ample carrel space for each student—a lot of things that had never occurred to me, a lot of demands. And she was not about to brook any recalcitrance on our part either. She put Chris Metzger, our buildings person, through a grueling time while we were constructing the library space, which was not in Sale Hall but in Brawley Hall, a hundred or so yards away. I know she tested his patience mightily. She tested mine too, though I never let on to that. Beverly might have annoyed me with all her demands and quirks, but she was putting together a damned good library, which I was quite pleased about.

We completed the renovations before the semester began, then got the books shipped in and put them up on the new shelving. Everything looked great as the Morehouse College students began to filter in—a week or so before our medical students. With the undergraduates' arrival, classes started, extracurricular activities started, the campus suddenly swung into life.

A few days later Beverly called and asked if I could come over to the library that afternoon, maybe around four o'clock.

"Fine," I said. "I can come by now, if you'd like."

"No, please come at four."

"Okay. At four then." I had no idea why she wanted me at four, but she was sufficiently quirky that I didn't think much about it. At four I went over and began going through the library with her. "Gee," I said. "This looks wonderful. Everything seems to be in order. How do you like the space?" I thought we had done an excellent job meeting all her many demands. But the woman obviously did know her business. It really did look wonderful. "This is great, Beverly. Do you like it?"

"Yes, it's fine," she said. "Except for one thing."

I couldn't imagine. What in the world was she going to complain about now? All of a sudden a huge din broke out, shockingly loud. It sounded like a band warming up: drums, horns, strings, the whole works. A cacophony. "Jesus, Beverly. What the hell is that?"

I wasn't in the habit of cursing in front of faculty—or anyone else for that matter. But this was enough to knock your socks off. The noise swelled. It seemed to be curling down from above, where we had hung ceiling tiles from the bare concrete.

"Mr. Dean," Beverly said. "You have put us right next to the band practice room! How do you think we are supposed to have a library here?"

My head was swimming. We had spent all this money, all this time. How were we supposed to know the band was going to be practicing next door? We didn't have the money to do this over. We didn't have the time either. I went to Gloster, who had better control over the bandmaster than he had over Miss Lamar. The next day they started practicing somewhere else, which kept me in Beverly Allen's good graces, fortunately for me.

Our first class arrived in 1978. At that point we were a two-year, not a four-year, medical school. We provided the basic science education that all medical schools do in the first two years. But then our students had to transfer to another school for the clinical work required in the last two years of training. For them to do this we made contractual arrangements with Emory, Howard, the Medical College of Georgia, and the University of Alabama. Our students who went on to these places received Emory, Howard, Georgia, or Alabama medical degrees.

Two-year schools were not uncommon at the time. Dartmouth was initially a two-year school. Brown was too; North Dakota and others were. But in the early 1970s the LCME decided they were no longer going to accredit two-year schools. All such schools would be required to develop a plan and timetable to become four-year institutions. Any new two-year schools, as we were, would also need to have a contract with one or more four-year schools to guarantee placement of their students in the third year.

To meet this requirement the Morehouse College trustees had passed a resolution at the medical school's inception committing themselves to the development of a four-year school. In addition, we signed contracts with Emory and the other medical schools guaranteeing acceptance of our students. Meanwhile, we worked as fast as we could toward developing our own third- and fourth-year clinical programs.

Our goal was to have our transition completed by 1983. To help accomplish this I recruited Stan Olson, who had been dean at the University of Illinois College of Medicine, then at Baylor, then founding dean at Northeast Ohio Medical University. Stan helped formulate the strategic plan, then assisted in implementing it. As a result we made such rapid progress that the LCME granted us approval to proceed to four-year status in 1981.

That set the stage for us to become an independent institution. We had begun as the medical education program of Morehouse College, without a sure sense of exactly what our affiliation status might be with the college once we had met the accreditation and other requirements for independence. But by 1981 we were ready to stand on our own. We negotiated an agreement with Emory School of Medicine to share their affiliation with their teaching facility, Atlanta's Grady Hospital. We also received permission from the Morehouse College trustees to continue using the Morehouse name, which Gloster and I firmly believed would benefit both the college and the medical school. It enhanced the college's prestige as a serious premedical and science-oriented school and expanded its footprint in the world of education generally. For the medical school, it gave us the continued ability to build on the college's strong reputation. At least as important, the Morehouse name provided us with connections to alumni in positions of influence in business, science, and government. It also gave us a potential donor base, a hard-to-exaggerate benefit for a school with no alumni of its own.

We were now, finally, our own institution, and I became its president as well as its dean. To this point our graduates had received their medical degrees from other schools. But our 1981 class was going to stay with us for all four years; they would be leaving as Morehouse School of Medicine MDs. It was a major milestone.

At the same time we were working toward another milestone. Now that we were our own school, we badly needed our own home. Across the street from Morehouse College was a sixteen-acre plot of vacant land. I had enough money to buy two and a half acres of this as the site for our first building, and I was already planning to acquire additional acreage. In my mind's eye I could see the whole sixteen acres as a campus full of buildings.

To raise the money for the first building we turned to the federal government. In 1978, as soon as we had our provisional accreditation, we began crafting congressional legislation that would provide funding for new medical schools. The Georgia delegation worked on a bill with us. Louis Stokes, the African American congressman from Ohio, shepherded it through the House; Arlen Specter sponsored it on the Senate side, with support from Mark Hatfield, who was chairman of the Senate Appropriations Committee. The bill passed; it provided for a four-to-one matching grant, four federal dollars for every private dollar we could raise.

Don Keough, who was now CEO of the Coca Cola Company, took the lead in our drive to solicit private funding. Coca Cola was by far the largest business in Atlanta, and with Keough in the chair, along with the attraction of federal matching dollars, it took us only a little over a year before we had enough to break ground on what would become our basic medical science building.

We had initially hoped to dedicate the building in December 1981. But various construction delays put completion back to July 1982. The usual building frustrations aside, when it was finished we had what everyone thought was an extremely impressive building. Our efforts in Washington had born fruit, and Don Keough's fund-raising leadership had been invaluable. I was deeply grateful for his efforts, which had brought in substantial contributions from local donors, including from Coca Cola itself.

Two weeks before the dedication ceremony we organized a luncheon at the new building as a thank you to Don and his fund-raising committee. The luncheon was scheduled for noon, and I had made sure that we had dotted the i's and crossed the t's on all the arrangements. I was in my office getting ready to leave for the new building when I got a call from our chief of maintenance. Keough had arrived early, he said, and was strolling around the building. The walk from my office to the new building ordinarily took about ten minutes. I made it in five. But by the time I got there, Keough had already taken his own tour.

"It's a beautiful building, Lou," he said. "Interesting the way you've done things. I'm extremely pleased with it . . . except, I did see one strange thing."

"You did? What was that, Don?"

"There was a vending machine back there, Lou. It seemed to be a Pepsi-Cola machine."

"Don, I can't believe it. I have no idea where that came from. Let me tell you, that thing will be out of here before sunset." What a faux pas, not that Don Keough didn't have a sense of humor, but a Pepsi machine? As if that wasn't enough, something else happened at the lunch itself. The food was delicious; the waiters attentive; the wine they were pouring from bottles wrapped in white linen napkins was excellent. Everything was going swimmingly until Keough asked a waiter to unwrap the bottle he was pouring so he could see the label.

He looked. It was a Beringer chardonnay. "Lou," he turned to me, "let me ask, have you ever heard of Sterling Vineyards?"

I hadn't.

He turned to his aide. "John," he said, "why don't you get with Dr. Sullivan? Next time he's out in the San Francisco area I'd like you to organize a tour of Sterling for him." He turned back to me. "Lou, Sterling's in Napa. They make a prizewinning wine. We've owned them for some time now. I'm positive you'll enjoy seeing how they do it."

I don't know if he could tell that I was blushing with embarrassment. First the Pepsi machine, now the wrong wine. Our most important fund-raiser. Lord, I thought, what else can go wrong? Fortunately, nothing did. And Don Keough wasn't a person to take offense. It did teach me, though, about the importance of caring for donors, corporate donors in particular, who are eager to shine the best light they can on their companies in small ways as well as large.

By the time the basic science building was completed, Ronald Reagan had been elected president. By then I was closely attuned to the significance of having allies in Washington, also to the importance of beefing up our support across party lines. What better way to do that, I thought, than to invite

President Reagan to speak at the new building's dedication? So we sent out an invitation.

We extended the invitation in January 1981, but the response was slow in coming. Meanwhile, one of the first things Reagan did when he took office was to slash the education budget. That was a bad surprise. Most damaging was his evisceration of the National Health Service Corps scholarship program that provided full tuition and living stipends for medical students who agreed to practice in medically underserved areas. In our first class, nineteen out of twenty-four students had these scholarships. Without them they never would have been able to afford their medical training. Reagan's action damaged us; it hurt all medical schools, but black schools were particularly affected.

Then in August Bob Jones University was in the national news for its policy of prohibiting interracial dating. Bob Jones was (and is) a private Christian university in Greenville, South Carolina. In recent years it has apologized for its past racist policies, but back then it was still doing everything it could to keep segregation alive and well. Only a few years earlier the university had argued in court that God intended segregation of the races and that scripture forbade interracial marriage. Under Carter the IRS was intent on rescinding the university's tax-exempt status. But when Reagan assumed the presidency, he came out in support of Bob Jones and had the Justice Department drop the case.

The political fireworks this ignited forced Reagan to backtrack, but meanwhile his support for Bob Jones went through the black community like a lead shot, which left me thinking what a terrible mistake it had been to invite him. If Reagan did come, I thought, I'd have to get on the plane out of Atlanta with him. I would have loved to disinvite him, but how do you withdraw an invitation to a sitting president? It took four months before the White House gave us an answer to the invitation. And the answer, to my vast relief, was no.

At that time I was working with Ray Cotton, a Washington attorney who was advising us on legislation. I called him up. "Ray, thank God he can't come. We're off the hook."

"Wait a minute," Ray said. "You should try to get the vice president."

"What? What are you talking about?"

"Listen, it's still important for you to develop these relationships. You should see if you can't get Bush to come. You can write to the White House how disappointed you are that the president won't be coming, especially after having waited for such an overlong period for a response from him. Perhaps in light of the circumstances the vice president might be able to take his place."

So we invited George H. W. Bush. And he accepted.

We held the dedication ceremony on July 18, 1982. This was a giant leap forward for us. For the first time we could see the school physically materializing in front of our eyes. We weren't any longer going to be in a trailer and rented rooms scattered around the college. Prior to this, visitors had to search around to find us. Now we were going to have our own home.

Five or six hundred guests were standing on the plaza in front of the building at nine in the morning when Vice President Bush began to speak. We had been told that he would be able to stay for only fifteen minutes at the reception following his speech; his staff said he had a commitment in New Orleans for a luncheon event. There was no reason to think that wasn't the case, though it also occurred to me that maybe they were allotting such a short period in case Bush's reception proved less than positive. He was, after all, Ronald Reagan's vice president, braving a very Democratic and black welcoming party.

I was a little worried about that myself when I looked out over the crowd and saw a group of demonstrators with picket signs on the other side of the street. But the speech went off without interruption, and afterward Bush was accosted by a cluster of African American Atlantan dignitaries, all of them Democrats, one after the other eager to have his picture taken with the vice president: Andy Young; John Lewis; Atlanta's mayor, Maynard Jackson; and Augusta's mayor, Ed McIntyre; among others. It was a highly ecumenical, bipartisan scene.

Bush's staff kept trying to move him out to his limousine, but he was brushing them off. It was obvious he was enjoying himself. We had been told fifteen minutes, but it was an hour before they were able to hustle him away. As he left, one of his aides put something into my hand, saying, "The vice president wants you to have this." It was little box of some sort. When the crowd began to dissipate I took a look; it was a set of vice presidential cuff links.

Two weeks later my assistant buzzed me with a call. "The vice president's on the line," he said.

"The vice president? What vice president?" I was in the middle of talking with the heads of the Atlanta University Center schools.

"*The* vice president!"

Oh, I thought. *That* vice president.

When I got on, Bush said, "Lou, I'm planning a trip to Africa in November. We're going to be visiting a number of sub-Saharan countries. I'd like it very much if you could come with me as part of my delegation."

This was a complete surprise. It was a moment before I could say anything. Why in the world would he be approaching me for this? "Gosh, Mr. Vice President, I'd be honored to go. I really have to look at my schedule to see if I can adjust it. But since I'm not in the government, can you tell me what my role would be?"

"To be honest with you," he said, "we don't have an Andy Young in our administration (Young had been Carter's UN ambassador). But I don't feel that I can go to visit Africa without some prominent African Americans in my delegation. You would be doing me a big favor personally, and you would be doing the country a service if you'd be willing to go."

I appreciated his candor. And after I had shifted one or two things around I called his office to accept. It turned out I was not the only African American in Bush's delegation. Ben Payton was there, the president of Tuskegee Institute— Bush had spoken at his inauguration a year earlier. Then there was Art Fletcher, who had been assistant secretary of labor in the Nixon administration and was now an adviser to Reagan. Art was a lifelong Republican, but he was a powerful advocate for affirmative action, as opposed to many of his political compatriots. Art had also been president of the United Negro College Fund; he was the one who had coined the phrase, "A mind is a terrible thing to waste."

Even if he often bucked his party on racial issues, Art was still a sincere Republican. As such he was alive to the ironies of representing men who, like Reagan, were not popular among African Americans, which had been true of Nixon as well. And here the three of us were, in black Africa accompanying Reagan's vice president.

Art wasn't the only one of us alive to the ironies. Ben and I were the perfect audience for his stories about the dangers. At one point, Art told us, he was addressing the annual NAACP meeting as Nixon's representative. Sensing their skepticism, he made an effort to be as polite and respectful as possible. "Ladies and gentlemen," he had said, "I bring you greetings and good wishes from the president of the United States, Richard Nixon."

At which an elderly woman sitting in the front row said, in a foghorn voice, "Sheeee-it!" For the next five minutes the place was a chaos of laughter. Art said he tried to hold back, but it was impossible. He couldn't help but join in the general uproar.

At each of the countries we visited on this trip the routine was more or less the same. At some point Bush himself would go off to meet with the president or prime minister, and the delegation would be shunted around to other events of varying importance. Barbara Bush was also in the delegation, and with all the time we were spending together, she and I got to know each other fairly well. We found we had plenty to talk about, and we both felt the beginnings of a friendship.

I didn't know much or anything about her background. I assumed she came from an old-line white family, which wasn't wrong. Her ancestors went far back in American history. But I also got the sense that she was highly sensitive to racial issues—this was before I found out how deeply the Bush family was involved in African American educational affairs. One afternoon in Senegal while Bush was meeting with the president, our delegation was attending a function, and Barbara, Art, Ben, and I were standing next to one another, listening to a band that was playing in our honor. As we stood there, they struck up the unmistakable strains of Stephen Foster's "Old Black Joe." Art, Ben, and I looked at each other incredulously. Were they kidding? Barbara's face had turned beet red. I'm sure she was thinking, what's next, Camptown ladies singing doo dah? Of course, the Senegalese had no idea. They were trying to honor us with a rendition of American music. Stephen Foster was one our greats, wasn't he, and "Old Black Joe" must have seemed appropriate, considering.

We were still in Senegal when we got word that Soviet general secretary Leonid Brezhnev had died. Exactly who would represent the administration at the funeral wasn't clear at first. Reagan himself wasn't going to go, but who would? Ordinarily, the vice president served as stand-in. Bush had done this quite a bit already. "My motto," he told us, "is 'You die—I fly.'" I was learning that Bush was a loose, relaxed person among friends, with a sense of humor—very different from the wooden appearance he made in front of cameras.

If Bush did go, we thought that might mean canceling the rest of the trip. He did go, but they didn't cancel. Instead we were all flown to the American military base in Frankfurt, Germany, for what seemed to be security reasons. From there George and Barbara and a few others flew to Moscow. Two days later they were back, and we took up our Africa trip where we had left off.

One of the things I learned about Barbara was her strong interest in adult literacy, which was a major challenge in many of the countries we visited. I listened to her presentations in front of different groups in different places. I was impressed by her knowledge of the subject and her touch with ordinary people. She would talk, then people in the group she was addressing seemed drawn to testify about what it meant to them to be illiterate, or literate, and how learning to read had changed their lives. Among other things, she was the keynote speaker at the dedication of Belvedere College in Zimbabwe, which had been modeled on Tuskegee Institute and built with USAID funds. Robert Mugabe had been in power for a year and a half; he was a hero then, the man who had liberated his country. He hadn't turned into the despot and disgrace he later became. Hope was in the air.

Barbara's dedication speech was fluent and strong. She was as good at addressing notables as she was at talking to common people. I began to hatch a plan. On the long flight back to the States we got to talking. "You know," I said, "you and I are in the same business, just different parts of it. You're as interested in education as I am. You know that we have a new medical school. We need someone like you on our board of trustees. Would you consider it?"

"Well, Lou," she said, "I really can't do anything without checking with White House counsel. But let me do that. I'll see what they say."

I thought that might just be a nice way of telling me no.

But a few days later she called. "Lou," she said, "I can do it." She sounded delighted. But she couldn't have been nearly as delighted as I was.

Barbara Bush came on our board in January 1983. She made it clear from the start that she wasn't going to be there in an honorary capacity. She came prepared to work, which I was happy to take full advantage of. Having Barbara with us added serious fund-raising firepower. It's not possible to exaggerate what that meant. Although we had been successful in our way at generating funds, our finances were still fragile. We were raising part of our funding from private sources, but without federal educational grants we would have been dead in the water, and politics made government funding a nervous affair at best.

That was one reason it was so essential to have senators Sam Nunn and Herman Talmadge on our board. But in 1980 Talmadge lost his seat to Mack Mattingly, who became the first Republican senator from Georgia since Reconstruction. When Mattingly was elected, I invited him to take Talmadge's board seat, which he accepted, fortunately for us. We had worked hard to include a provision in the higher education reauthorization bill that would provide funds we badly needed, especially to fund our transition to a four-year school, with the new clinical faculty and facilities that would require.

The language we managed to insert stated that dollars to support programming would be available to any new two-year school of medicine that had a letter of reasonable assurance of accreditation on September 30, 1978. We had crafted that provision with the help of Bud Blakey, who later became a senior staff person for Paul Simon, the chairman of the House Appropriations Committee. Only one school in the country actually met the provision's criterion—ourselves.

But in 1981 Congress had trouble agreeing on the appropriations bill, so they put everything in an omnibus budget reconciliation act. There were so many earmarks in there, though, that Oklahoma's David Boren moved to strip out what he called "nonrelevant amendments," which included section 326, our appropriation. "This bill has become a Christmas tree," he said. He was going to make sure it didn't pass.

If that happened we would very simply have come to a dead halt. So we urged Mack Mattingly to resist Boren's efforts. Mattingly in turn enlisted Thad Cochran of Mississippi, another Republican, and together they filibustered Boren's attempt to bring his version of the legislation to a vote on the Senate floor. The bill with our appropriation eventually passed, but it had been a dicey situation.

The result was that we got our funding, $3 million a year for five years. But the political drama had me biting my nails. In one way or another we were going to be relying on government funding in the future, just as every educational institution does. But this near fiasco drove up my motivation to raise our level of private donations. I was planning our first national fund-raising campaign, and having Barbara Bush at my side was a potential game changer.

The first order of business here was to find someone with a big national presence to chair our fund-raising committee. Equitable Life Insurance Company had a strong history of supporting black colleges, and I had a contact there, Darwin Davis, an African American who worked in that area with them. Darwin put me in touch with John Carter, Equitable's chairman and CEO. Barbara and I went to New York together to meet with him.

Carter knew what we were coming for and listened attentively to our pitch. "This is really exciting," he said. "I'd actually love to do it. But I've just accepted a request by the governor to serve on another board. That will be extremely demanding. I'm afraid I just wouldn't be able to devote the time."

I was thinking, oh boy. Carter was the best prospect we had.

"But," he said, "if you're willing to consider someone else, I have my executive chairman, Bob Froehlke, the former secretary of the army. He's been with us a year. He's got a great fund-raising track record. If you're willing to consider him, I think he'd be quite interested."

That was how Bob Froehlke became our committee chairman. He had been secretary of the army under Nixon and was a lifelong friend and associate of former defense secretary Melvin Laird. He had managed all of Laird's congressional races and was, as Carter said, an expert fund-raiser.

Our goal for the national campaign was $15 million. Froehlke, Barbara, and I worked together to develop a formula for how to do this. We set up lunches in various cities around the country: Boston, New York, Chicago, Minneapolis, Miami, San Francisco, Houston, and others, big cities where we had the best contacts. In each place we asked a well-known local businessman to be host. In Chicago, for example, we were able to enlist Don Clark, CEO of Household International, the country's largest credit card–issuing company. We always wanted to hold events in conducive venues. In Boston it was the Commonwealth Club, in Chicago, the Mid-America Club at the top of a skyscraper overlooking the lake.

Our host would open the gathering, welcoming people and telling them the Morehouse School of Medicine story, what an important venture it was, what it was doing to bring medical care to underserved areas, and so on. Then, as the guests were starting on dessert, our host would introduce Froehlke, who would tell them about the campaign to raise funds for facilities, faculty, laboratories, and scholarships. After his speech he would introduce Barbara, who was, of course, the person everyone had really come to see. Barbara would tell her personal story, how she had gotten involved with Morehouse and why, how we need more black physicians, how much she had learned from working with us, and how exciting it was to be part of this nationally important endeavor. It was impossible to miss the heartfelt commitment in her presentation.

After Barbara, I would come on to give the pitch. This much would pay a faculty salary; that much would give scholarships to five deserving students; such and such would equip a cardiovascular research laboratory. After me, Froehlke would come back to tell people that he hoped they would consider giving, as he himself had. "We'll be coming back to touch base with you," he said. "So please give it your most serious consideration." A week later I would go back to the city and make the calls.

Typically, in a city like Chicago we might raise $300,000 or $350,000. We did this in city after city, using more or less the same approach. It became so familiar that we started calling ourselves the Traveling Troubadours. We kicked off the campaign in the spring of 1984, a year after Barbara joined the board. We ended it in December 1985. Our goal had been $15 million. We raised $17 million.

Barbara was the key person in this campaign, for which I was deeply grateful. The fact that Morehouse School of Medicine was dedicated to the mission of serving the "underprivileged" (as she put it) in rural and inner-city areas was hugely important to her. A sense of fair play was embedded in her character and, as she saw it, minorities and minority schools had not been accorded fair play. Helping us raise money was her way of doing something about it.

As I got to know Barbara, and George Bush too, I discovered that there was nothing new about their commitment on this front. Their concern for African American education in particular went back to George Bush's days at Yale. While he was a student there, he had met William Trent, the founding executive director of the United Negro College Fund. Trent recruited the young Bush as the UNCF campus coordinator at Yale, and the Trents and Bushes (George and Barbara were already married) became good friends, a long-term cross-racial friendship that was not at all common in those days, especially in the Bush social set. Their relationship raised more than a few eyebrows.

As Barbara and I worked together, she and Ginger got to know and like each other as well. Ginger and I were frequently invited to Washington to functions and parties at the vice president's residence, which we greatly enjoyed, and when Barbara came to Atlanta for trustee meetings and school commencements she would come to luncheons and receptions at our home.

In addition, from the time Barbara joined the board, every year I received a personal check from the Bushes for the medical school, a substantial amount, unsolicited. Barbara was doing such a wonderful job raising money that I never considered asking for a donation, but they were not people who needed to be asked if they saw something they thought warranted their help. Ben Payton told me they were doing the same for Tuskegee.

In 1988 Bush ran for the Republican presidential nomination, with Ronald Reagan's support. By early June he had wrapped that up and had started planning for the nominating convention, scheduled for New Orleans in mid-August. One night I got a call from him. His name was going to be formally placed in nomination the Friday of the convention. On Thursday the program would highlight Barbara as the potential first lady. They had talked with people about who might introduce her, possibly Bob Dole or Bill Brock, or some other high-profile Republican. "But Barbara really doesn't know these people," Bush said. "She knows you, though. She likes working with you, and she likes what you're doing. I don't know what your politics are, Lou. I don't even know if you're a Republican or a Democrat. Or an independent. Frankly, I don't care. If you're willing to do this, introduce her, she would be flattered."

I agreed, of course. Ginger and the children came to New Orleans with me for the event, which was held in the jam-packed New Orleans Super Dome. I gave the short introductory speech, very much aware that most of the convention attendees were thinking, who in the world is this guy?

During the presidential campaign itself I told Bush that Ginger and I would like to host a reception for him and Barbara at our home in Atlanta. "Mr. Vice President," I said, "the reality is that the black community doesn't really know you. I think it would help them to do that if we had this reception. Also, Atlanta is really the center of the civil rights movement. It would be important if you got to meet some of the leaders personally. You saw most of them briefly years ago when you gave our building dedication speech. You may not remember, but they were all taking pictures with you."

Bush hadn't known when he asked me to introduce Barbara at the convention, but I was in fact a registered Republican, though I wasn't active in any way. My father, of course, had been a Republican. He identified with Lincoln, but even more important, he was a Republican because the people who were tying to prevent him from voting were Democrats. He had been quite upset back in 1960 when I told him I was voting for Kennedy. There were a lot of things I didn't like about some Republicans, people who lacked compassion, who had a mean streak and had no interest in helping those who needed it. But I did espouse certain Republican core principles: initiative, creativity, innovation, independence, responsibility.

Bush reflected the kind of values I was comfortable with. Bob Dole, his adversary in the primaries, also did to a degree. I thought they adhered to the positive conservative values, but they also had an interest in working with people and helping them when it was called for. Bush's interest in and support of black colleges was an example. That was one of the biggest secrets around. He, and other Republicans like him, understood that we have had a terribly troubled history of race relations in this country, and they knew that we still suffered from it, that there was an aggregate impact of decades of segregation and discrimination. They didn't have the attitude of some others, who said in essence—I had nothing to do with that, so I don't have any responsibility, even though they had been the beneficiaries from their inheritance.

So my own politics were a mixed bag, but I liked Bush; I liked his decency and his basic principles. I didn't mind if people knew I was a Republican. I had never

Me, one year old

Mom (Lubirda Sullivan), with me, age 1, and Walter Jr., age 2½, 1934

Me leading a meeting as senior class president in high school, 1949–50

Me, as a senior student at Morehouse College, greeting Morehouse president
Benjamin E. Mays and Mrs. Sadie Mays at the dedication of the lounge
in Merrill Hall, spring 1954

Medical school graduation, 1958. From left: Mom, me,
Mrs. Constance Moseley (family friend), and Dad

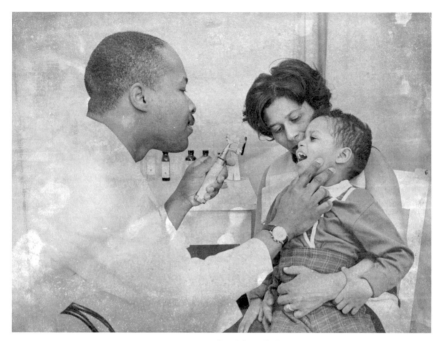

Boston City Hospital sickle cell clinic, 1971

Family, 1967. Counterclockwise from left:
Paul, Ginger, Halsted, Shanta, and me

Europe, 1963. From left: Paul, me, and Mom.

Boston University medical faculty, Boston City Hospital, 1967–68

First meeting of Morehouse School of Medicine (MSM) Board of Overseers, April 1976.
First row: James Palmer; Edgar Smith (chairman); me (president); Sarah Austin (secretary).
Second row: James Story (associate dean); Calvin Brown; Edward Mazique; Sally Guerry;
Pierre Galletti; Robert Berliner. Third row: Nolen Ellison; Carlton Goodlett;
Constance Menninger; Dale A. Kendrick. Fourth row: William Castle; William Hubbard;
Ephraim Friedman; Hugh Burroughs; Alphonso Overstreet

MSM inaugural convocation, September 1978. Left to right: Carlton Alexis, vice president for Health Affairs, Howard University; me; Arthur Richardson, dean of Emory University School of Medicine; Paul Rogers, chair of the Health Subcommittee of the Energy and Commerce Committee, U.S. House of Representatives; Thomas Kilgore, chair of the Board of Trustees, Morehouse College; Donald Frederickson, director of the National Institutes of Health; Senator Sam Nunn; President Hugh M. Gloster (Photo: Bud Smith)

President Hugh M. Gloster and President Emeritus Benjamin Elijah Mays of Morehouse College at the MSM inaugural convocation, September 1978 (Photo: Bud Smith)

Georgia governor George Busbee (center) at the groundbreaking for the
Basic Medical Sciences Building, MSM, 1980 (Lybensons Photo Service)

President Gloster speaking in March 1980 at the groundbreaking ceremonies for the
Basic Medical Sciences Building, the first building constructed for the school of
medicine (renamed the Hugh M. Gloster Building in 2000)

Chairman of the Board Clinton Warner presenting me the
presidential mace at my inauguration, April 1984

Groundbreaking for the Second Medical Education Building, April 12, 1985.
Left to right: Clinton E. Warner, MD, Atlanta surgeon and MSM board chairman;
Robert F. Froehlke, MSM trustee and chairman of the Equitable Assurance Society
and of MSM's $15 million campaign; L. Leon Dent, president of the class of 1985;
me, MSM president; and Cyril L. Moore, PhD, professor and chairman of the
Department of Biochemistry

Testifying to the U.S. House Committee on Education, 1988
(Ankers Photographers, Inc.)

Talking about the Department of Health and Human Services
with Vice President George H. W. Bush, November 1988
(George Bush Presidential Library and Museum)

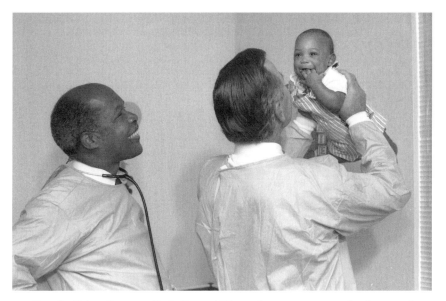

Boarder Babies Program, D.C. General Hospital, 1989, a program for the care of healthy babies of drug-addicted mothers undergoing drug-withdrawal therapy (George Bush Presidential Library and Museum)

Health and Fitness Day, South Lawn of the White House, April 1990, with President Bush, Barbara Bush, and Arnold Schwarzenegger (chairman of the President's Council on Sports and Fitness) (George Bush Presidential Library and Museum)

Senior management of the U.S. Department of Health and Human Services
at strategic planning retreat, National Institutes of Health campus, 1990

President Bush's first cabinet meeting after being sworn in, January 20, 1989.
From left to right: Lauro Cavazos, secretary of education; me; Marlin Fitzwater,
White House press secretary; Manuel Lujan, secretary of the interior;
James Baker, secretary of state; Fred McClure, liaison to the U.S. Congress;
President George H. W. Bush; Michael Boskin, chairman of the Presidents Council
of Economic Advisors; John Tower, secretary of defense designee
(George Bush Presidential Library and Museum)

Reception at the National Portrait Gallery for the unveiling of a bust of Rosa Parks, 1991.
From left to right: Dr. Hazel N. Dukes, president of the NAACP New York State Conference;
Artis Lane, artist; Rev. Joseph Lowery, chairman emeritus of the Southern Christian Leadership
Conference; Delores Jordan; Cicely Tyson, actress; Rosa Parks; Coretta Scott King; Ginger Sullivan;
Carmen Turner, former head of Washington Metro Area Transit Authority; Wayman Smith III,
former vice president of Anheuser-Busch; Alan M. Fern, former director of the National Portrait
Gallery (Photo: Jason Miccolo Johnson)

Dr. Robert C. Weaver, secretary of housing and urban
development under Lyndon B. Johnson; me; and
William Coleman, secretary of transportation under Richard
Nixon, 1992. Weaver was the first black cabinet secretary;
Coleman was the second; I was the fifth.

Meeting with Ibrahima Tounkara and Dr. Erick Gbodossu at
Malango Traditional Healers Center, Fatick, Senegal, May 3, 1995

Barbara Bush visiting MSM's Neuroscience Center, December 1998,
accompanied by Peter MacLeish, director of the center, and me

Africare's Bishop Walker Dinner, 2001, where I received Africare's Bishop T. Walker
Distinguished Humanitarian Service Award. Left to right: Susan Rice, Ambassador
Koby Koomson of Ghana, me, Ginger, Dr. Vincent Anku, and Mrs. Koomson
(Photo: Gustave Assiri)

Visiting former president of South Africa Nelson Mandela at his home in
Johannesburg, South Africa, October 1999, while serving as chairman of the
Board of Medical Education for South African Blacks

Me, Laura Bush, President Ellen Johnson Sirleaf of Liberia, President George W. Bush, and Ginger, 2004 (Official White House Photograph)

Georgia governor George E. "Sonny" Perdue presenting me with the 2005 Leadership Award from the Georgia Civil Rights Commission (Office of the Governor of Georgia)

Receiving the National Foundation for Infectious Diseases Jimmy and
Rosalynn Carter Award for Humanitarian Contributions, March 2008

First Obama inauguration, January 20, 2009, with Ginger and Shanta,
on a clear, cold 18-degree Fahrenheit morning

Early County 2055, an economic development program for Blakely and
Early County, 2010, for which I serve as an advisor, funded by the Charles and
Catherine Rice Foundation (former residents of Blakely)

David Chanoff meeting with black residents of Blakely and Early County,
arranged by Rev. Fred Daniels (standing)

The family: Paul, Halsted, Ginger, me, and Shanta

Laura and Paul, grandsons Paul Jr. and Brent

advertised it, but I wasn't keeping it a secret either. So Ginger and I did host a reception, even though I knew it might ruffle some feathers. But from my perspective, Barbara had been a great trustee. She had given her time, her political capital, her celebrity, in helping to raise money. I had great admiration for both her and Bush. So I was going to work to help him, knowing that questions would be raised. But I thought—I can't really be boxed in by those kinds of things, otherwise I'd never get anything done. As long as I feel comfortable with what I'm doing, if I think it's the right thing, then I'm going to do it.

So we hosted a reception. Bush himself couldn't come because of his schedule, but Barbara did, and many prominent people in both the white and black communities turned out to meet her, including most of our trustees. One who didn't was Monroe Trout, my vice-chairman, who lived in Connecticut and couldn't make it.

Monroe had been executive vice president at Sterling Pharmaceuticals and had recently taken over as chairman of American Health Services. He and I got along extremely well. Monroe had an unusual background; he came from an impoverished family with many children but had managed to put himself through college, medical school, and law school. Along with Edgar Smith and Sarah Austin, the board's secretary, he was the person I most relied on.

Monroe was active in Republican Party circles, and in 1985 when Health and Human Services secretary Margaret Heckler had gone off to serve as ambassador to Ireland, he had been in the running to succeed her. Three finalists remained then, all of whom were interviewed by Don Regan, Reagan's chief of staff. Monroe told me that the interview hadn't gone well. He and Regan had clashed. When he left the White House afterward he knew he didn't have it.

"I came close back then," he told me. "I'm still interested. I'd actually love it. Do you think you could support me with Bush?"

"Sure, Monroe," I said. "I'll be happy to. I think you'd be a great secretary."

The idea of Monroe as secretary raised all sorts of possibilities. As soon as he mentioned it, I started thinking, with Bush in the White House and Monroe at HHS I'd have unprecedented access. The funding potential would be tremendous. My mind was already jumping to some of the things I'd be able to do.

So I told Bush about Monroe. Bush had met him during one of his fund-raising receptions; Barbara had introduced him. So Monroe wasn't completely unknown to him. When September came around I pushed a little. "You know, we talked earlier about Monroe Trout, who I think would be a great secretary."

"Good," said Bush. "Be sure to get me all the information."

A week or so before the election I was in New York City. Walking along Fifth Avenue I passed the Aquascutum store, and something in the window caught my eye, a beautiful blue tie with small red elephants on it. I bought it and sent it to Bush. "Wear this on election day," I wrote on the note card. "It'll bring you good luck."

Sure enough, when the cameras focused in on him on election night, I could see he was wearing the tie. And he won.

The next morning I called to congratulate him. "I see you followed my recommendation and look what happened. Congratulations, Mr. President."

We had a laugh.

"Remember, we talked about Monroe Trout, who I thought would make a great secretary? I still do."

"I haven't forgotten, Lou," Bush said. "But to be honest, I haven't gotten the reaction I think I need to have in order to go forward with him. I was thinking, in a couple of weeks when things have quieted down, if you would be willing to come up to Washington, I'd like to talk with you about that."

I said, "Sure." But when I hung up I thought, what the hell did he mean by that? Did he mean, what should we do to get Monroe positioned right? But it sounds as if he wants to talk to me—about me. I discussed this development with a couple of people, quietly, including my chairman, Clint Warner. "No point in drawing conclusions yet," Clint said. "Let's just see what happens."

CHAPTER 9

President Bush Calls

I had spent my life in the academic world, not politics. I didn't begin to have Monroe Trout's political qualifications. I knew he'd make a great secretary. I had never even thought about myself in that regard. This whole idea was going to take a lot of consideration—if that was actually what Bush wanted to talk to me about.

This development was a surprise, but it wasn't completely out of the blue either. A couple of weeks earlier I had gotten a call from Roy Keith, the new Morehouse College president; he had come in after Gloster retired the previous year. Keith told me he was submitting my name. I had told him not to bother. "Don't waste your time, Roy. I'm not political. I don't have any interest. I love the job I have."

That had led to a ten-minute argument, until Roy finally said, "Listen, Lou, I didn't call you to ask your permission. I'm just informing you."

"OK. Fine. Do whatever you want, but there's no point. I'm not a candidate."

Then, maybe ten days later, Frank Royal called. I had first met Frank back in 1975 when he was chairman of the National Medical Association Board, and he and the other board members had been so worried that a new Morehouse medical school would divert funds away from Meharry and Howard. Since then, though, we had worked together well. Morehouse and Meharry had benefited from the

Association of Minority Health Professions Schools we had formed in 1977, and I had assiduously pursued initiatives that joined rather than separated us. Frank and I had long ago become friends.

Frank Royal was a lifelong Republican. He had a practice in Richmond, Virginia, and he was close to Virginia's powerful Republican senator John Warner. In addition to his NMA position, Frank was still the chairman of Meharry's board. He too was putting my name in.

"You know," I said, "Roy Keith said the same. I told him I have no interest in going to Washington. I don't want it. One of my trustees is very interested, though. He's highly qualified and he does want it. Monroe Trout. I'm supporting him."

"That's fine, Lou," Frank Royal said. "But I think we need somebody like you there, and I think you have a great chance. I'm going to put your name in."

"Fine. Whatever."

It wasn't worth another argument. I dismissed this kind of talk, anyway. These things happen all the time, I thought, people suggesting somebody or other. They're essentially meaningless. But then my name surfaced in a couple of news articles: "Dr. Everett Koop has been mentioned as being under consideration as secretary for Health and Human Services, also Dr. Louis Sullivan of the Morehouse School of Medicine." I attributed that to either Roy or Frank. As someone more or less naive then to how Washington works, I didn't know that one of the ways an administration vets names is to give them to the press, to see what kind of reaction they get, what might come out of the woodwork. Reporters will investigate. They might turn up that the potential nominee is a wife beater or a tax cheat or has something else nefarious in his background.

I wasn't prepared for this. I especially wasn't prepared for the call I got from our librarian, Beverly Allen. "Dean Sullivan, what is all this?"

"What is all what, Beverly?"

"Who are these people? Showing up here in my library wanting to see all your writings and publications."

"My what?"

"They want to see everything you've written about abortion."

"What?"

I had never written anything about abortion, or talked about abortion, or even given any particular thought to abortion. But the antiabortion people were bound and determined to find out if I had. My name had been mentioned. I was unknown to them. They were going to get every scrap of information on me they could.

Just before Thanksgiving I went to Washington to see president-elect Bush. My appointment was for ten thirty. I flew up the night before and stayed at the Sheraton Carlton Hotel at Sixteenth and K, two blocks from the White House. The next morning I had a leisurely breakfast and read the newspaper. At about ten o'clock I walked over, through Lafayette Park to Pennsylvania Avenue, where I presented myself at the security gate on the west side of the White House. I showed my license and my letter of invitation. "I have an appointment with the president-elect," I told the guard.

"Yes sir, we have it down in the schedule. But we have some visitors here"—he gestured toward the limousines parked in the circular drive. "Would you mind going down to the next gate, sir, the Old Executive Office Building. They'll take care of you there."

I started down the sidewalk toward the next gate when I heard, "There he is! There he is!" People were running toward me, some with cameras. "You're Dr. Sullivan?"

"Yes."

"You're meeting with the president-elect?"

"Well, yes."

"What are you meeting with him about?"

"You'll have to ask him."

"Is he going to offer you a job as HHS secretary?"

"I've been requested to meet with him. I'm here for that."

I was totally surprised, ambushed. I had no idea anybody knew who I was. I wasn't someone people recognized on the street. And this crowd of reporters included *Atlanta Journal-Constitution* people. Cameras were all over the place, television cameras too. Suddenly I was aware some of this was going to be on television, so I was trying to act dignified. But at the same time I was trying to walk as fast as I could to get to that damned gate down there.

They kept asking me questions as we walked. "How do you know President Bush?" "Why are you here?" "Who else is under consideration?" "Will you take the job?"

"I can't answer. I can't answer your questions."

Finally I got to the gate.

"When you come out, will you come out this way?"

"Yes, yes."

"Will you speak with us then?"

"Well, we'll see."

I got to the OEOB. They typed me into the computer. Inside they gave me a badge. Then, "Sir, the original gate you went to is now open. If you don't mind, could you go back to that gate? They'll let you in there."

I went back out, and, of course, the reporters were still there. It was only seven or eight minutes later. The quickest meeting ever.

"What happened?" they asked. "What did they say to you?"

"I'm simply going for an appointment." I wondered if I should try sprinting to the gate. "It's just an appointment. That's all it is."

When I finally got in and was waiting to see president-elect Bush, I told Bob Teeter, his press secretary, what had happened.

"You did what?" he said. "You're telling me you walked here?" He was incredulous. "Why in the world didn't you come by car?"

"Well, my hotel's just a couple of blocks away, so I walked."

"Don't even think about doing that! You walked? We'll have a car take you back. Nobody walks to the White House."

When I met with Bush, we talked for about half an hour.

Sure enough, he wanted to talk to me about the position. Would I accept it?

I said, "Well, I'm deeply honored. I hope you don't mind if I take a little time to sort this through. I have all these things going on at the school. I know you know that I've never been in public office. I have some people whose advice I need to get."

"I understand," he said. "It goes without saying—you need to think about it."

"I haven't given this prospect any consideration," I told him. "But maybe we should at least discuss a couple of things. I do know that if I were to be secretary there are a number of areas that would be important to me."

Bush and I had known each other now for six years, ever since that 1982 trip to Africa. But we had never had any discussions about policy; that hadn't been the basis of our relationship. Before he asked me to introduce Barbara at the convention, he hadn't even known if I was a Republican. Well, I was a Republican, but he still didn't know what kind of a Republican or what my priorities were. And I had no idea what kind of support I'd get from him if this secretary business did become a reality.

"Of course. What kinds of things are you thinking of?"

"One is that we need to have more diversity among doctors and other health professionals. Minorities are grossly underrepresented. We need to have more women in senior positions. I'd want to strengthen health programs like Medicaid. Strengthen them and extend them."

"Lou," he said, "that's fine. I agree with you fully. I'd support you in those things. But you should think very carefully about whether you want to do this. I'm not sure I'm doing you any favor here. My staff tells me the average HHS secretary's tenure is about eighteen or nineteen months."

Afterward I met with Teeter and Craig Fuller, another of Bush's staff people, who briefed me about the process and the job. I was with them almost two hours. "Above all," Teeter said, "you should keep an extremely low profile. Do not under any circumstances talk to the press. If someone asks you a question, you say, 'I know nothing about this. If you need to know anything, ask the president's staff.' First and last, *do not* answer any questions! In particular, don't make any statements."

On my way back to Atlanta I was thinking, how did this happen? I somehow didn't believe that either Roy Keith or Frank Royal had enough access to make a serious case for my nomination. It must have been Barbara, I thought. She had been a hardworking trustee; we had spent all that time together. She knew the medical school well and liked how we handled things there. I was fairly convinced that was it. She must have suggested it, and George must have thought, here was somebody he liked well enough personally, who could bring some diversity into his cabinet. And, of course, he liked the medical school too. But Barbara had to have played a strong role. Many years later I asked her directly, but she denied having had anything at all to do with it, which I took with a large grain of salt.

Back in Atlanta I really did have to sort things out. My ongoing responsibility was to the school. I had been dean or president for thirteen years, but I certainly hadn't accomplished everything I was planning to accomplish. We had had twenty-four students in our first class. Now we had thirty-two. Our goal was sixty-four, so we were only halfway there.

We hadn't developed some of our subspecialty areas yet either. We had the major specialties: medicine, surgery, pediatrics, public health, community medicine, and so on, but not the smaller ones like ophthalmology, dermatology, otolaryngology, and anesthesiology. I expected to bring these in over the coming years. The last thing I wanted to do was leave the school in the lurch, where we might lose some of the goals we had achieved or had on the horizon.

On the other hand, any successor I might have would be working toward the same goals. And there was no denying the attraction of becoming secretary. The biggest was that I would have the opportunity to address in a much broader way the very kinds of things I was already doing at the medical school.

Morehouse's mission had always been to train more minority physicians to alleviate the truly urgent needs of the minority community. We were promoting research on health problems that affected minorities and attempting to pioneer programs in community health. As secretary, I could have a substantial influence on the dollars being spent in these areas and on the programs being generated for this. And, of course, if I were secretary I'd be able to do this not just for minorities, but for the entire underserved population. I would have an influence on issues that affected hospital care, community center care, health insurance, Social Security (which at that time was part of the department), retirement, Medicaid policy, and health care coverage. Health and Human Services touched the lives of every American every day.

This was all new; I hadn't thought about it comprehensively. I didn't grasp the whole scope of it yet. But one thing was clear. If I did do it, I'd be universalizing the goals I came to the medical school with. I'd be turning my life around once again, more than a little overwhelming to think about—but what an opportunity!

The other side of it was that there could be some real negative consequences for the medical school. I needed to think it through and get some reactions. I talked again with Clint Warner, my chairman. He thought it would be a good idea, even though my leaving would pressure him and the others to find a new president and make a transition, never an easy job. I talked with Roy Keith, the Morehouse College president. But Roy had no qualms; he was one of the people who had forwarded my name in the first place.

I was concerned about what might happen with the Georgia legislature, though. We had substantial funding from the state, and the legislature was mostly Democratic. It was one thing if I was a soft-spoken, minding-my-own-business kind of Republican. It might be another if I was the Georgia Republican in George Bush's cabinet.

To test the waters there I went to see Tom Murphy, who had been speaker of the Georgia House for twenty-six years. In terms of political power in Georgia, he was it; the governor ran a distant second. Murphy was a big man, tall and heavy. He wore cowboy boots, a cowboy hat, and a belt with a big buckle. He chewed tobacco. He had been a good friend to the Morehouse School of Medicine for years.

I went in and said, "Mr. Speaker, I really need your advice. I've had this meeting with president-elect Bush. He wants me to serve as his Health and Human

Services secretary. I'm thinking about that, but I wanted to ask your opinion. You've been extremely supportive of the medical school. I wouldn't do anything at all that might jeopardize that."

Murphy reached in his pocket and pulled out a wad of Redman Tobacco. He took his pocketknife, cut off a piece, and stuck it in his cheek. Then he stared at me. The whole act probably took two minutes; it felt like two hours.

"Well," he drawled, "if Mr. Bush wants you to be his secretary, I don't think you have much choice. Do you? You'd be serving the country. You don't turn down a president. Plus, so far as I'm concerned there's not a dime's worth of difference between Bush and Dukakis anyway."

I knew Murphy did not like Dukakis in the least. He was telling me that my being Bush's secretary would be fine by him. After talking with Murphy and Keith and some of my board, I was satisfied that my leaving wasn't going to harm the medical school in any way. But it bore in on me that if I did leave, that would be it. I would truly be severing my ties. The federal ethics laws dictated that I could not maintain any sort of relationship. I couldn't even have any understanding or agreement that I would come back when the job in Washington was over, whenever that might be. Ethically, I simply could not have anything to do with Morehouse. This would be a huge change of life, similar to what had happened when I took the deanship and left hematology behind.

I'm not quite sure how Ginger had felt about coming to Atlanta initially. It was unknown territory for her, a different culture and an entirely different set of people. I might have been an honorary Yankee after twenty years in the North, but she was born and bred. When I took the Morehouse job I was, in reality, coming home. She most definitely was not. But she had made a life for herself there. She had gone to law school and clerked for a superior court judge. She had helped tremendously at the medical school, founding the Friends of Morehouse School of Medicine. The Friends raised money for scholarships and worked hard to heighten the profile of the school. After thirteen years she had made herself at home in Atlanta. But how would she feel about pulling up stakes again and starting over someplace else?

I needn't have worried. Ginger was excited by the prospect. I felt honored that Bush had asked me. She felt honored as well. All the children were out of the house by then: Paul in a radiology residency in New York; Shanta just coming back from a Guggenheim art history fellowship in Italy; our youngest, Halsted, finishing up his bachelor's degree at the University of Virginia. We were on our own, and Ginger was looking forward to being on our own in the capital. Whatever I decided, she was up for it.

For thirteen years now my identity had been wrapped up with the Morehouse School of Medicine. I wasn't feeling any little prickles of desire to change that, any small voice whispering to me that it was time to get on with something new. But being HHS secretary would open up a world of possibilities. I had always enjoyed challenges, and this would certainly be a tremendous challenge. But that wasn't fundamental. Being head of a medical school had enough challenges to satisfy anybody.

What really drew me was the potential. At Morehouse we were striving to address one part of the basic requirement people had for medical care they needed and did not have: doctors who would take care of them. But as secretary I would have in hand the entire array of health care needs. The Health and Human Services budget was $600 billion, by far the largest of any federal agency, including the Defense Department. HHS oversaw 250 programs, including NIH, CDC, FDA, the Public Health Service, and even, at that time, Social Security and Medicare/Medicaid. There was, in the end, no way I could turn my back on the opportunity the secretary's job would give me to influence the nation's overall health care instead of just one problem, fundamental as it was, of health care for the underserved.

At the same time I would be a visible representative of the black community in the president's cabinet—the only black member, for certain. My presence by itself would make a statement about priorities, about care for the underserved, and about the legitimacy of African Americans in the mainstream of American life.

Putting all that together with my respect and affection for Bush and the weight, by itself, of a president's request, and this was not something I was going to turn down. So I called. "I've given it some thought, Mr. President," I said. "I'm pleased to accept your offer."

In early December I was in Washington again, this time for an extended briefing. Bush's staff gave me big three-ring notebooks addressing all the major and many of the secondary yet still-important issues facing HHS. They briefed me on substantive matters and such (to me) arcane Washington concerns as etiquette requirements. I was told, for instance, that at any gathering with high-level attendees I had to know where I ranked so that I would not leave before it was socially permissible. The secretaries of state, treasury, defense, and so on preceded the HHS secretary in ranking, and so I would need to stay put until they exited the premises.

More pertinent, perhaps, I was briefed on how to deal with Congress and with the press—most especially with the press, representatives of which I was not to talk to.

As events soon proved, that was a lesson I did not take sufficiently to heart. Back in Atlanta a *Journal-Constitution* reporter named Kevin Sack contacted me. Reports that I was likely to be nominated were now circulating freely. Could he, he asked, do a profile on me for the paper? He knew there was an embargo on press contacts and that I didn't want to talk to reporters yet. But he wanted to have a story prepared in the event that I was nominated. If that happened it would be big news in Atlanta and it was important for people outside the health establishment to know my story. If I permitted him to interview me for the profile, he would promise not to publish it until after I was formally nominated, assuming I was. Nothing would see print until then.

That sounded okay to me. I had enjoyed a good working relationship with the Atlanta press for years. I was constantly, in fact, trying to get them to pay more attention to Morehouse, its growth, its impact, its importance. At Morehouse we were always trying to flag the press down—"Hey press! Look, we're over here!" I had a dedicated PR person whose main job was to find effective ways to say, "Look at us!" or "Look at me," since I was the school's public face. I thought my briefer's insistence about the press was more than a little overdone. So I said, "Okay," and Sack interviewed me.

The next morning I opened up the paper, and there was the profile. He had totally sandbagged me. As if that wasn't devastating enough, one of the questions he had asked me was about abortion: what was my position on it? And there was my answer, right out there in public. "Personally, I'm not in favor. I've never been involved with abortion one way or another. But the law of the land gives a woman the right to choose. If I'm nominated and sworn in, part of my constitutional responsibility would be to see that the laws are enforced."

Wrong answer. Wrong. Wrong. Wrong.

That answer was so wrong. The Far Right didn't trust Bush to begin with, and the antiabortion people didn't trust him most of all. Bush had been pro-choice earlier in his career. He changed that when he ran against Reagan in the 1980 primaries. But his true-blue commitment was highly suspect. Barbara had never stated her position, but people surmised she was really pro-choice.

So here was this incoming president they didn't trust. And now here was this unknown character who appears out of nowhere and makes a statement like this, giving what to the antiabortion people was a pro-choice answer. For them the only right answer would have been, "I think abortion is evil. I'm totally and irrevocably against it. If I'm confirmed I'll do everything I can to eliminate it."

Not more than an hour or two later I got a call from Craig Fuller of Bush's staff. An irate call: "What the hell is this?" he said. "We told you not to talk to the press!"

Not only was I embarrassed and chagrined. I felt like I was from East Podunk. Here they had told me. Then I had gone and done it, even if it was under false pretenses from the journalist, not that I'd ever talk to him again. But who cared about that?

"We need to have you come up to Washington for several days," Fuller said.

I went up. They gave me a room in the Hubert Humphrey Building and had staff come in to brief me on a whole range of issues, this time far more thoroughly. Abortion, welfare, disability, all the issues, most especially the controversial ones. Marlin Fitzwater came by to talk. He had been Reagan's press secretary, and he was going to be Bush's. He was especially unhappy about what I had done. I was going to need a thorough orientation on how to deal with the press and also how to handle testimony in front of Congress. That *Journal-Constitution* interview had all but sabotaged my nomination. But Bush had tremendous loyalty toward his people, which apparently included me since he had offered me the position. So they were going to do their best to salvage the situation.

They did, obviously, have other potential candidates. Nobody said this, but nobody had to. One was Everett ("Chick") Koop, Reagan's surgeon general. Koop was a prominent public figure, and after seven years in Washington, extremely well versed in the politics of health care. Otis Bowen, Reagan's HHS secretary and Koop's immediate boss, was happy to stay in the background and let Koop have the limelight—and attract the lightning, which Koop did. In the process Koop had built up a substantial national constituency. He was a candid, attention-getting spokesperson on health care. Everybody knew him.

Koop, I think, believed he would be Bush's appointee. He considered himself extremely experienced and extremely qualified, both of which he was, and some of the news articles speculated that he would get the nomination. It didn't seem reasonable to him that his candidacy might be dismissed in favor of a small medical school's dean with no experience of the political world and no presence whatsoever on the national stage, someone who seemed to have materialized out of the blue.

The other side was that Bush may not have been particularly enamored of Koop. I didn't know anything about this personally, but Bush was likely concerned that

Koop might go off the reservation. He had done exactly that with Reagan. Koop had a strong and highly public antiabortion position. But when Reagan had asked for a report that stated abortion affected the health of pregnant women, he had refused on the grounds that there was no evidence for it. That had caused a turmoil. Koop had been vocally antitobacco, which alienated a powerful segment of Reagan supporters, and he was in favor of sex education, which alienated another core Reagan constituency. Bush needed to build a team. It's questionable whether Koop's brand of outspoken autonomy appealed to him.

Beyond that, Bush had been living in Reagan's shadow for eight years. Now he needed to distance himself and, finally, get out from under. He needed to assert his independence and make the presidency his own. Keeping too many of Reagan's people would do nothing to further that goal.

For Koop, the secretary's office was almost an obsession, this from the candid memoir he wrote several years later. For my part, I never thought about who might be my rival. Bush had asked me; that seemed to be the beginning and the end of it. I had, in my naïveté, almost upended my nomination, and I did think a lot about that, but not about who might be waiting in the wings if I went under.

One event that in hindsight illuminated where both Koop and I were on this subject happened at the Bushes' 1988 Christmas reception. Ginger and I had been invited to these Bush parties for years; the only difference now was that I was the presumptive nominee. At this event Bush introduced me to Fred Malek, someone I'd never met. "Fred's a good friend," he said. "He'd like to get to know you. Why don't you spend a few minutes chatting with him?"

Malek was one of Bush's close advisers, but I had never heard of him and had no idea who he was other than a friend at the reception. But in retrospect, it was obvious that Bush wanted Malek to have a good look at me. Koop was at the reception too, but he did know who Malek was and he saw us talking, which signified a lot to him even if it didn't to me. He wrote in his book that when Bush said good-bye to him at that party, he knew it really did mean good-bye.

Until I read Koop's book, I wasn't aware of how much this had truly meant to him. Years later, after we were both out of government service, we developed a cordial working relationship. But my first sit-down with him once I had taken office should have told me how deeply he was feeling about having lost the job that he felt should have been his by rights.

In May, two months after my confirmation, Koop came to see me. He was still surgeon general then; his six-year appointment wasn't up until November. We weren't more than five minutes into the meeting when he stood up and said, "I'm sorry, I just can't go through with this. Will you excuse me?" And he walked out.

I never got an explanation for that. But my own explanation was that he really had believed he was going to get the position, and it was a shock that he didn't. I think he came in intending to have a conversation and establish a relationship, but the emotional stress of seeing this person he was now reporting to was just too much to take. Shortly afterward he submitted his resignation.

Before taking office I spent a good deal of time learning the ropes, what to say to the press and how to say it, most especially what not to say. I rehearsed at length how to handle congressional hearings. We did that in a special room set up to look like a Senate hearing room. Tom Korologos, a sort of lower-keyed Karl Rove type, played chairman and ran the mock hearings, which everyone called "murder boards," appropriately. Others sat in as panel members. They asked pointed questions, and they didn't spare the drama.

"Mr. Secretary, I understand the FDA is having a problem with tainted food. We haven't heard anything about what you are doing. Why is that? What are you hiding from us?"

I'd respond. Then after fifteen minutes we'd go back through it.

"Lou, you said X. No, please. That isn't the right way to respond to something like this. Here's how you handle this kind of question."

I learned. I learned that you don't have to take back words you have never spoken. But once a word does leave your lips, you've lost control of it. So you don't want to say anything you'll then have to go on the defensive over. "Oh, what I really meant to say was Y."

So, before you rush to answer, take your time. What's the best response? What's the answer to the question that's going to follow this question? The fundamental lesson they were teaching was not to get caught up emotionally, no matter how you might feel, no matter what kind of attack you might be under. Once that happens you've lost control of the situation. There are times you want to be seen pounding your fist on the table—but you only do that deliberately. You do it for effect.

Marlin Fitzwater talked with me. Tom Korologos worked with me. Then they gave me over to Alan Simpson. If I needed reassurance, that reassured me. Simpson was the Senate minority whip, very close to Bush. What this told me was that unless something else egregious happened, I wasn't going to be dropped. They were going to try to salvage and rehabilitate me.

Simpson himself was antiabortion, but he wasn't a militant. After my formal nomination, he was the one who escorted me around on the Hill, introducing me to senators, first of all to Arlen Specter, a pro-choice Republican from Pennsylvania.

Simpson brought me to Specter's office, but Specter said he'd rather have me over to his condominium to talk, which seemed a little unusual. Afterward I understood. Specter wanted to talk to me personally, in a relaxed setting, with no secretaries or handlers or any other distracting business. He wanted to get to the heart of my true position on abortion

"I really do think I would have a responsibility to enforce the existing law," I told him.

"Yes, of course you would," he said. "But you should know that that is not the answer the pro-life people want to hear from you. They'd rather have you doing everything you can to prevent abortion. But what is your actual opinion, confidentially, between us here?"

"Senator, the fact is that I've never been involved at all with this question. My entire background is in hematology. But, if you ask my wife, she'll tell you she's pro-choice. So if I get pushed to the wall . . ."

"Well," he said, "that's fine. Let's leave it at that."

Simpson would introduce me, telling people they could be very frank with me, then he'd leave and I'd talk with each senator. Typically I'd have fifteen minutes or so, then Simpson would be back. I found Bob Dole to be a very warm, very solid person, a fiscal conservative but a social liberal. Tom Harkin was very supportive, as were our Georgia senators, of course, Sam Nunn and Wyche Fowler, and others. I didn't sense any hostility from anyone—with the exception of Jessie Helms— not even from the old-time southern dinosaurs like Strom Thurmond.

For most of the senators I was a curiosity. They had never heard of me. Here was this black doctor George Bush had nominated, someone who headed a school many of them had never heard of either. And Bush's wife used to be on this person's board. That was interesting. What was that about? My credentials seemed good enough to them. They were interested and forbearing. The Republicans generally seemed pleased. With most of them it was as though we had known each other forever. The Democrats were correct and amiable, though not overly so. All things being equal, they were willing to give the president's nominee their support.

I'm sure a lot of that was because of the White House, which was no doubt getting the message out, and because the administration had Alan Simpson managing this. Even the antiabortion senators had been managed, as well as the southerners who might not have been overly enthusiastic about having an African American on the job.

People in this last category were not necessarily my friends, but things had been changing for some time now. African Americans were voting. Southern senators had to be careful about how they dealt with me. As a result, my interactions with even potential adversaries were polite, cordial. I wanted their votes. But I was also clear on what my priorities would be. I wanted to improve the health system for everyone, but the greatest improvement was needed for the minority community. And that meant a whole range of things, including increasing the number of minority physicians and other health professionals. And there was no argument on that at all, even from Thurmond.

Thurmond was somewhat similar to Herman Talmadge. He had a terrible racist background. In 1948 he had headed the Dixiecrat Party, with its "Segregation Forever" platform. But now blacks in South Carolina were voting, and that had persuaded him to adjust his opinions. Beyond that, Thurmond's private life cast him in an interesting light. Thurmond had a daughter by a black woman. I had a friend who was a student at the traditionally black South Carolina State College when Thurmond's daughter was there. Thurmond, he said, would come by every Thursday, drive right up on campus to her dormitory, honk the horn, and wait for her to come out. Then he'd take her off someplace for lunch or to buy clothes or for some other outing. He continued to support her after she graduated too.

At the time, this was no secret. Everybody knew, white and black, but somehow it had just never come up as a big issue. In some ways it was simply the Old South. White men fathering mixed-race children were no rarity, and sometimes they acknowledged and supported them. There had been a situation like that back in Blakely too, a man in the black community whose father was white and who acknowledged and helped him. It was common knowledge.

Thurmond supported me. When it came time, he gave me his vote. The one who didn't was Jessie Helms.

Helms was having none of it. He made it clear he didn't like me. Not only was I black, I had also made that statement about abortion. That statement wasn't acceptable. My position on tobacco wasn't acceptable either. As dean I had already been talking publicly about the dangers of tobacco, which he knew about. I had also said in that interview that I was going to work to reduce tobacco use. Helms was from North Carolina; he didn't like that at all.

"Why do you think you're the one who should run this department?" he said, not in a friendly way. His tone wasn't pleasant; his body language wasn't pleasant. He didn't intend to be pleasant. "Isn't your position on tobacco interfering with grown-up people's choice? Tobacco companies aren't interested in getting children to smoke. But for adults who choose to smoke? They have that right. They have that right as Americans. Why would you want to come in as Big Nanny, telling people what they should and shouldn't do?"

"I'm interested in Americans' health," I told him. "We've known for a long time, since 1964, that people who smoke have a much higher rate of lung and other cancers. I'm concerned about the health of our citizens. I'm also concerned about the effect it has on our economy."

"Well," Helms said, "we're not really sure that it's smoke that causes lung cancer."

This was 1988. Helms's argument was an outdated bunch of bull, which I was sure he knew. I tried to be courteous. I wasn't combative. But at the same time I told him, "This is what we know. We're going to continue to do research. If I'm secretary it's going to be my responsibility to use the best knowledge we have. We may not like it. But that would be my professional responsibility."

"Well, ahem. I don't know about that, Dr. Sullivan."

Helms had been in the Senate a long time. He had brought a lot of federal dollars into North Carolina. He had protected the tobacco industry. His arguments weren't necessarily cogent, and not only on the tobacco issue. But given what he had done for the state, people overlooked his lack of cogency, just as they overlooked his thinly disguised racism.

He wasn't sure at all that he was going to vote for me, Helms said. And he didn't. All that rolled off my back. It was what I expected from him. I also knew that his day was over. My confirmation vote was ninety-eight in favor, one opposed, with one senator absent for illness. I considered the one nay vote a favor. I would have had a hard time explaining to the black community back in Georgia why it was that Jesse Helms had voted for me.

CHAPTER 10

Mr. Secretary

When Thurgood Marshall was chief counsel for the NAACP, he traveled all over the country, including to Blakely, Georgia. I had seen him there when I was a child, at one of my father's Emancipation Day celebrations. When I was confirmed Marshall had been a Supreme Court justice for more than twenty years. Given what he had done and what he represented, I decided to ask if he would swear me in. I wanted someone identified with the civil rights movement, and, other than Martin Luther King, there was no one who had done more.

I called. I introduced myself and mentioned in passing that when I was quite small he had come to Blakely, that my father had founded the NAACP chapter there. "I would be very honored if you would consent to swear me in," I said.

"Well, doctor," he said, "I don't know. Might be a little awkward. Let me get back to you."

When he called back, the answer was no. "I don't think I can do this," he said. "You'd best get someone else."

I tried my hardest to convince him, but it was a no go. I speculated that he didn't want to have anything to do with swearing in a Republican secretary, the most liberal justice swearing in a conservative administration appointment. That may or may not have been the case; he didn't explain himself. Of course, Bush had been strongly criticized about the Willie Horton campaign ad issue. He was not in good odor with the black community.

But Leon Higginbotham did agree to swear me in. Higginbotham, a justice on the Third Circuit Court of Appeals, had also been a leading civil rights figure. With some part of me I felt that my appointment was a statement, and having Higginbotham swear me in meant a great deal.

I was the only African American in Bush's cabinet. I wrestled a bit with the idea that some people would inevitably perceive me as a token. That bothered me, but I wasn't going to be boxed in by it. I was intending to be an active force, and to some degree at least I had the president's ear. Somebody has to break the ice, I thought, and I've been given this opportunity. Why would I not take it?

In fact I was not breaking the ice. Four African Americans had served in cabinet posts before me. Robert Weaver was the first; Lyndon Johnson had appointed him to his newly created Department of Housing and Urban Development. Ford had Bill Coleman as his secretary of transportation, and Carter had appointed Pat Harris to both HUD and later to Health and Human Services. In Reagan's years Sam Pierce had been HUD secretary, a thankless job given that Reagan slashed the low-income housing budget and more or less eliminated funding for residential construction. Sam was so little heard from that in the black community he was known as "Silent Sam."

Bill Coleman, Ford's transportation secretary, was a Republican, much more conservative than I, but he had also been one of the chief NAACP strategists for *Brown v. Board of Education*. A brilliant lawyer, Coleman had clerked under Felix Frankfurter; he was the first black to clerk for a Supreme Court judge. I got to know Bill well, and he helped me find my way through Washington's various mazes.

I told Coleman at one point that I'd like to meet Bob Weaver, the first African American to serve. I had heard a story about how Johnson had appointed him, a groundbreaking political act. That had been a fairly historic event; it had paved the way for both Coleman and me. I wanted to know how it had really happened.

Coleman knew Weaver and took me to New York to see him. Yes, Weaver said, the story was true. What happened was that Johnson was embroiled in the civil rights turmoil of that time: marches, demonstrations, court cases, congressional alley fights. He had also just created the Department of Housing and Urban Development, and he was looking for someone to head it. He wanted the first chief to be African American, a precedent-setting move. But with all the conflict going on he didn't want it to be seen as if he was forcing that through. He wanted the choice to be thrust on him.

In the search process Johnson's people had proposed several individuals, including Weaver. When they presented the candidates' credentials, Johnson had said, "This Weaver looks like the man we need."

His staff said, "Well, sir, if you think so. But there is a problem."

"Problem?" said Johnson. "What problem?"

"Well, sir, he's, uh, colored."

"Colored? What color is he?"

"Sir, he's a Negro."

"Really? You don't say? . . . Well . . . hire the nigger!"

"Yes," Weaver told us, "that's just the way it happened."

Since 1953, when HHS's predecessor agency was launched under President Eisenhower, I was the seventeenth secretary. The department's budget was actually the fourth largest governmental budget in the world, larger than Germany's and the United Kingdom's national budgets, almost twice as large as the Defense Department budget, though few knew that. A total of 124,000 people worked for HHS in institutions and programs that affected every American. In terms of scale, this was a far cry from what I had overseen at Morehouse. It was a different universe, nothing like anything I had ever been part of. The question was, how would I manage such a behemoth? And not just manage it, how would I direct it? The folklore of the department was that the most effective secretaries had been Eliot Richardson, Cap Weinberger, and Joe Califano, all of whom had had a good deal of government experience. I was very much aware that I was a novice.

But while the scale of the department was vast, I believed that the management procedures I had adopted at Morehouse would also make sense here. I hadn't built the medical school by myself; I had done it by working with teams of people. I saw my major responsibility there as developing the vision, saying, this is what we want to do. This is where we want to go. Now, how do we get there? And I made sure that my colleagues were part of the process and, consequently, invested in the process.

I approached the secretary's job with the same principle. I first met with the senior members of the department, four or five hundred of them, in the department's auditorium. I introduced myself and told them about my background. "I'm honored to be your secretary," I told them. "But as you know as well as I, this is my first time in government service. I have a lot to learn. I want to work with you and ask for your help so I can really try to understand this department and manage the programs as best I can. But you have the information. You are the experts. You have to be sure that I am informed. I believe in open discussions. The important thing is to have the best idea—regardless of where that idea comes from. So I ask for your help. I want to meet as many of you as I can. And don't hesitate to write to me or otherwise contact me. That's the way I want to operate."

I also made a tour of the ten regional offices. My own fitness routine revolved around walking, thirty or forty-five minutes every morning. When I visited various cities I invited members of the department to walk with me. I was amazed at the positive impact that had. I'd often have a large group hustling along with me, but not so fast that we couldn't talk. To many of the professionals in the department, secretaries were political personages, people you couldn't touch, couldn't reach, couldn't talk to. The best thing was just to leave them alone. They'd be here for a short time. Then they'd be gone.

I often met people who would say, "Hello, Mr. Secretary. I'm So-and-So. I've been here for seventeen years. Welcome aboard." What was unsaid was, "I was here long before you, and I'll be here long after you too."

I had already been well briefed on substantive issues by Otis Bowen, my predecessor. We had met a number of times prior to my confirmation and had developed an easy and, to me, instructive relationship. Now I spent a great deal of time reading briefing documents, so I could go into meetings prepared. One of my challenges was to be a quick study, and one of my goals was to have a staff that could handle a lot of nonmomentous issues so that I could give my full attention to the more significant ones. They would make decisions and send me memos. It didn't take long before I felt I had developed such good lines of communication with people in the department that often we'd be able to get out ahead of any potential crisis that might be brewing.

I came to the department with a fairly well-formed vision of where I wanted to go. As I had told Bush, I wanted the department to meet the needs of all Americans. We needed to have a department that was oriented in that direction, which meant, among other things, that I was planning to put minorities and women in senior positions. "I'll support you in that," Bush had said. That was important. When I came in, HHS was almost all male and lily-white in its upper echelons, as it had always been. We needed more minorities and women overlooking programs. We needed more minority doctors; we needed more primary care and family doctors. The department's programs influenced all American lives, but Head Start, Medicaid, welfare, and others had a disproportionate impact on poor Americans. If we were able to get adequate resources for these programs and make sure the rules and regulations made sense, they would end up helping people rather than hobbling them.

From one point of view, my overall mission might have been seen as racially oriented, but the reality was that the people who were affected most were poor people, white and black, and far more whites than blacks, though of course the poverty rate was higher in the black community. I was concerned to maximize the well-being of everyone, but particularly of the people on the bottom. I wanted the millionaire to do well, but the millionaire had access to resources that weren't available to others. I was far more concerned about the poor. That was the direction I was going to go in; that was the tenor of my agenda.

Once I was oriented, I began pursuing these goals. But from the moment I stepped in we were also in the middle of other urgent issues, none more dire than the AIDS epidemic. By 1989 AIDS was in full swing. The first signs of the disease had surfaced seven or eight years earlier, but it had taken time before the virus was identified and the means of transmission tracked down. The Human Immunodeficiency Virus, HIV, was extraordinarily complex. Exactly how it worked we did not know. What we did know was that it was inevitably fatal. In devastating the infected person's immune system, the disease opened the way for a variety of grave and otherwise rare infections, one or more of which would result in the carrier's death, most often within a year of diagnosis. This was a true national health emergency, like nothing we had ever faced before. It needed to be addressed by an all-out assault by medical science on one hand and public education on the other.

To the country's immense harm, the Reagan administration had for years been ideologically incapable of doing either. AIDS was prevalent among homosexual males. Transmission, we had found, was through semen and blood. Unprotected gay male sex and intravenous drug use involving shared needles were the most common avenues. As a result, the disease was not only deadly but stigmatized as well. Gays engaged in conduct abhorrent to many of Reagan's advisers. Intravenous drug users were hardly better. These people "had brought it on themselves" through their immoral activities. Why the government should spend significant resources to help them was in essence a moot point. Even talking about the subject was anathema to many in the Reagan camp.

As surgeon general, Everett Koop had been frustrated beyond measure by his inability to bring the facts about AIDS to public attention. It had taken him forever to make the case to White House circles that the public had to be informed in clear language what the disease was, how it spread, and how to prevent it. That meant sex education. That meant describing the kinds of sexual activity that were dangerous. It meant advocating condom use for those at risk or those who may be at risk. All of this sent segments of Reagan's constituency into spasms. But Koop was determined. With HHS secretary Otis Bowen's support (Bowen was also a physician), Koop eventually published a surgeon general's report that was widely disseminated. With that, Koop's former allies on the Republican side redoubled their criticism of him, much of it vicious and unrestrained.

When Bush was inaugurated many saw him as a kind of clone of Reagan. He had served as Reagan's vice president for eight years, and people expected that he would more or less continue Reagan's policies. Regarding AIDS, it was assumed he would do everything he could to ignore the problem. As the new, unknown HHS secretary, I was expected to follow suit. Overcoming those perceptions was going to be a challenge.

The fact was that Bush's experience and expertise were in foreign policy. He had been ambassador to the UN, ambassador to China, and CIA director. He was far less at home in the domestic arena. But he did grasp the urgency of the AIDS problem. With the epidemic right on the front burner, we formed the first AIDS Advisory Council to advise us on what our priorities should be and how we should pursue them. David Rogers from the Robert Wood Johnson Foundation was one cochair; June Osborne, dean of public health at the University of Michigan, was the other. We had both scientists and laypeople on the council, the scientists to keep us current on research, the laypeople to advise on how to educate the public regarding delicate issues having to do with sexual orientation, intercourse, and so on. We knew we needed all the help we could get, and we searched it out. The atmosphere was quite the opposite of what had prevailed in the Reagan White House, when Koop had been muzzled at every step.

I had even tried to appoint Tony Fauci as director of NIH. Fauci was the country's leading AIDS researcher, the head of the National Institute of Allergy and Infectious Diseases, an excellent administrator as well as a superb scientist. I thought appointing him to lead NIH would make a statement about the priorities we were giving to the disease. When he declined, I arranged an Oval Office meeting for him with President Bush. But Fauci still declined. He was appreciative and honored, he said, but he believed he could make his greatest contribution by staying in his current job and pursuing his research on a vaccine. That was going to be a long-term project (we still don't have a vaccine, twenty-two years later), but we had already made the first medical breakthrough, AZT, a drug that retarded the proliferation of the virus. We fast-tracked approval of the drug, and I had approved federal reimbursement for its use.

Bush's first budget, proposed that spring, called for $4.5 billion for AIDS research, screening, treatment, prevention, and education, three times the Reagan budget. Bush wasn't going to lead the charge himself, but he was giving me running room to take the steps I saw as necessary, and he was making sure the medical scientists had the wherewithal to ramp up their efforts.

By now, though, there wasn't just concern about AIDS, there was outright panic. Eight years into the disease, the AIDS activist groups were well organized, and they were in an uproar. Reagan had done nothing, they claimed. He had ignored those who were suffering and dying. His administration was packed with homophobes whose attitudes were akin to murder. And now comes Bush, Reagan's protégé. To the activists, this administration was nothing more than an extension of the last.

Almost from my first day in office, the Humphrey Building had been besieged by demonstrators of one kind or another. So many of the issues the department dealt with were incendiary: AIDS, abortion, animal research, Social Security, all of which had their own emotionally charged interest groups. Through 1989 and 1990, by far the loudest and most aggressive of these were the AIDS-activist groups. They picketed my offices; they held demonstrations on the NIH campus. They were determined to paint us into a corner as a bunch of right-wing fanatics who didn't care about anybody and weren't doing a thing to address this mysterious, deadly epidemic.

This was simply wrong, a carried-over perception. The efforts we were making were not being recognized. The vast difference between this administration and the last was lost in a welter of fear and anger. I wanted to do everything I could to correct this, to say, here's what we've done, here's what our approach is, these are our goals. We are not the enemy. Our common enemy here is the disease. We are making progress. We need cooperation and support, not opprobrium.

In 1990 the International AIDS Conference was held in San Francisco at the Moscone Center. I thought this would be the perfect forum to convey the administration's message. I invited Bush to go with me. Reagan had been silent in the face of this epidemic. Bush's presence by itself would do more than anything else could to convey his commitment.

Bush agreed it would be a good idea, but his schedule didn't allow him to go. These were volatile waters. I wasn't surprised that he wasn't going, and I wasn't disappointed either. If there was a bad public scene, I was obviously the one to bear the brunt of it, not him.

I worked hard on the speech I was going to give, highlighting the work we were doing and the resources we were devoting. At the plenary session I was on the stage with several other speakers. The ones who spoke before me were received courteously and applauded. Then I was introduced. As I stood up to go to the podium chaos broke out. The place seemed to explode with sirens, whistles, bullhorns, and chanting. The roof of the Moscone Center was a cement vault, which amplified the sound. The volume of noise was like nothing I had ever heard. The crowd was showering the stage with pennies, condoms, and other objects.

I had gotten up, but now I went back to my chair to sit it out. By then I had experienced quite a few demonstrations at speeches I gave. Typically, people would shout and jeer for several minutes, then quiet down when others in the audience got irritated and started yelling, "Sit down! Shut up!"

But this demonstration didn't stop. Ten minutes went by and the place was still in a frenzy. I got up and went to the podium. I realized that they were not going to let me speak. But by then I was royally pissed. I had come with a message of conciliation and outreach. I had really gone to great lengths to put together a statement. I had met with people in the department and the researchers at NIH, including Fauci, to make sure I understood everything. My job here was to break us out of the perception left by the Reagan administration, and I was bound and determined to do that any way I could.

With all the noise, nobody in the auditorium was going to hear me. The sirens, whistles, bullhorns, and chanting were growing louder. But the mikes and cameras were right in front of me. This was going to be televised and broadcast on radio. I thought, okay, these people here are not going to hear me, but the rest of the country will, and I launched into my full fifteen-minute speech.

The podium was at one end of the stage. When I finished I walked across to the other end and waved at the crowd, as if my speech had just been a great triumph with them. No matter what I had been taught about not giving way to emotion, this reception had me upset. Then I went off with my security to the airport.

I was in the Crown Room at the airport when I got a call from John Sununu,

Bush's chief of staff. He was excited. I had done a great job representing the administration, he said, not letting those "pinkos" and "homos" stop me. I had a seriously mixed reaction to that. I was pleased to have done a good job for the administration, but not pleased with Sununu's reasons for being excited. The people in the Moscone Center were exactly those we were trying to win over, to develop communication and positive relations with.

Sununu's comment was at odds with the attitude I was experiencing from Bush. We were working to change the relationship with the gay community and also with the liberal constituency. Bush's philosophy was, the election's over. Now it's time to govern. He intended to be the president of all the people, not just of white, Republican heterosexuals. We wanted to change the tune from one of confrontation and conflict to one of cooperation and civil discourse.

The Moscone event showed how hard that was going to be. At almost every public event where I gave a speech, activists showed up to protest. Some were more or less respectful, in their own way. I'd start to give a speech. They would stand up and turn their backs until I was finished. Then they'd sit down. Others were more aggressive. They'd jump up and shout, "Liar!" "Homophobe!"

Over time I learned that graduations were one place where audiences didn't have any tolerance for these disruptions. Parents were there to see their kids graduating. Then suddenly people stood up and started shouting, "Murderer, murderer." If they kept that up others would begin yelling, "Shut your mouth!" "Who invited you?" The more obnoxious the demonstrators were, the more anger they generated.

I never did form an easy relationship with the militant groups, but in time many in the AIDS leadership did get the message. This was a new administration. We were constructive and concerned. I was addressing this terrible problem as a physician, charged to heal, not to heal some and not others, heterosexuals but not homosexuals. Even in my previous life as a hematologist, as relatively quiet as that had been, I had dealt constantly with alcoholics whose lifestyles had brought on fatal anemias. It had never entered my mind to judge them, only to try to cure them. AIDS had to do with sex and, as far as we knew then, mostly gay sex, forbidden distasteful subjects in Reagan's administration. I was trying to bring a physician's orientation to bear on the work of the department. We weren't in the business of propagating an ideology; we were trying to address a health problem that seemed each day to grow more threatening.

Abortion was another issue that could just eat you up. I seemed to be always dealing with it in one way or another. My assistant secretary for communications, Kay James, was a pro-life person, very active and very respected by those who shared her ideals. Kay and I got along well, and she oriented me on the subject. To me, abortion was more or less a new subject. I'd never dealt with it, and I hadn't given it much thought. But I quickly learned a lot about the issues around it, the emotions, the politics, the activist groups—and also how to answer questions. Kay taught me a great deal of that. She explained that the answer I had given to that reporter in Atlanta was a red flag. The antiabortion people were saying—he's pro-choice. He's going to favor abortions.

This was a real problem for Bush, who was himself suspected of being at heart pro-choice. But Bush was ensconced in the White House, behind layers of protection. I was an easier target, more accessible, so I was the one they went after. We tried to play it down the middle as well as we could. We were not promoting abortion. But the law of the land was that it was a woman's right to choose. That was the bottom line. We were not promoting abortion or supporting it, but this was an issue that had to be dealt with in the courts and legislature. As secretary I did not have the latitude to address the issue.

That was the official line, but it wasn't acceptable. The pro-life groups wanted declarations condemning abortion; they wanted us up on the moral barricades. Barring that, they were going to make as dramatic a public case as they could. They tried their best to entrap me into damaging statements. Their level of militancy was beyond anything I had seen before, far more sophisticated and determined than that of the AIDS groups, for instance. They tracked my schedule and followed me around. I'd be giving a speech somewhere on food-labeling policy or new cancer research, and activists would pop up with questions about abortion. I'd leave the venue and on the way out reporters from antiabortion newsletters would accost me.

"Mr. Secretary, our readers need to know, what is your true position on abortion? Do you believe it is moral to kill babies? Do you believe killing babies is moral or do you not?"

I'd talk to them as I walked. "I'm here to talk about the importance of proper food labeling, not abortion. If you want to know more, please read my statement of such and such. Tomorrow you can talk to my assistant Kay James. She'll have whatever information you're looking for." I was bobbing and weaving as fast as I could.

I felt badly that I couldn't protect Bush better. But this was a no-win situation.

On this front he might have been better off to have chosen a strong antiabortion person as secretary. There were certainly viable candidates who held that position. The fact was that he and I had never had the discussion, even after my newspaper gaff. The omission may well have been deliberate on his part. It was true—I had never given any serious thought to the abortion question, but once I did I came to believe that a decision about abortion was something that should be between a woman and her doctor. But that was my private opinion, and it remained private.

I looked at issues like the abortion argument as a distraction, the kind of thing that could eat us alive in terms of time consumed. We tried to handle it and other volatile subjects in ways that would provoke as little public controversy as possible. I had a long list of priorities I wanted to promote: food and drug safety at FDA, biomedical research at NIH, prevention programs at CDC, funding for medical training at the National Health Service, better health care access for the poor. And getting trapped in the quicksand of religious and quasi-religious arguments about the right to life or the right of women to control their bodies was not going to further the nation's health, not as I conceived it at least. But volatile and often enraged interest groups were not easy to get away from. The HHS secretary was, as I was now learning firsthand, the most picketed of all the cabinet secretaries.

There was, for example, People for the Ethical Treatment of Animals (PETA), the most militant of the animal rights organizations. Some years earlier PETA-affiliated individuals had broken into a research lab in Silver Spring, Maryland, that was using macaque monkeys to study wound healing from injuries to the nervous system. The researchers were inflicting surgical wounds to the spinal cords and brains of monkeys, then looking at the recovery and adaptation process to get information that could be used for the rehabilitation of stroke victims and soldiers with battlefield injuries.

As far as the animal rights people were concerned, the research was cruel and inhumane. The monkeys were suffering from debilitating injuries and, according to the undercover PETA individual who was working at the laboratory, they were being kept in substandard living conditions. PETA members had broken into the laboratory, stolen the monkeys, and deposited them at the front of Building One at NIH, calling the press in at the same time. This was government-sponsored research treating animals inhumanely. They demanded that it stop. Police then raided the lab. Charges were brought against the researcher, who was first convicted of animal cruelty, then had his conviction overturned on appeal. Celebrities got involved. PETA brought suit to get custody of the monkeys, which went all the way up to the Supreme Court.

This had started off at the beginning of the eighties, but when I came in as secretary the Supreme Court was in the process of making its decision, so the Silver Spring monkeys were a hot issue. PETA was always clever at finding ways to publicize their position. In the summer of 1989 they built a papier mâché monkey and put it up on a pole in front of the entrance to our offices in the Humphrey Building. The monkey had a motor in it, which gave it movement. The thing seemed alive.

I was certainly in favor of treating animals humanely, but I didn't have any reservations about using them for research. In my own research on how vitamin B_{12} binds to receptors in the gut I had used the ileal mucosa of guinea pigs, which meant sacrificing them. The fact was that if you could explain why studies were necessary, what they hoped to accomplish and how that was significant to human health, a lot of the resistance to using them melted away. But PETA's position was that animal rights were equal to human rights; it was immoral to use animals for medical science, period. That argument got no sympathy from me at all.

As far as the monkey outside our building went, we couldn't stop them from putting it up, but we could make sure the display didn't disrupt access to the building, which meant we could legally force them to put it farther out on the sidewalk, toward the curb. We could also make sure it had an attendant, so that if it fell over no passerby would be injured. Then it turned out they needed a power source for the motor that made it move, so they asked to plug it into one in the Humphrey lobby. We refused because, as we told them, it was inappropriate to use public resources for a private demonstration. An immobile monkey out at the curb in the full blast of Washington's summer heat and humidity did not stop much traffic, and after a few days the monkey disappeared.

For PETA and activist groups generally, the object, of course, was to gain media attention. If possible, they wanted to provoke a confrontation that would find its way to television audiences. When it came to health issues, that meant they would try to provoke me, to catch me on a TV bite losing control.

I had to get used to having malicious questions or insults thrown at me, and responding in a measured way. "I understand your anger, but let me tell you what we are trying to do, what the facts are." Another thing I learned was always to stay on message. You can ask your question, but my answer is going to be what I want the public to hear. Never let the interviewer control the interview; you control it.

All this took some getting used to, even after my murder-board training with Tom Korologos. It was so different from what I was used to in an academic environment, where the idea was to speak honestly, have a debate, get all the information out, then measure and analyze it. But in the public arena people aren't really interested in a debate; they're interested in making a point. If they can use you to make that point, so much the better.

No group demonstrated that better than the activists for people with disabilities. Why I should ever have been involved in a controversy with them was beyond me, but Washington is an alien world where the laws that you think should govern your life are often turned upside down. The problem here was funding for nursing homes. Advocacy groups wanted one-third of the funds allocated to nursing homes to be redirected to home-care assistance. The fact was that although I headed the department that administered these funds, the allocations themselves had been set by Congress. Redirecting the funds would require legislative action; it wasn't in my authority to do it administratively.

We informed the advocacy groups of this. But it made no difference. I was the administration's face on health matters. Lobbying in the halls of Congress was a stodgy, out-of-the-spotlight affair. I was a far more attractive target than even some committee hearing. Direct confrontations with me would inevitably draw media attention.

Looking back on these confrontations, I can hardly believe they really happened. They were so bizarre. I'd be giving a speech somewhere, and a large group of wheelchair-bound individuals would show up, very polite and quiet. The ushers would bring them to the front of the auditorium, where there was typically room and where the sight lines were unimpeded. I'd begin speaking, and suddenly the whole line would throw themselves on the floor and start crawling toward the stage, chanting in unison, "Why won't you meet with us? Why won't you meet with us?" The audience would have no idea what was going on. Why were these people with disabilities confronting the secretary, and why so wildly? Was he doing something terrible to paraplegics and quadriplegics? What could he have done to them to make them act like that? After a while the ushers would remove them, not that easy a job. But it was difficult to emerge with my dignity intact after a demonstration like this, which also made any sort of dialogue impossible. But, of course, that wasn't the point anyway.

In Chicago once I was delivering a speech at the Drake Hotel when my security told me that a large group of people in wheelchairs was gathering in the lobby.

When I finished I'd never be able to get through them. So security was going to create a distraction of some sort, then they'd hustle me out a side entrance into my car. We tried this, but my escape was noticed. The car sped off, but only for a hundred yards or so. The light at the end of this short block was red, and there were cars in front of us. We were blocked. I looked behind and there was one demonstrator wheeling as fast as he could down the middle of the street. "He's going to get in front and block us off," my security person said. "Then they'll lie down in front of the car." But just before he caught up, the light turned and we were off, until the red light at the end of the next short block. I looked behind and the demonstrator was closing in, with others behind him. To my immense relief, this light too changed and we were off to O'Hare Airport, leaving the demonstrators behind.

Some of the most contentious confrontations had to do with political third rails: AIDS, abortion, sex education, and others, issues a Republican White House had to treat with great tact. Interestingly, although this was true, I never received any direct political instruction from Bush or his staff on these matters. Of course the White House staff and my staff met regularly, and I developed a far more nuanced understanding of the politics as we went along. I also felt a general philosophical compatibility with Bush, and I tried to be sensitive to his political needs, as long as they didn't conflict with what I considered important health considerations. I knew that I was enjoying an independence that some of my predecessors definitely had not. But I did have to be careful.

Since Surgeon General Luther Terry's report on smoking in 1964, the facts about tobacco's effects on health were well known. After that there was a continuing push by health officials to inform the public and reduce the smoking rate. At the same time the tobacco industry wielded huge political power, driven by massive political contributions and a well-oiled lobbying machine and spearheaded by representatives and senators from tobacco-growing states. Industry lobbyists didn't just marshal tremendous resources; they had developed a high level of sophistication in using it, mobilizing the tobacco farmers, the companies, and their political allies. Efforts to fight smoking were always a battleground.

Smoking is the number one cause of preventable death in the United States. No single thing is more harmful to the nation's health; nothing comes close. When my tenure began, 450,000 people a year died of smoking-related causes, in dreadful ways. I pressed this issue, giving speeches and press conferences about the need to reduce tobacco use. That was good, as far as it went, but these kinds of activities didn't generate widespread media coverage. By 1989 there was a continuing drumbeat of reports on the links between tobacco use and cancers of various kinds as well as cardiovascular disease, emphysema, and other respiratory illnesses. Against this background my pronouncements were not making the news. I needed something that would highlight the message.

In January 1990 I spent two weeks in the Middle East—a week in Israel, a week in Egypt—reviewing research programs we were supporting that required collaboration, such as mosquito control. These scientific projects also had an underlying political purpose, to encourage communication and cooperation between the two countries.

On the plane ride back I read a small article in the *International Herald Tribune* about protests in Philadelphia's black community against a plan to test-market a new cigarette called Uptown. This new, high-tar cigarette was mentholated and unfiltered. That, and its name, "Uptown," shouted out that it was aimed squarely at the African American market. The test-marketing was going to be done in Philadelphia, and that city's black leaders were up in arms. I was scheduled to give a talk at the University of Pennsylvania the following week. I showed the article to Ginger. "I think I can make a big issue of this," I told her.

In Washington the next morning I was in the office for my daily meeting with my senior staff, twenty or so people from NIH, FDA, CDC, Social Security, and other agencies. I came into the meeting with a copy of the newspaper and asked if anyone was aware of this. As I started speaking I realized everyone in the room was smiling. "Okay," I said. "What's so funny?"

What was funny was that they did know. Not only did they know, but while I was away they had been discussing among themselves how best to convince me that I should come out strongly against this, just what I had decided to do myself.

The first thing I did was send off a letter to the R. J. Reynolds Tobacco chairman objecting strenuously to their plans to test-market this cigarette. I told him it was unconscionable that they were aiming this at the black community, which already suffered a heavy burden of illness and death due to a number of factors, including smoking. This new cigarette would add to the burden. I demanded that they cease their plans to test-market it. Then I prepared my speech.

The routine with any of my speeches was to send the text over to the White House in advance so that the staff there could look it over and make sure that nothing was at odds with the president's position or in conflict with what other secretaries might be saying publicly. All the secretaries did this. The system was designed to make sure we were all consistent and not out of line with the administration.

But I knew this speech was likely to get some reaction at the White House. This was going to be a public flogging of a major contributor with powerful congressional allies. And while Bush gave me a good deal of running room, on tobacco he wasn't eager to back me up. He didn't interfere, but that was the extent of it. I wasn't at all sure that they would go along with this speech. I didn't want Sununu or the president calling me up and telling me I couldn't give it. I didn't want to be insubordinate, but I didn't want to be muzzled either.

To avoid any interference I instructed my staff to send the speech over to the White House at eight o'clock the morning of the speech itself, which was scheduled for ten thirty in Philadelphia. I knew that by the time the White House staff even looked at it, I'd be on my way back to Washington. After that the chips would fall wherever. I wondered if I might not be buying myself a one-way ticket back to Atlanta.

I was going to the University of Pennsylvania to dedicate a new medical research building that had been built partly with NIH funds. But I started my talk not with the research potential of the new facility or the government-university partnership in medicine, but with the letter I had sent to R. J. Reynolds. The tobacco companies, I said, were fully aware of the health impact of smoking. They knew that smoking was slow-motion suicide. Yet they continued to market their products, putting profits above health. Worse, they were preying on the youth. It was particularly pernicious that they were targeting African American young people in a city like Philadelphia, whose black community was already suffering from an abundance of social ills. My talk was eighteen minutes. For the first short segment I excoriated R. J. Reynolds and the tobacco industry in general. The rest of the speech, which was most of it, was about the new building and its advantages in adding to our research capacity.

The press was there. We had made sure they were informed beforehand. They loved the material; they ran with it. Here was the secretary of a Republican administration, naturally assumed to be in bed with tobacco interests, lambasting the industry. That day and the next there was zero coverage of the new building part of the speech but massive national coverage of the three minutes devoted to how R. J. Reynolds was trying to ensnare the black community into further tobacco use.

The White House did not call me in, but I found out later what had happened there. The cigarette people had spoken with Sununu. They were furious. They wanted to have the president discipline me or, better, terminate me. Sununu listened to them. "I'll go to the president if you want me to," he said. "But you'll have to agree to abide by his decision, whatever it is." They thought about the pros and cons of that and backed off.

I never did hear from the White House about that speech, though in a subsequent meeting Bush told me that he was aware of what had happened. He was following our antismoking efforts. "We're behind you, Lou," he said, then, a little wistfully, "Maybe we're a little too far behind you." He was not going to get into a political fight if he didn't have to, but he wasn't going to rein me in either.

Although the Bush White House had its ideological underpinnings, in essence George H. W. Bush was a pragmatist. His approach generally was to let people argue questions out freely before he came to a decision. The new food labeling I was proposing was a good example. That debate played out in the Oval Office in front of Bush himself. My adversary there was Ed Madigan, secretary of agriculture.

On food safety issues HHS shares responsibility with the Department of Agriculture. For canned food the Food and Drug Administration (part of HHS) is responsible; for meats and fresh vegetables, it's the Department of Agriculture. But there's a lot of overlapping authority, which can cause confusion. For a long time people have argued that everything should be in the hands of one agency or the other. The new food-labeling proposal put Madigan and me at loggerheads.

For years food labels had noted the amounts of various nutrients and other substances per serving. If you looked at a can of tomatoes, the label told you it contained a certain number of milligrams of sodium per serving, another number of milligrams of potassium, and so on. But what did those numbers mean? Most people had no idea whatsoever.

Scientists at the FDA had now worked out a system of providing nutritional information that people would understand. They proposed that labels should show the percentage of the daily requirement for a particular nutrient instead of just milligram amounts. That can of tomatoes provided fifteen milligrams of sodium per serving, or 1 percent of the daily requirement based on a two-thousand-calorie diet. The new label would give percentages of fat and fiber as well. If consumers were on a low-sodium diet they could figure out their daily intake. If they wanted to limit fats or sugar or increase their fiber, they could calculate percentages from what they were eating.

The new label was rational, understandable, and important. Today these labels are taken for granted; they're a feature every food-conscious buyer looks at. Who could argue against it? In 1990 the Department of Agriculture could. The agriculture department secretary's constituency included the cattle and dairy industries, and they were vehemently opposed. Their concern was that if people knew what percentage of the daily requirement of fat, for instance, was in their products, it would hurt sales.

The position they took with Ed Madigan was that the new label would cause confusion. It would be costly to change what we were already doing, and the information was not that valuable in any case. Here, they claimed, was yet another foolish government regulation that would cost money, help no one, and impede the ability of business to function in a free and fair commercial environment. The new label was meaningless, wasteful, and antibusiness. Why do it?

That case had some traction with an administration that was probusiness and against excessive regulation. In addition, the meat and dairy industries had their own strong lobbying organizations, and they were working overtime to defeat this. I, on the other hand, was committed to it. I had reviewed it carefully with my FDA colleagues and others in the public health service, and I was convinced the new labeling would be beneficial. It would increase people's awareness of what they were eating, and that would have a significant positive impact on the nation's health. Despite what I thought were overwhelming arguments for instituting this, I couldn't come to agreement with Madigan. So I took it to the White House. Madigan and I were both there.

My typical meeting with Bush in the Oval Office was about fifteen minutes. This meeting lasted an hour and a half. The debate went back and forth, Madigan arguing strenuously that the new labels would simply be useless, expensive, and of no actual value.

I knew this was going to be his position, of course. So in the end I pulled out a paper place mat from a McDonald's chain that had a dietary description very similar to what we were proposing: for example, it listed the fat, protein, and sugar in a Big Mac. What the FDA had in the works was no secret, and since McDonald's was always being criticized for the nutritional content of what they served, they were trying to get out in front of the issue with these place mats.

"Mr. President," I said. "Here's the company that serves more meals and more beef every day than anyone. Why would they be using place mats like these? McDonald's spends a great deal on consumer research. Why would they go to the trouble of doing this if it were meaningless or confusing?"

Bush said, "Here, let me see that." He took it. "Look at that, that's interesting."

At the end Bush said, "OK, thanks fellows. I've heard both of you. Let me take a couple of days. I'll reflect on this some and give you my decision. And remember, however we come out, you've made your arguments here. Whichever way the decision goes, we're going to be together on it."

The next day Sununu called me. "The president accepts your position, Lou. We're going to go with the new labels." And then the catechism: "Remember, when the press calls, we're a team."

I called the FDA commissioner, Dave Kessler, to tell him the good news. The new labels had originated with him. Unfortunately, he was traveling, so I spoke with his deputy for communications, Carol Scheman. "We're making the announcement tomorrow," I told her. Be ready to field calls from the press. And remember, we're one team. No gloating."

"I understand," she said.

The next day we made the announcement. The day after that Carol was quoted in the *New York Times*. "How do you feel about this new food label?" she was asked.

"Oh, we're very pleased," she said. "And we're trying very hard not to smile."

An illustration of the fact that you can only do so much even with bright people. That comment was Scheman's way of signaling to the world that the FDA had won—which they had. But then we all had.

That was how Bush tended to operate. He encouraged free-flowing discussion with little imposition from above that might deter some possibly left-field or off-message argument or approach. The atmosphere of his cabinet meetings reflected that. They were run by a loose, relaxed man who encouraged his subordinates to say what they thought. I looked forward to those meetings; I think all the secretaries did.

I had cordial relationships with all my cabinet colleagues, but especially with Jack Kemp, who was the housing secretary. HUD and HHS shared substantial concerns, so Kemp and I frequently found ourselves working together. He was an enthusiastic person, extremely energetic. Kemp was what I thought of as a truly compassionate conservative. His instincts were progressive, but his arguments would typically be economic rather than social. I had a close, easy relationship with him. He'd often kid me at the beginning of cabinet meetings— "Lou, before the president comes in, let's have a quick meeting of the black Republican caucus, since both of us are here." Kemp had been a professional football player before launching his political career—he was quarterback for the

Buffalo Bills. He had spent his life on teams with black players, being protected by black players, having friendships with black players. I never felt awkwardness or hesitancy with anybody in the administration, but Kemp was as at home with blacks as he was with whites. In that regard he was unusual among the people Bush had around him.

When we'd have cabinet meetings, we'd all gather in the cabinet room, which is right off the Oval Office. Bush would come in. We'd chat and banter for a few minutes. Then Marlin Fitzwater would say, "Okay, photographers." And he'd bring them in.

At that moment a change would come over Bush. It happened at every single cabinet meeting, always in the same way. There he had been, a moment before, relaxed, laughing, kidding around, and suddenly he was tensed up, wooden. And that's how he came across to the public. Wooden and flat. Not the jovial person with the colorful personality that he was in private. Then the cameras would leave, we'd start the cabinet meeting, and he would revert to who he really was. The result was that what the American public saw of him as president was extremely different from what we saw when the cameras were not around.

That was interesting from a psychological viewpoint. From a political viewpoint it was frustrating. We knew that the person in the public's mind was not the person we were used to working and dealing with. We understood that Fitzwater and others were probably trying to coach him. But whatever they were doing just didn't work. He simply was not able to adapt, surprising to all of us, given how long Bush had been in political life.

So, in place of the authentic George H. W. Bush, what the world got was the wooden George Bush, also the effete, snobbish, aristocratic George Bush, the one who then Texas governor Anne Richardson described as having been "born with a silver foot in his mouth." To make matters worse, there was also the occasional staff-inspired attempt to make him appear more like a down-to-earth, regular, manly kind of guy. The pork rinds business, for instance. A reporter who asked what snack food he enjoyed got the answer: "Pork rinds." The press made a big deal of that. This wasn't a man who snacked on potato chips or, God forbid, French Brie. He ate pork rinds, something only a real man could relish.

I was riding on a plane with him to New York shortly after this episode, when the steward brought out a big bowl of pork rinds. Bush eyed them suspiciously, looking a little queasy. "Thanks," he said. "I think I'm full. Take those things away, will you?"

The pork rinds business was nonsense. But the perception of Bush as effete or wooden or snobbish was equally nonsensical. Bush's manliness could hardly be called into question. He had been a torpedo-bomber pilot in World War II (the youngest in the service at the time) flying slow, awkward planes that the Japanese shot down at an alarming rate—including his—in an engagement for which he won the Distinguished Flying Cross. Of course, that was far in the past, but then in 1990 Saddam Hussein occupied Kuwait, and Bush put together the coalition that threw him out of there; the event that may define his presidency in the history books, since he afterward refused to go into Iraq itself to root out the dictator and his regime—a decision that will be contrasted with his son's on the same subject thirteen years later.

More to the point, for me anyway, was that Bush ran the cabinet with a sense of security that allowed for the free back-and-forth of debate and the emergence of new ideas—essentially the same approach I was using to run my department. As a leader you don't have to be the expert on everything. But you do have to have a vision of what the problems are about and how to support the departments that deal with them. At Morehouse in subsequent years we established the first neuroscience institute in a minority institution. I knew little about neuroscience, but I heard from the head what they were doing and what they needed, and once I had made a decision I made sure their needs were recognized in the institution.

What I found at HHS was that the same approach paid off in spades. I think a number of my predecessors hadn't bothered to do that, to keep in close touch with the different department and program heads. Just the simple act of inviting people to walk with me and chat made a difference. That formed an image and a bond with people throughout the department. As in any organization the grapevine at HHS worked at the speed of light. The person in Atlanta called his colleague in New York, saying, "The secretary was here yesterday. Let me tell you what he was like. Let me tell you what we did."

That really helped me form working relationships and bonds with people in the department. They were the ones managing the programs. They would bring their problems to me, and often not just their problems but their proposed solutions. My job was to help work through those problems, but never to try and pretend I knew more than they did, or that my answers were better. My job, once I was informed and had made a decision, was to go and get those resources, whether that meant arguing with the White House or up on the Hill or talking with the American Hospital Association, or whatever else.

And one of the advantages of being secretary was that I could always get a lot of free advice. Many advocacy groups have their own particular perspectives. They try to win you over, but of course you're aware of that and, meanwhile, you're learning. Then you meet with another group, with a different perspective, then another. You can get yourself educated quickly.

I tried to establish an environment where I was going to make the decisions, but people knew they were going to be heard. If they didn't win the day it was not because they didn't get to make their argument. That meant they may not have won, but they didn't necessarily lose either. They were part of the process. They knew they had the same shot next time around.

That was Bush's philosophy too. We argued inside and supported the decisions outside. Listening to people, having them know that you respect their points of view—even if you come out somewhere else—is helpful to both you and them. It was especially helpful to me as I moved into gear with my own underlying agenda.

CHAPTER 11

Reforming Health Care

Thirty-seven million Americans had no health care coverage when I came into office; these included workers in small businesses and poor people, many of them minorities. I didn't arrive with any kind of a ready-made plan, but there was no question: we had to find a comprehensive way to address this problem. We needed health care reform.

Early on we started working with a team to come up with concepts that would go into legislation, but it was clear from the start that this was not something the White House was ready for. When I brought it up with Bush, the response was, yes, we could possibly look at this, but now isn't the time. Other issues need to be addressed first.

Despite the lack of enthusiasm, I assumed there would, in fact, actually be a time, so I kept the wheels turning, though I wasn't expecting that we'd be moving into high gear on reform any time soon. But in the meantime, we needed something that was going to address the health of the nation in some kind of comprehensive way, something that wouldn't rely on political leadership to get accomplished.

As luck would have it, that something was already in the works. In 1979 Jimmy Carter's surgeon general and assistant HHS secretary Julius Richmond had issued a document titled *Healthy People*, a survey of where the nation stood on a broad array of health markers and issues, what each meant, and what could be done to improve behaviors and outcomes. Blood pressure, for example. The report explained what it is, what the statistics look like, what we would like it to be, and what can be done to improve it. It listed usable, current information and goals to meet for a hundred other items as well.

Julius Richmond was a professor at the Harvard School of Public Health, a highly respected figure. The idea behind his document made great sense. It had been well conceived and well carried out. But very little had been done to publicize it. *Healthy People* had drawn some attention among people in the health establishment, but not nearly as much as it should have. The public could certainly have used it had it been publicized and disseminated aggressively, but it hadn't been.

Before I came in, HHS had decided to update and expand *Healthy People*. The Public Health Service was involved in setting objectives and researching and coming up with recommendations, and they had brought in state public health agencies and private organizations, such as the American Cancer Society, the American Heart Association, and the Red Cross, among others, to help them. They were all working toward putting together a revamped, comprehensive, up-to-date document.

After I arrived as secretary I gave this effort my full support. When the report was ready, in September 1990, I launched it with a big press conference and a 5K run through Washington's Rock Creek Park. I wanted the highest-profile publicity bang we could get. We called the report *Healthy People 2000*. This is where the nation's health is now; this is where we want it to be ten years from now.

We emphasized that these were *national* health goals, not *federal* health goals. We weren't trying to impose anything on anyone. We weren't passing a law; it was an educational and inspirational effort. Our aim was to raise the issues, to influence people and organizations, to show how individuals could affect their own health.

We had learned plenty of lessons from the ongoing war against smoking. You can have the best scientifically based data and conclusions for some aspect of healthy living, but as soon as you try to mandate a behavior, somebody is going to start screaming, "Why do you want to come in here like Big Nanny," as Jessie Helms had told me, "telling people what they should and shouldn't do?" I had been on an outdoor speaker's platform once with California governor Pete Wilson. When he got up to speak a wave of wild demonstrators stormed out of nowhere throwing eggs and fruit. My security person got in front of me just in time to take an egg in the chest. I saw Wilson catch an orange and rifle it back. The day before he had signed a bill making motorcycle helmets mandatory. The demonstrators wanted to take back their freedom to suffer traumatic head injuries. And a short time later they got it; the legislature repealed the law.

"These are national health goals," I said. "Not federal." *Healthy People 2000* was an effort to improve health and enhance health literacy, to have people take more control of their own well-being. I wanted to start instilling a recognition that health means more than having doctors and nurses, facilities, and research. The most basic necessity is for people to manage their own lives to a far greater degree than they were. That was absolutely necessary if we were going to improve health generally and bring health care costs down.

We wanted to get the message out that prevention was sound, that it had a scientific basis. Exercise has specific, strong health benefits. Abstaining from smoking does. Wearing seatbelts does. Eating properly does. You can manage these things yourself, *Healthy People 2000* said.

Twenty years ago much of this was considered soft science, or just soft. I wanted to change that perception. I wanted to start instilling an attitude toward health that would take hold. I wanted it to become a movement—a healthy people movement. I wanted organizations and state health departments and legislatures to use our data and recommendations as a platform for actions they could undertake.

Here was a national status report on almost every aspect of the nation's health, from nutrition, to substance abuse, to heart disease, to maternal and infant health. Where we were, where we should be in ten years, and how we should monitor our progress. Even if I'm not able to move the president on health care reform, I thought, if some of this takes root, I'll have made a lasting impact. One way or another, my tenure was going to be measured in a few short years. I would resign, I would be fired, or Bush would leave office. But *Healthy People 2000*, I hoped, would have an effect far into the future.

I also asked myself, what ongoing positive impact could I have on HHS itself, as an institution, that would live beyond my presence as secretary? Benjamin Mays had placed his stamp on Morehouse College. Gloster had too, in his own way. What could I do that would move the department in the direction I thought it should go in and create a lasting impact?

When I came in, part of my agenda was set for me, but part was my own. My own priority was to improve the health of the poor, minorities, the underserved. That was my theme. That meant programs and leadership. Part of my strategy was to increase the role of women and minorities in leadership positions, to break down barriers to advancement and make the department more representative of the people it served. That would change the face and the culture of HHS so there would be more recognition of the need for diversity and much more commitment to it. But having minorities and women in leadership positions would also help ensure that the programs I was planning to bring in would work, that they wouldn't be relegated to the shadows by an unresponsive bureaucracy. I wanted to bring in people who shared my philosophy and would be in their positions long after I was gone.

Traditionally, an African American had headed up the civil rights office at HHS, but in terms of senior leadership in Washington that was it. The highest-ranking black career civil servant in the regional offices was an individual named Bill Toby, who worked in New York. I didn't know Bill Toby, and he didn't know me. But when I came in, suddenly his stature and influence seemed to grow. He talked about this later, long after we had gotten to know each other.

"It was funny," Bill said. "I had been working in the department for twenty-five years, so although I was in the New York office and not in Washington, I was known. When Dr. Sullivan came in everyone assumed that I knew him well. I never said I didn't know him, although I didn't. I was mum about it. But people just assumed we must be good friends. Everyone was calling me, from all fifty states: 'Bill, would you talk to the secretary about this or that?'"

Blacks just weren't part of the normal picture. There were so few that people thought there must be some kind of direct connection between me and whichever other of us might be out there. I was going to do what I could to change that picture. One of my first acts when I came in was to appoint a group to look at all the advisory committees to see to what degree they were integrated and to build up a potential list of nominees for us to recruit. The department ran 250 health and welfare programs: children's health, Head Start, child-abuse prevention, elderly programs, Social Security, Medicare, Medicaid—and we had advisory committees for almost all these. That was a lot of people.

I appointed Bill Bennett to chair that group. Bill was the African American officer from the Bureau of Health Manpower who had been involved with the planning for the medical school, someone who was committed to getting more diversity into the department. The idea was to develop a bank of names so we'd have people available when opportunities came up.

Then I looked at senior positions. I brought in Bernadine Healy from the Cleveland Clinic to be the director of NIH, the first woman in that position. I tapped Gwendolyn King as Social Security commissioner, also the first woman there. Bernadine was white, Gwendolyn black. Later I brought Bill Toby, an African American, from the New York office to head the Health Care Financing Administration. I talked with Toni Novello about coming on as surgeon general to replace Koop. She was at that time deputy director of the National Institute for Child Health and Human Development at NIH. I had interacted with her on various NIH committees, so we knew each other already. Here was a woman already in government, an engaging personality, a Latina. There had never been either a minority or a female surgeon general.

I presented these names to Bush, who then nominated those who required confirmation and sent their names to the Senate. Bringing in more women and minorities was one of the subjects he and I had discussed in our meeting after his election. I knew we were in sync on this.

I also consulted on these nominations with senators Mark Hatfield, Arlen Specter, and Tom Harkin, and with Paul Rogers of Florida on the House side, along with others, to get their ideas, to see if they had candidates themselves, and to get their support. Their help was important for the confirmation process and also down the road. Health was a volatile area, full of controversy. If one of the nominees ran into problems at some point, I wanted to have allies to turn to.

All of those we tapped were accomplished people. I especially hoped that Toni Novello would be a star, which, unfortunately, did not happen. Part of the reason was that I had a high profile as secretary. Otis Bowen, my predecessor, had no desire to be out front and was quite happy to have Koop as the public figure. But that wasn't me. I felt strongly about issues. I wanted to be involved in them, and I felt it was important for people to get to know me. To some extent that may have hurt Toni. In any event, we ended up with a group of minority and female leaders. HHS took on a different complexion from what it had been. I felt good about that.

But I didn't bring them on just to integrate the department. I wanted to get more resources for NIH altogether (NIH had a budget of $8 billion when I started; when I left it was $13 billion), but I also wanted to change NIH's orientation.

Women and minorities were dramatically underrepresented in clinical research. As a result, many of the illnesses and conditions they suffered from were not understood adequately. Very simply, no one was paying sufficient attention.

To start remedying this situation, we established the Office of Research on Women's Health at NIH, bringing in Vivian Pinn to run it. Vivian had been one of the first black graduates of the University of Virginia School of Medicine. I had gotten to know her back in 1969, when she joined the faculty at Tufts medical school in Boston. She subsequently had become chairperson of pathology at Howard, perhaps the only female pathology chairperson in the country. Under Vivian the Office of Research on Women's Health undertook a long-term, large-scale study of the major chronic diseases affecting women: heart disease, breast and colorectal cancer, osteoporosis, and others.

I also established the Office of Research on Minority Health (now the National Institute of Minority Health and Health Disparities). We tapped John Ruffin for that, a PhD biologist who was then dean of graduate studies at North Carolina Central University. I charged Ruffin with what I hoped his office would accomplish, a twofold mission, as I saw it. Blacks had a significantly shorter life expectancy than whites—six to eight years for men. They, we, had higher death rates from heart disease and cancer. Why was that? And what could we do about it?

We also did not have enough minority investigators. If we had a larger number, perhaps we could get more attention focused on these issues. So how could we identify, recruit, and train more minority medical scientists? Every quarter, I told Ruffin, I wanted a status report, telling me what the activities were and what the results were. I wanted to know if he needed more support, if he needed to rethink his strategies. I wanted him to run with this. I wanted something accomplished.

I was especially concerned about what was happening with young black men. They were in terrible trouble. The litany of problems was enough to make your head spin. So many youngsters were ending up on drugs or in jail, their prospects diminished toward zero by the economic and social circumstances in which they lived. The poverty rates in their communities were astronomical, the unemployment rates likewise.

Identifying ways to address these problems was urgent. With $100 million in discretionary funds I had at my disposal, we set up the Minority Male Initiative. We looked at the problems in prison, the disgraceful state of health care there and the environment that facilitated the spread of hepatitis and AIDS. We looked at the high recidivism rate; so many of the young men had no job skills, and when they were released they had a prison record too. For them to get work, they needed help.

What could be done? We called an all-day conference that included the heads of community organizations that were dealing with one part or another of these problems. We brought in various chapters of the Urban League, Boys and Girls Clubs, and others. We asked, what part of this problem can you help provide strategies for? We wanted to try to find some answers so that we could give guidance to the relevant agencies. We looked at proposals and ongoing programs. We awarded grants for stay-in-school, male mentoring, and tutoring programs. If you had a good idea, you could come in and get it evaluated. If it looked promising, you could get funding for it. We spread our net and monitored results to see what made sense and took root. We were searching.

The Office of Research on Women's Health, the Office of Research on Minority Health, the Minority Male Initiative, the integration of HHS's upper echelons— these were all elements of my effort to direct the department's energies toward what I considered areas of primary concern. I drove to increase NIH's research budget and worked to improve our flagging childhood immunization rate. In *Healthy People 2000* we inventoried the nation's health and set goals for improvement. I covered all the bases I could. But most important to me was dragging this great ship of a department around so it could bear down on the health needs of the poor and underserved.

One essential element of our plan was the need to bring medical services into places where they were so lacking. This was exactly the challenge that had led to the creation of the Morehouse School of Medicine: the need to train physicians who would establish primary care medical practices where they were most needed.

That had been my mission at Morehouse. The question we faced was how to finance the training of young physicians who were going to dedicate themselves to this kind of practice. Many of the applicants who want to do this are poor themselves. They come out of these kinds of communities, which is why they are motivated to go back to them. But they cannot afford medical school.

To help address this problem, the National Health Service Corps provided scholarships—full tuition and living stipends for students who agreed to serve in medically underserved areas, rural or inner city, one year of service for each year of scholarship support. This program had been developed in the 1960s and grew during the 1970s. It had become an important avenue of student support for medical and other health profession schools. At Morehouse nineteen out of our first class of twenty-four had these scholarships.

When Reagan came in, he drastically cut these scholarships. When he took office the program had a budget of $400 million. When he left it was a third of that. His cuts had badly hurt all medical schools, and both white and black students were affected. But of course the black schools were wounded disproportionately. My goal was to get that program ramped up again. I worked hard and by the end of my tenure I had managed to bring $100 million more into the scholarship fund. It wasn't up to pre-Reagan levels, but it was a start.

———

The one area where I made a terrible mistake when it came to African American affairs had nothing to do with health care. It is something that still bothers me badly today, more than two decades later. Secretaries don't just run their departments; they are members of the administration, which can call on their support at any time for anything. In the summer of 1990 Thurgood Marshall retired after serving twenty-four years on the Supreme Court. To replace Marshall, Bush nominated Clarence Thomas, an African American who had served for the previous sixteen months on the District of Columbia Court of Appeals. Prior to that his primary experience had been as an administrator. Thomas was from Georgia, but our paths had never crossed. I didn't know him at all, nor had I followed his career. He was an unknown quantity.

When Bush nominated Thomas it caused a huge reaction—this was before the Senate confirmation hearings. Here was this relative unknown, a person of no outstanding accomplishment, being tapped to take the place of the great and revered Thurgood Marshall. To many that seemed simply insupportable, a slap in the face. Bush hadn't consulted me about the nomination, not that that meant anything in particular. Neither had he consulted the other senior African American in his administration, Connie Newman, who was head of the Office for Personnel Management, the independent agency that manages the government's civil service. Connie had been on my board at Morehouse for several years, so we had gotten to know each other then.

With all the noise about Thomas's nomination, Bush invited Connie and me up to his summer house in Kennebunkport. He explained to us that he thought the criticism was unfair. The confirmation hearings were coming up. He needed our help to get endorsements for Thomas's nomination from some of the major black organizations: the Urban League, SCLC, CORE, and so on. Would we be willing to help? We both said, yes, of course we'd do that.

On the basis of Bush's request and my regard for him and my desire to support him, I agreed, as did Connie. But she and I also decided that if we were going to be effective in selling this guy, we needed to know more about him. What was his orientation? What were his views? So we told the White House handlers that we needed to meet with Thomas, and they arranged for him to come to Washington.

We used Connie's town house on Capitol Hill, and the three of us sat down together for a long talk. Thomas told us that he realized how important this appointment was. He was going to be the only African American on the court. He knew people would be looking to him, especially on civil rights and other fairness cases. He convinced us that not only was he sensitive to these issues, he supported them. Connie and I both came away from the meeting buoyed up. Thomas had given both of us a level of comfort.

The first person I visited to try to secure an endorsement was John Jacob, president of the Urban League. "Well," he said, "Let me think about it. Let me talk to members of my board." Five or six days later he came back. "Lou, I'm sorry. I can't get support for it. We'll have to sit this one out."

I went to Houston to a convention of CORE, James Farmer's organization. Farmer didn't even have to think about it. "Absolutely not!" he said. Connie was closer to the NAACP leadership, but she got turned down as well. No endorsement there. It wasn't that people necessarily felt that negative about Thomas, per se. But they didn't know him, and when they looked at his record they thought he was not qualified. Part of their reaction was disappointment. Marshall was an icon. It was hard to think that his seat would be taken by a person with very little history of accomplishment. So the reactions were partly disappointment but also partly suspicion of a Republican administration. Someone like Leon Higginbotham would have been acceptable. But he was not the nominee.

In the course of all this I approached the Reverend Joseph Lowery. A close companion of Martin Luther King, Rev. Lowery had been one of the founders of the Southern Christian Leadership Conference. He was now the SCLC's third president. I knew him. He was a major presence in Atlanta. When I asked Lowery if he would consider supporting Thomas, he said, "I don't know him. I'd like to meet this person." So we arranged for Lowery to come to Washington and interview Thomas at Connie Newman's.

Lowery brought a couple of his lieutenants with him, and they, Connie, and I spent several hours talking with Thomas. They asked direct questions: What was Thomas's thinking about affirmative action? What was his position on voter registration? Thomas had all the right answers. He was all for equal opportunity; he was all for voting rights. He said, as I recall it clearly, "Rev. Lowery, I promise you this. If I am confirmed I will not disappoint you. I will not let you down. I know how important these things are."

Lowery heard Thomas out, and he was persuaded. "I've been around a while," he said. "I'm getting to be an old man now. I just want to go to my grave feeling secure about the man who's sitting there making decisions on the Supreme Court. I need to know that the things that are important to me and my people are the things that are important to him."

Thomas said, again as I recall, "Rev. Lowery, I'm from Pin Point, Georgia. I know what oppression is. You can rely on me." It seemed heartfelt. It was a moving statement.

Lowery said, "Well, okay. You have my support. We're having our convention in Birmingham in two weeks. I'm going to see if I can get an endorsement." And Lowery did get it. The SCLC, Martin Luther King's organization, endorsed Clarence Thomas. It was the only black organization of national stature that did. In the end, of course, Thomas was confirmed and took his seat on the bench, where he very soon showed himself to be almost a carbon copy of Antonin Scalia.

One day after Thomas had been on the court for some time, Lowery called me up. "Well," he said, "you got me."

"What do you mean?"

"What the hell is that guy doing up there on that court?"

"Rev. Lowery, I'm just as surprised and disappointed as you are. I was right there with you. I heard the same things from him that you did."

After that, for many years, every time I'd see Lowery, he'd just shake his head. He was angry, but fundamentally he knew I'd been had too. I really felt I'd been used. I think that Bush was probably surprised as well. Thomas has turned out to be not only a disappointment but almost an embarrassment. He never engages in the discourse of the court. He seldom says anything. I watch the votes he casts—against affirmative action, against voting rights, against health care coverage for the poor, in favor of allowing corporate money to dominate our political processes. I look at these votes, and I cannot credit that he truly believes that these positions help those in our nation who most need help. His votes are certainly inconsistent with the assertions he made to me and to the Reverend Lowery. And having grown up poor and having suffered from discrimination and segregation himself, it is astonishing to watch him vote against programs designed to attempt to rectify damage and create an equal playing field for all.

One of the most maddening things is that he's against affirmative action. Here the contrast between Thomas and his fellow justice Sonia Sotomayor is revealing. Thomas is famously bitter about affirmative action, which may have helped with his admission to Yale Law School. To him, affirmative action was degrading; he felt it stigmatized him, that because of it potential employers looked at his (excellent) grades and refused to credit them. Because of affirmative action, he believes, his Yale law degree was, as he put it, "not worth fifteen cents." Sotomayor, in contrast, is grateful that affirmative action opened Princeton's doors for her. But how she got in was not the most important factor for her. It was what she made of the opportunity, in her case, the opportunity to graduate summa cum laude and earn admission to Thomas's alma mater, Yale Law School, where she was an editor of the *Yale Law Review*. You would think that pride in his accomplishments would dominate Thomas's reflections on his law school experience, not that he would harbor such a profound sense of insult and grudge. To me there's something deeply disturbing about that.

Thomas might well have been confirmed without any of my activities. But SCLC was a highly respected black civil rights organization. An endorsement from them was about as good as getting one from the NAACP or the Urban League. That was a big, big letdown. He represented himself to us in one way, something he did, in my opinion, simply to garner the endorsement, knowing that his judicial inclinations were exactly the opposite of what he was telling us they were. I consider him a person of dubious integrity.

That bothers me: Thomas, an arbiter of justice, on the court of last resort. Thurgood Marshall's replacement. And he's a young man; he'll be there a long time. It's been years now since Thomas's confirmation. I think Joe Lowery has forgiven me by now. It's been harder to forgive myself.

———

While all the work was going on at HHS to plan, launch, and implement our various initiatives, there was still that eight-hundred-pound gorilla sitting in the corner, waiting: health care reform. Thirty-seven million people had no health insurance.

The system needed to be reformed. These people needed to be covered. The question was, how best to do it?

But the issue wasn't just the number of uncovered people. There were other basic problems in the system as it stood. The reimbursement rate for medical services was askew. Specialists received higher rates than primary care and family practice doctors. That meant, for example, that we were assigning a higher monetary value to an orthopedist fixing a fracture than to a primary care doc giving a series of vaccinations. This reimbursement scale meant that we were not incentivizing primary care medicine, whereas from a policy perspective, we needed to be doing the opposite. At the same time the pay scales favored procedures at the expense of preventive care, also the opposite of what we should have been doing. Other big problems were built into the system as well. It badly needed fixing.

Overriding the gamut of problems was the spiraling cost. In 1965, when Medicare/Medicaid was passed, 6 percent of the GDP was going to health care. When I came in, the figure was 11 percent. Our actuaries were projecting that the rate of increase would accelerate so that by the year 2050 it would be 35 percent (now, in 2013, it is 18–20 percent). We had to rein in these costs. At the same time we had to increase coverage. In a sense it was like squaring the circle, but one way or another both had to be accomplished.

I didn't come in with a developed concept on how to do reform. Rather, I understood that we had these problems, and we needed to find ways to address them. Our initial approach was to start up discussion groups inside HHS. If we did have a plan, what were some of the things we would want to be in it? What would it look like?

I also began talking with Bush about the need for a comprehensive health care plan. But these discussions were relatively brief. Among the many demands on his attention, this clearly was not a priority. Part of that was the Republican instinct that health care meant big government—not something you wanted to embrace if you could find a way not to. But also, health care was a complicated subject that fell outside Bush's comfort zone. His expertise was in foreign policy. He had been ambassador to the UN and ambassador to China. He was at home in the world of diplomacy and international affairs, as he showed when Saddam Hussein invaded Kuwait a year and a half into his term, and Bush put together a global coalition to drive him out. There he took charge. He knew what he was doing. But that wasn't the case in the domestic arena, in education or housing or welfare. In domestic policy he relied on his close advisers, Sununu and others, who were telling him to stay clear of health care. Health care to them was a swamp, a losing proposition.

In August 1990 Saddam invaded Kuwait. By the time that was wrapped up, another six months had gone by. Afterward, Bush's positive ratings were off the charts, as high as 92 percent in some polls. He was at the zenith of his popularity. The political necessity for health care seemed negligible. Bush wasn't dismissive when I brought the subject up, but he clearly had no energy for it. From the White House perspective, there were only so many battles they were able to take on. This would be a major one, and there seemed no overwhelming reason to spend the political capital.

In the meantime, though, we continued to develop ideas. My sense was that before the election, Bush would have to submit a plan. I wanted to clarify the main issues and have solutions prepared. We had two main priorities: we wanted to cover the thirty-seven million who did not have health insurance, and we wanted to attack the problems that were driving costs relentlessly higher.

We began to do this seriously in early 1991. I put together a working group that included Gail Wilensky, who was heading the Health Care Financing Administration overseeing Medicare and Medicaid. Gail was a PhD economist who probably had as detailed a grasp of health care issues and their financial concomitants as anyone in the country. I also brought in Jim Mason, an MD/PhD from Harvard who had been head of the CDC and was currently my assistant secretary for the Public Health Service. Gwen King was also a core group member. She had been Reagan's deputy assistant for intergovernmental affairs and was head of the Social Security Administration. We had eight or nine people in all, supplemented by consultants we brought in from the outside to provide advice, especially on the financial and clinical elements of the plan.

To increase coverage we looked first at small businesses, which employed a large segment of the labor force but for whom providing insurance coverage was often not affordable. Here we proposed the creation of health care networks or pools that small businesses could join. Going to the marketplace by themselves to buy insurance was expensive. But making it possible for small businesses to form purchasing cooperatives spread the risk and gave them the leverage to negotiate for lower premiums, making it feasible for them to provide coverage for their employees. For self-employed individuals, we proposed either a tax credit or a sliding subsidy that people could use to buy their own health insurance, while at the same time making sure that limited cost programs were available for them to buy.

Portability was another problem. People were often fearful of moving to different jobs because that meant needing to enroll in new plans that might have different eligibility criteria. They might be excluded, for example, because they had some preexisting condition or disease that put them outside the eligibility guidelines. Our approach would prohibit denial of coverage for preexisting conditions. To help bring medical care to underserved areas we wanted to expand community and migrant health care centers and further the growth of the National Health Service Corps. At the same time, we were proposing to limit malpractice costs, which were growing relentlessly and creating upward pressure on the overall cost of delivering health care. We also wanted to simplify record keeping and administrative costs and reduce insurance paperwork, all of which would produce savings of many billions of dollars.

By May 1991 we had completed the plan. Now I pressed to meet with White House officials to round it out, to make sure it was consistent and in-line with the president's views. But we did not get that meeting. We were in essence told not to bother. They were not interested. I was, to say the least, frustrated. But the message was clear. The president was riding high in the polls. Health was an issue with twists and turns and surprises; it was a lot of potential trouble. Fundamentally, they didn't want to have anything to do with it.

But I was not given a definitive no either. And during that summer, Dick Darman, director of the Office of Management and Budget, put together a group to consider the plan on an intergovernmental level. As head of OMB, Darman was the individual who would decide what would be feasible economically and politically. How do we fund this? How much is it going to cost? How did it fit in with other needs? Darman was a financial expert, an economist, but he also had extremely sophisticated political skills, which was an unusual combination. He was the key person.

My relationship with Darman was cordial but complicated. With Darman you knew where you stood. He wasn't duplicitous. He'd tell you if something wouldn't work because of either the finances or the politics. He tried to be an honest broker. He wasn't an ally or an adversary. But he was not the soul of warmth. We'd sometimes kid him about that. "Hey Dick, there are actual people out there who are suffering the consequences of your decisions. People!" But we did need someone who could take a very dispassionate look at things, which was what he did.

I can't say exactly why Darman initiated a working group at that point. My speculation is that the administration was responding to my advocacy about getting health reform on the agenda. They didn't want a big internal rift on the issue, and whatever did come of it, they wanted to exert some control over what a plan would look like.

That was the sense I had, because despite the working group, there was still no enthusiasm from the White House. In my discussions with John Sununu I'd hear, The president is doing well. His ratings are high. Why mess it up embarking on risky propositions? Sununu would say privately, "Health is a Democratic issue. They always outmaneuver us on this. We have everything to lose and nothing to gain." A lot of Sununu's positions, I felt, were political as opposed to ideological. He was focused like a laser on what was necessary to get the president reelected, and by this criterion health reform did not qualify.

I pushed, but continued to get nowhere. I met with President Bush. "Mr. President, we have a real problem we need to address, and we can't get your staff to help us get this going. It's a serious problem."

"Lou, we're anxious to get something done, but we really have to get our allies lined up in Congress."

And so on. We really felt we had been left at the altar in terms of the legislation we had developed. I was saying, to the best of my ability, if this is going to get anywhere we need to have you out there. But it did not happen. At the same time, it's worth saying that this kind of thing goes on regularly. Cabinet secretaries have programs they want to move forward. Sometimes they succeed; sometimes the stars aren't aligned. You have to wait for the right circumstances.

In the most difficult case, if there's an issue that cabinet members feel is so urgent that they would not be meeting their essential responsibility to the country if it's not addressed, then they can make a demand and let the chips fall, which means putting their job on the line. A dramatic example is the Saturday Night Massacre, when Attorney General Eliot Richardson and Deputy Attorney General William Ruckelshaus resigned after Nixon fired Special Prosecutor Archibald Cox. I was frustrated, but I was hardly at that stage. I continued to believe that we would get support when the circumstances were right.

In November the circumstances suddenly did turn right. Six months earlier Senator John Heinz from Pennsylvania was killed in a helicopter crash. The governor made an interim appointment; then in November a special election was held. The Republican candidate was Dick Thornburgh. Thornburgh had been a popular two-term governor in Pennsylvania before being named attorney general by Ronald Reagan, a post he retained under Bush. The Democratic candidate was Harris Wofford, who had held various civil rights positions in the Kennedy administration and had been Pennsylvania's secretary of labor.

As this race began, Wofford was so far behind Thornburgh in the polls that nobody gave him any shot at all of winning. But James Carville and Paul Begala ran Wofford's campaign—this was what first brought them to national attention—and they found a wedge issue in health care and "the right of every American to see a doctor." Wofford beat Thornburgh by ten points. It was a stunning upset.

Wofford's victory shocked the White House—not only that he had won but that his main platform had been health care. At that point our plan went from something that was withering on the vine to something that was suddenly high priority. "Where's that plan that you've been working on?" I heard. "Send that thing over; let's take a look at it."

President Bush introduced the plan in a talk he gave to the Cleveland City Club in February 1992. He submitted the plan to Congress, but both houses were Democratic then and we simply could not get it onto the congressional agenda. We couldn't even get it on the calendar of the Senate Finance Committee.

In a way I felt vindicated in having gotten the plan rolled out at all. But I also thought that we could have made a hell of a lot of progress if we had gotten behind it publicly in the fall of 1991, before the political season started. If the president had spoken to the American people and said, We have a problem. We have a solution for it. We have to get it debated and see where it needs strengthening or changing, and then we have to pass it. But we never got that. It was too little, too late. In an election year the president was not ready to go to the mat for it, and the Democrats had no interest in giving Bush a board to hit them with. So in the end it went nowhere.

Nobody worked harder on the health care reform plan than Gail Wilensky. Gail was, and is, a health policy guru, not an essentially political person. In 1994, after Bill Clinton's health care plan went down in flames, many of her Democratic friends called her. She still recalls it well: "They said, 'That was a pretty interesting health care reform program that President Bush had proposed. Maybe we should have taken it more seriously.' I thought, Yeah, thanks a lot guys. You did everything you could to torpedo it, minimize it, and mock it."

All of this had happened, and it was a shame. Our plan to get everyone covered, plus our assault on the underlying drivers of health care costs, was a program that should have received bipartisan support. It would have drawn the poison from the debates that eventually blossomed into such vicious partisan antagonism. It would have spared us that and accomplished what we are obligated to do for those Americans who have the least access to the medical services that are so essential in all our lives.

But 1992 was an election year, and Bush, a little surprisingly, was in trouble. He had come out of the Gulf War crisis looking unbeatable, but in 1990 and into 1991 the country was experiencing a significant recession. There was some cabinet discussion about the political impact this was having, usually led by treasury secretary Nick Brady and OMB director Dick Darman. They followed the numbers closely and talked about what might be done to shorten the recession's duration. This was a naturally occurring economic phenomenon, but they were concerned. We didn't want this around very long because of its potential to impact the election. But it did stay around. By early 1992 the situation seemed to have flattened out, and the economy was starting to recover. But in spite of the signs that the downturn had ended, people weren't yet feeling it. It became evident that this was going to be a real problem.

During the campaign several of the secretaries found ourselves out on the hustings. I paired up frequently with Jack Kemp and Lynn Martin, the secretary of labor. The president and vice president would go to the big rallies, and we'd attend the smaller ones, addressing chambers of commerce, Rotary groups, farm groups, or sometimes local Republican political organizations and campaign workers, trying to keep them energized.

But as the election approached we were more and more concerned. The polls were showing Bush falling behind Clinton. Kemp and I talked about what we might do to turn this around. It seemed to us that one major problem was that Bush wasn't focused enough on the fact that people were hurting. He didn't give the appearance of someone who cared deeply about ordinary people and their problems.

In one of my talks with the president I said, "You know, you have a strong commitment to education, including minority education. You have a history. You were important early on in the United Negro College Fund. You still are. You're major benefactors. Your family has always had a member on the board; there have been four or five Bushes there by now. People ought to know this."

"Lou," he said, "I don't do that for political reasons."

"I understand that. But what people really want is to know you: who you are, what you stand for, what your values are. And this is one of those things that is so positive and very important in the black community."

But I could never get him to talk about it. He backed away from it. He thought it would be inappropriate to draw attention to it. Unseemly. As Barbara Bush told me later, looking back on the situation, "George was absolutely right. That would be tooting our own horns. And we do *not* toot our own horns."

When it came down to the wire, we were hoping there would be some election day miracle. But that kind of thing rarely happens. The economy was improving, but that hadn't made an impression yet. Bush was never a match for Clinton's eloquence, and he was never comfortable around the press. He was behind in the polls at the end, and the election proved the polls all too valid. We were out, and the new administration was preparing to come in.

After the election I told the department that we needed to prepare comprehensive briefing books for the new secretary designate, Donna Shalala. We spent quite a bit of time and energy on this, but I could not get Shalala to come in. She simply would not do it. Finally, she did put in an appearance around January 10, a week and a half before Clinton's inauguration. I set aside three hours for our discussion. She spent twenty minutes. She made it clear that she had little interest. She told Bill Toby later—"How can you stand working with those Republicans?"

To this day I do not have a relationship with her. I did not think of myself during that transition as a "Republican." I thought of myself as the secretary of health for the country, trying to transfer knowledge and information to the incoming secretary. From a professional standpoint her attitude constituted a serious failing. To her mind we were suspect, as was the experience and understanding we had accumulated in the department over the previous four years. With Shalala it was politics first and last. She was an intensely partisan person. History will judge how well that enabled her to function during her own tenure.

———————

My immediate problem, of course, had nothing to do with Shalala. When I accepted Bush's offer of the secretaryship I had severed all my ties with Morehouse. I understood then that my future after this plunge into the political world would be an open question. In the rough-and-tumble of Washington, I had neither the time nor the inclination to give it any thought. As the election results sank in, I wasn't at all sure about what might come next.

CHAPTER 12

Morehouse, a Model Black Institution

It wasn't that I was worried. I was sure that after my experience at Morehouse and my time now as secretary, there would be opportunities, either in academic medicine or industry or possibly in a think tank. I wasn't concerned about making a living. My concern was whether I could find something satisfying.

In fact, during the spring before the election I had gotten a call from Jim Hayes, the new chairman of the Morehouse School of Medicine board. Hayes told me that Jim Goodman, who had succeeded me as president, had decided to retire at the end of June. "We'd very much like to talk to you about returning to Morehouse," he said.

I said, "Jim, you know, the rules are that I can't talk about anything like that. I'd be compromised. Secondly, I don't know how this election is going to turn out. But if Bush wins, some of us will probably be asked to stay on. I don't have any idea what might happen. So I think you really ought to go ahead with the process." I didn't know any of the details, except that after that the board constituted a search committee and began the business of looking for the next president.

I got another call as the election campaign was heating up, this one from my old friend, the Reverend Leon Sullivan. "What are your plans?" he said in his unmistakably large voice. "You leaving?"

"Leon, I haven't made any plans. I'm doing everything I can to help the president get reelected."

"Okay. But if you decide to leave, you call me first!"

Leon Sullivan and I went back ten years or so. He was a phenomenon, a large, energetic, elegant, gregarious man with a powerhouse mind and a voice that could wake the dead. At six feet five or so he usually towered over everybody in the room. He was an imposing human being. Leon was a minister in Philadelphia, Pennsylvania, and a social activist with a worldwide reach. One of his organizations was IFESH, the International Organization for Education and Self-Help, which operated in sub-Saharan Africa to stimulate economic growth, democratic political development, and education. Leon had asked me to join his board in 1984, and I had accepted.

Like many African Americans, I wanted to learn as much as I could about Africa, and I wanted to contribute to health and other aspects of development. Here we were, living in the world's wealthiest country, with our ancestral ties over there. What could we do? At the same time Leon, Andy Young and others, myself included, were concerned—disappointed and frustrated by what was happening in many of those nations. They had gained their independence, then the liberators had given way to dictators and corruption. Was there any way we could help move that situation toward something better?

Leon's approach was to encourage the widest contacts possible between Africans and African Americans. He pressed constantly for more communication and collaboration. He tirelessly promoted American economic investment in Africa. Every other year he held a big conference in one African nation or another, with four thousand or so participants, half Africans, half African Americans. I had been to several of them.

While on his board I also became aware of another of his organizations, OIC, Opportunities Industrialization Centers, whose mission was to stimulate economic and social development in America's inner cities. The NAACP was focused on political development and civil rights. Leon Sullivan focused on economic development.

Leon was also the first African American board member of General Motors. He had been relentless in pursuing the boycott of apartheid South Africa, and as a senior member of GM's board he had significant leverage. He led that fight, and eventually GM did pull out. Beyond that, he authored what came to be known as the Sullivan Principles, which stipulated that American corporations working in

South Africa had to ensure that all employees were treated equally in an integrated environment. He lobbied businesses to adopt the principles and instituted shareholder battles to accomplish the same end.

We used to kid each other about our names, both of us Dr. L. Sullivan, which did lead to some confusion. When I became secretary, he called me up to congratulate me.

"I need to come in and talk with you." When he came in he said, "Man, you don't know what kind of problems you've caused me, becoming secretary. I've had calls from around the world"—in his booming voice—"Around the *world*! Congratulating *me*!"

"Well," I said, "now you know how I feel. For years I've had people calling to tell me how much they admire me because of my *principles*!"

On one occasion the confusion was memorable. I was the keynote speaker at a fund-raising dinner and Bill Cosby had been called on to introduce me. His introduction was fulsome in the extreme. I was, according to him, one of the leading figures in the world attempting to right the terrible injustices of racism. I was one of the great moral leaders of this generation. I was a dozen other admirable things. At the beginning of this I was a little embarrassed, but impressed to be acknowledged so enthusiastically, until Cosby mentioned what a truly wonderful person this Leon Sullivan individual was, in addition to his many accomplishments. At that point someone came up and whispered something in Cosby's ear. Cosby didn't miss a beat. "Apparently I've made a mistake," he said. "I thought I was introducing Leon Sullivan. Turns out I'm introducing Louis Sullivan, whom I don't know from Adam." The audience was in stitches. Cosby knew me very well from Adam; he had introduced me at the previous year's fund-raiser. "Louis," he turned to me, "you're on your own."

After the election, the chairman of the Morehouse School of Medicine board, Jim Hayes, called again. Morehouse had been functioning with an acting president, Nelson McGhee, but they had not yet found a permanent replacement for the retired Jim Goodman. Bush had lost. Could I now give some serious consideration to coming back?

I did. I knew I could pursue other things, but four years earlier I had left Morehouse with reluctance. I felt I really hadn't finished what I started to do. I still had that feeling. And there was no denying my emotional attachment to the school. The great challenge of training young doctors who would serve where they were most needed hadn't lessened. The great challenge of building a black school that would establish its place as a national leader in medicine was just as mean-ingful now as it had been then. The achievement had already been substantial, and I was grateful to Jim Goodman and Nelson McGhee for nurturing it. But the Morehouse School of Medicine had been the great purpose and satisfaction of my life for thirteen years. When I considered all the other things I might do, nothing else held a candle to it. Morehouse was where I could make the greatest contribu-tion and where I could derive the greatest personal fulfillment. So I accepted the trustees' offer.

My tenure as HHS secretary ended at noon on January 20, 1993. That afternoon I flew back to Atlanta and started at Morehouse. The next day I spoke to a general assembly of students, faculty, and staff. I was so very pleased to be back, I told them. I congratulated them on where the school had gone and what had been done. I spoke about where I believed we were as an institution and what our chal-lenges were for the future. Afterward a great many people came by to shake hands. Secretaries I had known four years ago hugged me. I felt embraced, as if I had truly come home.

Jim Goodman had left six months earlier. Nelson McGhee, who was associate dean for clinical affairs, had been serving as acting president. But in his caretaker role Nelson didn't feel he had the authority to commit the institution to an ongo-ing path. In those circumstances things had been moving sideways. Now I could feel a sense of expectation in the air, which I shared. I could see where I wanted us to go and at least part of how we might get there. I couldn't wait to get started.

———————

At the same time other things began cropping up as well. Even before I left Washington, Leon Sullivan had called. "Bush lost. What are you going to do now?"

"Well, maybe go back to Morehouse."

"I want to come in to see you."

"Okay."

"I want to bring Jack Smith with me."

Jack Smith had just been named CEO of General Motors. GM was having all sorts of problems. They were losing market share; the quality of their cars was deteriorating; their labor relations were in terrible shape. They were in real trouble. The board had gotten rid of Robert Stemple in a directors' coup and had brought Smith on as CEO. They had a new chairman of the board as well, John Smale, who was the former CEO at Proctor & Gamble. Leon brought both of them in to see me. They wanted to recruit me to the board.

In February, a month after I resumed the Morehouse presidency, I accepted and joined. Leon and I were now the two African Americans on GM's big eighteen-person board, each of our nameplates reading "Dr. L. Sullivan," no doubt to the bemusement of other board members.

At GM I thought I could help address some of the health-related cost problems embedded in the company's union contracts. I put forward proposals to institute copays for doctors' visits and to switch to a mail-order pharmacy system for prescriptions. GM's labor costs had made the company increasingly uncompetitive on the world market. But getting the union to budge on any kind of containment proved impossible. Still, I had had four years of experience in a giant bureaucracy. I knew that significant changes didn't happen quickly. The prerequisite was keeping your shoulder to the wheel.

Leon Sullivan had precipitated my recruitment to the GM board. But I quickly discovered that I had landed in the middle, or actually at the beginning, of a radical shift in corporate thinking about governance. Corporation boards had traditionally been club rooms for white males. It was almost unheard of to find any minorities or women on the boards of major corporations. But by the early 1990s companies were coming under fire for their lack of diversity. Something of a wave had started, moved partly by a gathering sense of the need for fairness and inclusion, but more by the growing awareness that diversity was good for the life of companies. Board diversity brought a wider range of thinking and a greater sensitivity to the marketplace, especially important as globalization began to take hold. Companies began looking seriously to broadening their approach, and diversified boards were a means for doing that.

In the weeks after I joined the GM board I found myself being courted by Richard Gelb, the chairman and CEO of Bristol-Myers Squibb. Dick Gelb was a good friend of the Bushes. I had recruited him while I was at Morehouse to be head of one of our campaign committees, so I had gotten to know him well. Now he called to talk to me about joining his board. At almost the same time I got a similar call from Cigna. Shortly after that a small train of companies approached me about joining their boards. At Bristol-Myers Squibb, Household International, and Equifax, I was the first black board member. At 3M I was the second. It was clear to me that I was being courted for several reasons. I was now the former secretary and large companies liked to have Washington experience on their boards.

I was an academic, which had a bit of prestige attached to it, and I brought something of a network with me—all this in addition to being an attestation of sorts to a company's commitment to diversity.

At most of these companies I served on human resource committees and nominating committees. I was heavily involved in bringing in the right mix of skills and broadening the makeup of the boards I served on. At 3M, for example, we brought on three women and one Latino. In a way I found myself doing the same thing that I had done at HHS, where one of my overarching objectives had been to include women and minorities in the department's upper echelons.

I worked hard on these boards. I joined eight of them before I decided I was in danger of overloading myself, even though I had the go-ahead from the Morehouse trustees. My work for these companies gave me, I thought, good justification for requesting donations for the medical school, which I did freely. And they were always forthcoming. When I asked 3M's Desi DeSimone, for example, he wrote a check for $1 million. I also wasn't shy about asking the chairmen, vice-chairmen, and CEOs to lead fund-raising campaigns for us or at least to serve on committees. DeSimone gave time and leadership generously, as did others: William Taylor at Cigna, Lewis Platt of Hewlett Packard, Charlie Heimbold at Bristol-Meyers, Don Clark at Household International, and others. I sometimes thought back to my early attempts to ask for money, how embarrassed and reluctant I had been. I had pretty clearly gotten those feelings out of my system.

My experience as secretary also raised my ability to bring government resources into play, not just for Morehouse but for other minority institutions and the health of minority populations in general. One opportunity of that sort opened up as a result of a hearing that Senator Arlen Specter held on NIH funding. Specter had a strong commitment to health and to minority issues, which had precipitated this particular hearing.

What happened was that the Institute of Medicine had put together a committee to review how NIH was handling cancer research regarding minority communities. The Institute of Medicine is an independent agency that was established under the charter of the National Academy of Science to provide advice, information, and direction on health matters. It serves basically as a nongovernmental national academy of medicine. As an independent body, it has great credibility and prestige.

The IOM committee came up with some troubling findings. With a research budget of $3 billion (this was in 1990) the National Cancer Institute had allocated

$120 million to study cancer in minority populations, a strikingly small percentage. Not that the finding was that surprising: research dollars for minority health generally tended to be more or less inconsequential. I had attempted to address that exact issue with a number of the initiatives I took as secretary—for women as well as minorities.

Specter's Senate subcommittee had called Al Haynes to testify. Haynes was dean at the Charles Drew medical university; he had chaired the IOM committee. Specter had also called the head of the National Cancer Institute. He asked me to come in as well to comment on the report.

In his presentation, the National Cancer Institute director maintained that all the research they sponsored was benefiting minority as well as mainstream populations. That was true, Al Haynes said. But it left out a great deal. In general, because of the lack of research, we often did not know the course or impact of cancers on minority groups. Death rates from cancer were almost uniformly higher for blacks than they were for whites. Even for breast cancer, where white women had a higher incidence than black women, black women's death rates were higher. We did not know how to explain either of those statistics. Were they due to differences in biology? In genetics? In access to health care? Was it something we could address? "We think this is the kind of question NIH should be looking at," Haynes said. "We need more than just generic cancer research. We need to know what's happening out there in the real world, which is the world of diverse peoples."

Afterward, Specter called on me. "Dr. Sullivan, we have this Institute of Medicine report, and we've heard from the director of the Cancer Institute. What are your thoughts?"

"We have an Office of Minority Health at NIH," I said. "But it's an office, not a center, which means it has to negotiate through the NIH bureaucracy in order to make grants. Were it a center it would have its own grant-making authority and mechanisms. If we had a center we could more readily respond to such questions. So one recommendation would be to elevate the Office of Minority Health to a center."

"Send me a memo," Specter said. "We'll look into it on my committee."

That started the process. We received support in both the House and Senate. On the House side Louis Stokes took the lead; on the Senate side Specter did. We crafted legislation, and eventually the bill passed. It was one of the last bills Clinton signed before leaving office in 2001.

Previously, the Office of Minority Health had to go through the relevant institutes—the National Cancer Institute; the National Institute of Allergy and Infectious Diseases; the National Heart, Lung, and Blood Institute; and so on—to award grants. After it was elevated to a center, though, minority health had its own funding to support research, $30 million initially. Compared to the $3 billion for the National Cancer Institute, $30 million was a rounding error. But it meant dedicated funds; it meant that interested researchers had a home they could look to for grants. It stimulated thinking about the health of minorities.

Making the Office of Minority Health into a center also set the stage some years later for elevating it to an institute. Within the NIH hierarchy, the greatest resources are in the institutes. Again, this required an act of Congress. Our strategy here was to get that included in the Obama Affordable Care Act. I advocated strongly for this, as did the presidents of Meharry and Morehouse (I was president emeritus by then) and the acting president of Drew. The Association of Minority Health Professions Schools that we had founded back in 1977 provided a lobbyist and advice on strategies.

We did not get any support from Francis Collins, who had become the head of NIH. His position was that an NIH center has all the authority an NIH institute has, so there was no point in changing the designation. My response was that a center might have all the authority of an institute—yet an institute has a higher profile and greater prestige. So if the Center for Minority Health does function like an institute, let's call it an institute.

Collins was noncommittal. But I had allies in the federal health establishment. I also had support on the Hill I could call on, Democrat and Republican. So I had leverage, which Collins knew, though I kept that in the background. "Francis," I said, "we've come to you because we are going to work to get this done. We think this gives you, as the new director of NIH, an opportunity to be on the side of making changes that will enhance the focus and abilities of NIH to deal with issues of minority health.

But despite my efforts Collins was not persuaded. The best I got out of him was, "Let me think about it."

In the end we got the institute amendment tucked into the Affordable Care Act. Harry Reid put it in as a so-called leader's amendment. Given the raging controversy around major elements of Obama's bill, our amendment passed with hardly a notice.

As a final note, in 2010 when Specter was defeated after twenty years in office, the Association of Minority Health Profession Schools honored him, to express our gratitude for what he had accomplished for the health of minority communities and for the nation's health in general.

＝＝＝＝＝

Despite my work on various boards and the ongoing battles in Washington, the center of my attention was the health, welfare, and future of the Morehouse School of Medicine. There had been progress in the four years I had been gone, but one thing that struck me on my return was that the school was still housed in the same two buildings we had put up previously. Developing the campus was a primary need, and I began devoting myself to raising funds for new facilities.

Putting together money from a variety of sources, including funds we received from the 1996 Atlanta Olympics, we were able to add a multidisciplinary research center that housed outpatient clinical research and a neuroscience institute, the first of its kind at a minority school. Then we added what we called the Research Wing, along with a parking facility. Finally in 2002 we cobbled together $23 million, the largest amount from two government grants, for a federally designated National Center for Primary Care.

The person most responsible for our success in garnering the funds for the primary care center was Ronny Lancaster, whom I had recruited from HHS shortly after I left. Ronny was a lawyer in one of the department's regional offices when I came in as secretary, and he had been recommended to me as someone with exceptional analytic and administrative skills. I had brought him to Washington as deputy assistant secretary for planning and evaluation, and he had quickly become one of my key think tank people. I especially valued him for his highly developed political understanding and even more so for his independence and objectivity. I could always count on him to give me honest, straightforward advice, whether or not it might have been what I wanted to hear. As secretary I didn't always get that, and I treasured it.

I brought Ronny to Morehouse as senior vice president with primary responsibility for governmental affairs, which he excelled at. He managed our effort to bring in the federal money for the primary care center, which became our keystone building. He did all the preliminary work with the significant congressional representatives, so that by the time I went in to ask for their commitment they had already been prepared and won over. As far as building the campus went, Ronny deserves the lion's share of the credit.

In addition to ramping up the building program I also began pursuing endowments for professorial chairs. I was bent on making Morehouse into a school with national stature. To do that we needed good facilities, which we were developing. We also needed to begin attracting the highest-level faculty. Our first endowed chair, in family medicine, was funded by our trustee Sally Hambrecht and her husband, William, with a $1.2 million gift. William Hambrecht was, and is, a leading investment banker involved in bringing public such companies as Apple, Google, Genentech, Adobe, and Amazon.

The Hambrechts' gift was followed by a $1.5 million donation to endow the George and Barbara Bush chair in neuroscience, given by Will Farish, a friend and classmate of George Bush's from Yale. Farish's grandfather had been an early president of Standard Oil, which eventually became Exxon. Farish himself was a major philanthropist, but he kept well out of the public eye. Giving, as far as he was concerned, was a private matter.

When I came back to Morehouse, I went to Texas to visit Farish's family foundation and see if it might be interested in funding half the endowment needed for the chair. A couple of weeks later I got a call back, asking how much the whole chair would be. They had no interest in funding just half of one.

Our first Barbara and George Bush professor of neuroscience was Peter MacLeish, an internationally renowned professor at Cornell who had trained with Nobel Laureate Torsten Wiesel at Harvard and Rockefeller Universities. The Bushes came down for Professor MacLeish's inauguration. I asked the foundation to please extend our invitation to the Farishes; we would love to have them there together with the Bushes. But I was told, "Oh, they don't come to things like that. They like to keep a low profile." It was a great pleasure hosting the former president and first lady at the inauguration event. I wish we had been able to honor the Farishes as well.

———

Morehouse School of Medicine had sponsored programs in Africa since early on in the school's life. I had also been involved in Africa personally, with Leon Sullivan and his IFESH organization and also through a nonprofit organization we called MESAB, Medical Education for South African Blacks.

MESAB was founded by Herb and Joy Kaiser after Herb Kaiser retired from a long career as a U.S. Foreign Service officer. During his professional life he had been stationed in numerous countries around the world, including South Africa. It was while he was working in Johannesburg that Herb was diagnosed with melanoma. Fortunately, the cancer was caught at an early stage and successfully removed. That incident got Herb Kaiser to thinking, though, and what he thought was about the unavailability of health care for South Africa's blacks. Had he himself been a black South African, his melanoma would have been a death sentence.

That experience stayed with him, and after he retired he and his wife had founded MESAB. By then apartheid was being dismantled and black students were being accepted at universities. Few were going, though. No scholarship money was available, so for most of these potential students acceptance was an empty gesture. To help address this problem, MESAB undertook to raise scholarship money for black students who wanted to go into the health professions. That was its primary purpose. The secondary objective was to facilitate the integration of South African universities. Stanford's president Donald Kennedy came on as MESAB's first board chairman. I was an original board member. George Soros was one of our funders. It was at a MESAB fund-raising gala that Bill Cosby had mistaken me for Leon Sullivan.

Over the period of MESAB's existence, we raised something on the order of $8 million and supported more than ten thousand students, most of whom went on to become doctors, nurses, and other health professionals. One of our scholarships was established by United Therapeutics in 2007, in honor of Hamilton Naki, the great black South African surgical technician who had never himself been to college. "There was no doctor in my village of thousands of people," wrote the Hamiliton Naki scholarship winner, Moses Matlhadisa, describing what motivated him to want to become a physician. "But there was a doctor from a nearby town who came once a week." It was a story that could have come right out of Blakely, Georgia.

MESAB was a personal project of mine, but the medical school also developed its ties to Africa. Actually, long before the medical school, Morehouse College had close connections with Africa and Africans. When I was an undergraduate, my classmates included fifteen or twenty African students, including the drum-playing Babatunde Olatunji. So, right from the start, while the school of medicine was still the medical education program of Morehouse College, we had an interest in outreach. Howard and Meharry both had programs in Africa, and they were our models.

Nowadays NIH funds health projects centered in other countries, but earlier USAID underwrote these kinds of programs. I visited USAID in Washington to introduce the medical school. We were interested, I said, in participating in their African projects. I think the fact that we were a black school had at least some influence, since African American teachers and researchers don't carry the baggage that sometimes attaches to white Westerners in formerly colonized countries.

Through USAID we established HIV-AIDS prevention and education programs in Zambia, Lesotho, and Swaziland. In Senegal we worked to create communication and collaboration between the country's Western-trained physicians and its traditional healers. Senegal had two medical schools connected with schools in France. But relatively few trained doctors practiced in the country, while many traditional healers did. Moreover, people tended to trust the traditional healers more than the physicians. When it came to health, the healers wielded tremendous influence. At the same time the physicians ridiculed and belittled the healers. They felt toward them a little bit like American orthopedists used to feel toward chiropractors, practitioners whose bone and joint manipulations, they believed, were of little value and delayed or sidetracked patients from getting the real medical attention they needed.

In Senegal the government came up with the idea of creating linkages between the physicians and healers. If they could do this, they believed they could much more effectively bring at least a modicum of contemporary care into the countryside, where it was needed the most. Through USAID our faculty was involved in creating a program to bring the two groups together.

Our African connection was important in terms of filling an emotional space as well as giving our students and faculty a more expansive, global view of health needs. Our attachment to Africa, like the attachment of so many African Americans to Africa, constituted a part of our identity.

As the medical school matured, biomedical research became another element of our identity. We were, first and foremost, dedicated to training primary care physicians. But we also tried hard to recruit faculty with an interest in research, not only because they contribute to new knowledge but also because they create an environment of inquiry. Faculty want to feel that they are part of an entity that is creative and innovative and that plays a role in cutting-edge developments. It was a great satisfaction, especially given my own background in research, to know that our faculty was in the top quintile in terms of garnering research grants on a per capita basis. Many Morehouse students didn't arrive planning to make careers as medical scientists, but the research emphasis enriched their training environment and stimulated their sense of physicians as problem solvers, so significant to every clinician.

Nevertheless, the school's raison d'être was training good primary care physicians. I believed from the start that we could aspire to a national role in that area. When we started, the concept of primary care, including family medicine, was relatively new. The old idea of a general practitioner, someone who served the general health needs of families and the communities they lived in, had fallen sharply in regard, especially with the emergence of increasingly narrow specialties and subspecialties. Fewer and fewer medical students were going into primary care, yet the need for primary doctors was more and more urgent.

That was an area where, despite our small size, we could make a difference. We wanted to counter the sense in medicine at the time that primary care and family medicine did not have a strong science base. We expected our graduates to become board certified in family medicine or internal medicine or ob-gyn. Our overarching mission was to have a quality program so there would be no questioning the merit of the institution.

In 1996, three years after my return, Morehouse was first in the country in terms of graduating the highest percentage of primary care physicians. Jumping ahead, in 2010 a new "social mission index" was published by the George Washington School of Public Health. In this category Morehouse was ranked number one in the United States. It was a moment of pride for us, but the development caused more than a little consternation in the medical establishment.

The Association of American Medical Colleges was particularly upset. The AAMC is largely involved with medical education and the quality of care provided by teaching hospitals, with a major emphasis on research. Now suddenly this social mission index was published and schools that were always at or near the top in various surveys, the Columbias and Stanfords and Hopkinses, turned out to be near the bottom in terms of social mission. In response, the AAMC chief of academic affairs came out in the *Washington Post* criticizing the new index.

After the article the presidents of the black medical schools met with the president of the AAMC, Darryl Kirsch, to express our extreme displeasure with the AAMC's reaction. I was with them.

"Why would you attack something like this?" we asked. "You may raise questions, but why would you go to the trouble of talking in public in this critical fashion about social mission? Do you feel that has no importance?"

Kirsch was defensive. He agreed we were doing something important. The AAMC was really questioning the methodology, he said. They also felt that the author of the index, Fitzhugh Mullan, had an agenda, that he believed the only important medical discipline was primary care and he was using the paper to push his agenda.

I knew Darryl. He had been dean at the Medical College of Georgia. I also knew Fitzhugh Mullan. He had been deputy surgeon general under Koop and had stayed on in that position during my tenure. Fitzhugh was a distinguished professor of medicine and health policy at George Washington with a long record of public health service. He was a man of strong views and no reluctance to voice them.

Our response to Darryl was, "Why then aren't you critical of the *U.S. News and World Report* ranking of medical schools? Everyone will tell you how flawed that is. And yet you walk into the deans' offices at Cornell or Stanford or Hopkins, and they'll have reprints lying all over the place. If the methodology is so nonscientific, why haven't you spoken out about that?"

We weren't arguing about the importance of medical research or specialization. That would have made no sense whatsoever. But the idea of denigrating primary care was equally nonsensical. Morehouse or Meharry or Howard were not striving to be a Harvard or Johns Hopkins. But they and other schools whose mission was primary care were also making a strong contribution, and that needed to be acknowledged. And not just acknowledged, I thought; it needed to be emphasized. "The primary objective of medical schools is to train doctors to take care of people," we said. "Isn't that true? Training specialists is important. Training primary doctors is important. We need to have a big tent."

The upshot was that we received an apology from the AAMC. Then they formed a working group to look at the question. Given their central role in American medical education, it was a significant step. I couldn't have been prouder of the number one ranking, of course. By then I had been away from the Morehouse presidency for seven years, but I had an ongoing emotional investment in the school. Fitzhugh Mullan was a careful investigator, but whether or not his methodology was perfect, the index was a recognition, thirty-six years after we started out in those double-wide trailers, that we were fulfilling the hopes embodied in our founding mission.

That was important, not just for the black community, but for the country as a whole. In terms of numbers, Morehouse's contribution was and always would be relatively small. But we can contribute a great deal to the attitudes of people. If we can get other institutions to adopt the goals that are significant to us, that would have a tremendous multiplier effect. The social mission index is an example. Indexes like this one could have a strong impact on places like Hopkins and Harvard and Stanford. They are competitive institutions. How can they be number ninety-five when they're supposed to be the best school in the country? Flawed or not, these kinds of indexes and rankings provide recognition. We may dismiss them because of their methodology or underlying agenda, but at the same time they change behavior. We do proceed by signs and signals.

———————

When I first took on the deanship of Morehouse, I felt that the school, or the idea of the school, embodied my most deeply held hopes and motives. I wanted to help the black community, and from the very start I had seen medicine as my pathway. I was tremendously fortunate that Hugh Gloster had given me the opportunity to create a reality out of that elemental aspiration.

But I had another mission in mind as well. I had grown up in a segregated society. What that society was saying to me and to all African Americans was, "You are below par, mediocre, incapable." I wanted Morehouse School of Medicine to declare emphatically that we were capable of building an institution that was first-rate by anyone's standards. I wanted Morehouse to be a place that measured up on the most stringent criteria. I wanted it to be able to compete with any school in the country. That was my way of fighting back against all the debasement and condescension, of turning it back and revealing it for the lie it was. As far as I was concerned, Morehouse School of Medicine was an institution that was going to help transform long-held perceptions. That was the larger vision I had, and I was determined to realize it.

That motivation was far more than just an idiosyncrasy on my part. Morehouse College, which had given birth to the Morehouse School of Medicine, had a history of launching its graduates into the mainstream of American society. The college was a springboard for the recognition of African Americans as legitimate, fully equal, contributing members in the life of the nation.

I was a product of that myself. My peers and I had helped fulfill the expectations and hopes that Benjamin Mays and other Morehouse leaders had for us. But there was still an impression that we, those of us who had "made it," were somehow anomalies. Despite whatever one individual or another had accomplished, there was still the perception of black inferiority, a mindset cultivated over hundreds of years of slavery, segregation, and racism. You couldn't escape from that history, not in my generation at least, and maybe not in the current generation either. Its weight was simply too heavy.

I wanted Morehouse School of Medicine to help show that there was nothing anomalous about accomplished, skilled African Americans. I wanted our graduates to demonstrate that, and I wanted the school itself to demonstrate that the same was true for our institutions. It wasn't that we were alone in this effort, far from it. There were other fine African American institutions. But we were the first black medical school in a century, which meant that we drew special attention, which in turn meant that we needed to put a spotlight on the theme of black institutional as well as personal accomplishment.

These were not parochial concerns. Almost all the traditionally black schools were founded in the nineteenth century, at a time when African Americans were excluded from mainstream education. But in the aftermath of *Brown v. Board of Education* and the civil rights laws, inclusion and integration have been the general rule. Because of this, many people ask why we need to have black schools. We are an integrated society now, they say. What then is the point of black schools? What is their value?

The answer to that, my answer and the answer of other African American educators, is that black institutions make a unique contribution not just to the black community but to the mainstream of American life. At Morehouse College we were urged to set goals and take risks to reach for those goals. We were taught that if we made the investment of time and effort, we would be rewarded with accomplishment. That same dynamic is true of all the good black schools, Xavier, Spelman, Howard, and the others. They support the personal development of the individual so that their students' level of confidence expands, as does their motivation to make the most of their talents. They can have a profound impact on the subsequent life patterns of graduates and enlarge their ability to contribute to society as a whole.

As I write this a movie is in the theaters about the Tuskegee Airmen, the black fighter pilots who made an impact in the air war over Germany. When World War II started, it was widely believed that blacks weren't intelligent enough to fly or didn't have the courage necessary for air combat. But here was a group of African

American men who did everything they could to give that assumption the lie, and their performance changed perceptions. Once they had the right training, they ended by making a magnificent contribution to the national effort.

The good black educational institutions do something equivalent. They are specialists in preparing young African American women and men to take their place as contributing members of society. In doing so they play a role parallel to that of Catholic or Jewish or Mormon institutions. Catholic colleges provide solid educations, but they also convey a sense of Catholic history, values, and heritage. That is their value added. A similar thing can be said for a Mormon Brigham Young University or a Jewish Brandeis. These schools do not intend their graduates to exclude themselves from the larger society. On the contrary, they believe that graduates with a strong sense of their own identity will add richness and strength to the diverse fabric of our national life. That is precisely what black institutions do. And I wanted Morehouse School of Medicine to serve as a model in that endeavor.

CHAPTER 13

Missing Persons

In 2002 I had been head of the Morehouse School of Medicine for twenty-four years. I felt good about what we had done and where we were. For some years, though, I had been planning to step down. I was in good health. I was still enjoying the work. But I didn't think I needed to be president for life, and institutions are often reinvigorated by changes in leadership, which is what I had in mind. I thought it made sense to look for a new president while I was still in good shape, rather than waiting until I had a heart attack or something and throwing the school into the hands of an interim leader. I had seen Howard and Meharry suffer under interim leadership while they were searching for new deans or presidents. I wanted us to avoid that if we could.

In 1998 the medical school accreditation agency had awarded Morehouse a third straight seven-year accreditation, a recognition that we were stable and thriving. When their review came out, I gave a report to the school. I congratulated our steering committee that had been working so hard during the accreditation procedure. Then I said, "I've been president of Morehouse School of Medicine since the beginning. The institution has been growing. We've been successful. But I believe it's time we begin looking for new leadership." I asked the board to establish a search committee. I told them I would serve as president until a new leader was found, whether that was six months or two years, or whatever.

My goal was to achieve a seamless transition. I envisioned that when the new president came in, I would be available to serve as a supporter or mentor on fundraising, governance, or other issues. That was the kind of relationship I had with Hugh Gloster. He and I didn't always see eye to eye, but we had enough understanding and respect for each other that it worked to the school's advantage. I contemplated having that same kind of relationship with the new president.

By 2000 we had found somebody, James Gavin, a highly respected endocrinologist who was senior scientific officer at the Howard Hughes Medical Institute and past president of the American Diabetes Association. It took a fairly extended period before Gavin was able to finish up his work at Howard Hughes, which I was a little impatient about, but in 2002 he assumed the presidency with high hopes, his and mine. He was a prolific researcher, an excellent speaker, and a highly engaging personality. He hadn't had much administrative experience, but then neither had I when I came in. With Gloster's help, I had learned on the job. I was sure he could too, and I looked forward to our ongoing relationship.

Unfortunately, it didn't work out the way either of us had hoped, and after two years Gavin tendered his resignation. In retrospect, I believe he could have been more accommodating to my efforts to stay engaged and to assist him in building on what had already been accomplished. At the same time I might perhaps have been more sensitive to his desire to make a clean break and stamp his own identity on the school. What happened wasn't that uncommon in situations where founder-driven organizations transition to new leadership. But it was, without a doubt, a bump on the road of the school's development, one we might have avoided had we had the foresight.

In the meantime, though, I had in fact retired and was taking on other projects. In 2003, shortly after I resigned as president, the W. K. Kellogg Foundation approached me with the idea of chairing a commission to look at the state of diversity in medicine and other health professions. I had already been involved with Kellogg in a series of exploratory meetings on this subject that included other major health-oriented organizations, the Public Health Service, the Institute of Medicine, the IRS, and various community and academic health centers. A major finding of these exploratory sessions was that, as the concluding report put it, "The U.S. medical profession is on a demographic collision course with an increasingly diverse nation."

The paucity of black and other minority doctors had become an issue in the 1960s and 1970s, when the civil rights efforts of those days focused attention on the exclusion of blacks from mainstream upper-level professions. Since then we had improved diversity in the health field. But progress had been far less than what many had expected. The Association of American Medical Colleges (AAMC) had sponsored a number of commissions to study the problem, one of which I had served on in 1968. The latest was the "3000 by 2000 Commission," which called for increasing the number of minorities entering medical school from one thousand to three thousand by the year 2000.

Now it was 2003, and we had not come close to realizing that goal. In 1950 some 2 percent of American physicians were black. By the late 1980s that had risen to between 4 and 5 percent. But in the 1990s the percentage had stagnated. Why was that? What effects did the lack of minority physicians have on health care? And what could be done about it? Those were the questions the Kellogg Commission (which the foundation decided, somewhat to my discomfort, to rename the Sullivan Commission) was designed to investigate.

I wanted to make sure that whatever answers we came up with would gain political attention, so I asked Paul Rogers and Bob Dole if they would serve as honorary cochairs. Dole had left the Senate after thirty years to run for president in 1996, when he lost to Bill Clinton. He was still in Washington, a Republican elder statesman. Rogers, a Democrat known as "Mr. Health," had served in the House for eleven terms and had been the chairman of the Subcommittee on Health and Environment. Dole's and Rogers's involvement conveyed the seriousness we felt as we undertook this work and gave us a high profile on the political front.

Together with the Kellogg people, I selected sixteen commissioners from the health professions, the legal and business communities, and higher education. Louis Stokes; Eric Holder; Elena Rios of the Hispanic Medical Association; William Weldon, CEO of Johnson & Johnson; John Rowe, CEO of Aetna; Joan Reede, dean of diversity at Harvard Medical School; and others equally prominent agreed to take part. In addition to medicine, we planned to look at nursing and dentistry. We couldn't cover all the health professions; we would have ended up with a study a mile wide and a quarter-inch deep. What I wanted was a report that would be comprehensive, but not voluminous, so that people would actually read it. I wanted it to be read, and I wanted our conclusions to generate not just thought but action.

The lack of diversity in the health professions had a particular urgency to it. In the first place it indicated that despite our great advances toward equality, minorities who wanted to make lives for themselves as doctors, nurses, or dentists still faced high barriers. Access to careers in the health professions remained largely separate and unequal. In this area of national life, minorities simply were not present in any significant numbers. I began to think of them as "missing persons."

The problem had consequences that went far beyond the inability of our medical, dental, and nursing schools to include significant numbers of minorities, as bad as that was. The low number of minority physicians and other health workers was a major factor in the shocking inequality in health care that afflicted a large segment of America's population.

This was a subject I knew firsthand. A great deal of my own professional life had been an effort to address exactly this issue. Now, for a variety of reasons, concern about these disparities was growing in the medical establishment. Political figures and the general public too were becoming aware of just how stark and troubling this situation was.

In response to a congressional request for an assessment of racial and ethnic health disparities, the Institute of Medicine undertook an in-depth study, which was published in 2002 as a book titled *Unequal Treatment*. In careful, dispassionate language *Unequal Treatment* documented an underside of medical treatment that sent shock waves through the health establishment.

Unequal Treatment detailed how, even when corrected for socioeconomic status and insurance coverage, blacks did poorly when compared to whites in terms of access to care, type of care, and health outcomes. The black infant mortality rate was twice that of whites. Blacks received less in the way of medication for cardiac problems, fewer angioplasties, fewer joint replacements, fewer kidney transplants, and even less pain medication for broken limbs. The black mortality rate was 60 percent higher than that of mainstream whites. Almost every medical specialty had its own grim history of unequal treatment, a history that was still all too alive.

The IOM study was comprehensive and thoroughly researched. Coming from the Institute of Medicine it had great prestige; it drew attention and set alarm bells ringing. The question was, almost forty years after the civil rights laws, how could these things possibly be? The answers to that question were complex. They had to do with poverty, poor education, lack of coverage, the ingrained culture of medical training, and other factors.

A major element, *Unequal Treatment* suggested, was the undercurrent of bias that still affected the way doctors treated patients. Some of this may have been the remnants of overt racism. But a significant part had to do with deeply ingrained prejudices, largely unrecognized and exceptionally difficult to eliminate. We might believe that we are free of prejudice, but we might more accurately say we are unaware of our prejudices. Almost all doctors insist they give equal care to all their patients, white, black, men, women. But the statistics, as the IOM report illustrated so starkly, told a different story.

All of that spoke to the need for more diversity among doctors and other health workers. Despite the increasing sophistication and prevalence of diagnostic testing, the doctor-patient relationship was and is still "the bedrock of clinical practice," as one famous clinician, Jerome Groopman, put it. But given the scarcity of minority physicians, most minority patients are treated by mainstream doctors. Subconscious stereotyping, like overt prejudice, means that communication and affiliation between minority patients and mainstream doctors are harder to achieve. And health care is, in the end, the delivery of scientific knowledge and expertise given *in a social context*. That was a point I emphasized in every forum I could. And when the social context is neglected or relegated or when it is less than positive, outcomes almost always suffer.

One element of unequal treatment had to do with bias—or to put it more bluntly, racism—often institutional, often subconscious, but racism nonetheless. Another element was access. The practice patterns and locations of mainstream and minority physicians were different, as we knew so well. Minority doctors tended to establish themselves in the barrios and ghettos and rural enclaves of their communities. Far more often than white doctors, they were drawn to practice in the poor and disadvantaged communities they so frequently came from themselves. Given the limited number of minority physicians being trained, these communities simply did not have anywhere near the same level of access to doctors that more affluent communities did.

The Institute of Medicine had called for increasing the number of minority health professionals as a key strategy to eliminating health disparities. Moreover, the need to do this was becoming more pressing year by year, as the demographics of the nation continued to shift. The minority populations were growing at an ever-faster rate as a percentage of the whole. At the same time the percentage of minority doctors, dentists, and nurses was actually declining. Demographics and the ability of the health establishment to respond to needs were indeed on a collision course.

The Sullivan Commission's charge from the Kellogg Foundation was to identify the barriers to achieving diversity in the health professions and to formulate policy recommendations that would achieve solutions. The fact that we were doing this with foundation money meant that we didn't have to deal with the constraints that confronted governmental or quasi-governmental panels. We set our own agenda and had no political or other pressures on us. We also had an enthusiastic and energetic set of commissioners who were leaders in fields directly involved in the issues.

We gave ourselves eighteen months to accomplish the task. We examined previous studies on the problem, and we commissioned several of our own. But the main thrust of our effort went into holding public hearings in six cities, chosen partly because of their population diversity. In Atlanta, Denver, New York, Chicago, Los Angeles, and Houston we heard testimony from witnesses who included health and education experts, business leaders, community advocates, health professionals, and students. In each place we gathered oral and written recommendations about what to do and how to do it.

The hearings typically took a day or a day and a half. At the conclusion of each we'd distill what we had heard in a summary. This is the health status of this community. This is what the level of population diversity is. This is the level of diversity in the health workforce. These are examples of programs that are working and these are the kinds of programs that are not working. We began in April 2003. By March 2004 we had completed our hearings and other investigations and sat down to digest what we had learned and to formulate actionable recommendations. In September of that year we issued our report.

The report was titled *Missing Persons: Minorities in the Health Professions*. In it we articulated the rationale for increasing diversity in the health professions. We argued that increased diversity would not only benefit the members of minority groups but would raise the health level of the entire population. Better health meant better productivity in the workforce, less absenteeism, less cost for coverage, and increased ability to compete globally. For the well-being of Americans generally and the vitality of the workforce in particular, we needed to have a health care profession whose makeup more closely mirrored that of the population it served. We needed health care workers who were culturally and linguistically competent to attend to the needs of an increasingly diverse people.

Then we laid out our specific recommendations, thirty-seven in all. We confronted the reasons relatively few minorities entered medical school. We talked about the inferior education, specifically science education, minorities tended to receive. We spelled out how colleges and health professional schools could work with businesses and public schools to provide academic enrichment, counseling, and other support services.

We discussed the financial limitations on minority enrollment. I had graduated from medical school $500 in debt, which I paid off during my internship. Today a medical student will typically graduate with a debt burden of $200,000 or $250,000. For many minority students $200,000 is a frightening number. Psychologically, for them there's not a lot of difference between $200,000 and $2 million. It scares them off. What changed the picture so dramatically between the time I was a student and now was that in the mid-1970s many of the scholarship programs that funded so much of medical school tuition costs were replaced by loan programs. The argument was that taxpayers shouldn't pay for medical education; students should pay for it themselves out of future earnings.

That may have seemed logical at the time. In fact, it was a huge mistake. Today poor students are simply not going to medical school. What we see in incoming classes are kids from the upper-middle and upper classes. The poor have been largely squeezed out. In the process the fundamental American ideal of equal opportunity has been lost, and the health of the population has suffered accordingly. To address this problem we recommended increased private and public tuition funding, scholarships, loan-forgiveness programs, and tuition-reimbursement strategies.

We discussed medical, dental, and nursing school admission practices, curriculum changes, congressional action, and other salient aspects of the problem. We identified exemplary practices that had helped build minority participation. We emphasized the need for leadership, from the medical establishment, business, and the federal government.

We released the report at a press conference at the National Press Club, looking to get the biggest possible media bang. We sent out op-ed pieces to leading newspapers; we sent copies to the secretaries of HHS and education. We sent it to the White House and to all the professional health organizations.

Unequal Treatment came out a year before *Missing Persons*. We were fortunate in the timing. *Unequal Treatment* got everyone's attention. Health care of minority populations, it demonstrated, was shamefully inferior. Then we came out with *Missing Persons*, showing that to get adequate health care to underserved populations, we needed more minority physicians and other health workers.

Unequal Treatment woke the medical establishment up. *Missing Persons* rein-forced the message and put the spotlight on health care workers. Yes, we needed to address insurance coverage and the culture of medicine; we most certainly needed to address bias. But the bottom line was that we had to have enough doctors who would actually provide the care. The AAMC was projecting that the country would need thirty thousand more doctors than we were currently graduating. Where were they going to come from? I was convinced this was going to be recognized as a national priority that the government would have to step in and address. Given the projected shortfall, enlarging the pipeline of minority health professionals would be an important part of the resolution.

One of our Sullivan Commission recommendations was that there should be a federal commission to oversee diversity in the health professions, to monitor prog-ress and make recommendations for programs or funding. I submitted this proposal to Margaret Spelling, George W. Bush's domestic policy adviser at the time. We had several meetings about it. From Spelling I heard, "This is important. This is some-thing that needs our attention. We'll look into it and get back to you."

For the next six or seven months I kept pressing on that front, but it was a frus-trating business. "Yes," I'd hear. "We haven't forgotten. We're looking at it. These things take time." Ultimately I gave it up. It was clear to me that nothing was going to be done at that level. Nothing has yet been done at that level, eight years later. Now, of course, with so many more people coming into the system under the Affordable Care Act, the estimated need for health professionals to take care of them has grown dramatically. In 2012 the AAMC projected the need for 120,000 more doctors and nursing associations for a million more nurses.

At the same time we weren't sitting around waiting. What we needed was a means of generating national momentum—increasing public awareness and insti-tuting academic reforms and legislative initiatives. What I had in mind was some-thing like the 9/11 Commission, which didn't disband immediately after provid-ing recommendations but instead pressed Congress to act. Discussing this with the Kellogg people, I said it was my hope we would have some follow-up mecha-nism that would serve as a catalyst to push for action. We did not want *Missing Persons* to sit on people's shelves gathering dust. We didn't want to simply launch it into the empyrean with the hope that it might sow a seed that might somewhere, sometime, lead to doing something concrete. Kellogg agreed. They decided to set up an ongoing body to do this. Following on the Sullivan Commission, we named it the Sullivan Alliance to Transform the Health Professions.

At the same time that Kellogg funded the Sullivan Commission, they had also commissioned an IOM study to explore the benefits that racial and ethnic diversity in the health professions would have for both minority and nonminority populations. This study was chaired by Lonnie Bristow, the first black president of the American Medical Association, which was a significant milestone in itself. Bristow's committee had issued a report titled *In the Nation's Compelling Interest: Ensuring Diversity in the Health Care Workforce*, with its own list of recommendations. We invited Bristow and members of his committee to join us in the Sullivan Alliance; then we moved ahead.

In January 2005 we formally inaugurated the Sullivan Alliance. Our charge was to find ways to implement the recommendations in the two Kellogg-sponsored studies. In this endeavor we cast a wide net. Our aim was to enlist the participation and investment of health professionals, business leaders and corporations, the academic community, government, nonprofits, and community groups. Our goal was to increase minority representation in medicine, nursing, dentistry, psychology, and public health, with the expectation that efforts in these areas would spill over into the other health professions. Our long-range goal was to have this as a national priority on the federal government's agenda.

Two of the most significant barriers to increased enrollment in medical and other professional schools were the inferior education minorities tend to receive from kindergarten up and the lack of familiarity with the medical world and what's required to enter into it. After doing the studies and formulating our recommendations, we were ready to establish a national effort that would address at least one large dimension of the problem.

The core of the Sullivan Alliance program would be to provide research experiences for minority students during the summers of their junior or senior college years. This meant establishing relationships between ourselves and medical schools and research institutes. It meant raising money for stipends. And it meant publicizing our efforts so that students would know about our program.

We thought of these summer internships as a vehicle to get minority students inside the walls of health science centers to expose them to the whole range of health professions. They would attend conferences and learn the difference, for example, between a physician and a nurse practitioner and a physician assistant, understand what the admissions requirements were, and learn how to finance a medical education. Youngsters who have very little information but think they'd like to be doctors would learn what it really takes. They would form relationships with clinicians and scientists. Going back to their schools at the end of the summer, they would have someone professional to talk to. They would be able to pick up the phone and discuss things with a mentor in an academic health science center. Instead of being a forbidding foreign country, the world of medicine and research would become familiar to them.

We launched our program in Virginia in mid-2004, bringing together Virginia Commonwealth University and the five historically black colleges in the state. Subsequently, the University of Virginia School of Medicine joined the alliance, as did Eastern Virginia Medical School and the new Virginia Tech School of Medicine, essentially all the health science programs in Virginia.

In a serendipitous development, Nebraska also joined the Virginia Alliance. During an organizational conference at Virginia Commonwealth, the chancellor of the University of Nebraska happened to be present. Harold Maurer had previously been chairman of the pediatric department at the Virginia Commonwealth School of Medicine, so he knew people there and was interested in what was going on.

At the conference Maurer expressed his support for what we were putting together. "We also have a strong interest in diversity," he said. "Our constraint is that we have a very small minority population. If you decide to go forward with this, we would be interested in participating." So the Virginia Alliance became the Virginia-Nebraska Alliance. Students from Virginia began going into summer internships at the University of Nebraska Medical Center as well as at the Virginia medical schools.

Virginia was the first state where we organized a Sullivan Alliance. Subsequently, we established an alliance in Florida that included all of the medical schools in the state, along with Florida A&M and Bethune Cookman. In Florida we also brought in the Florida Medical Association, the Florida Health Department, and Florida Blue Cross/Blue Shield, which gave us additional scope, political strength, and funding.

At this writing we are in the process of forming alliances in North Carolina and Maryland. Ohio, Alabama, and Mississippi are also in development. One of our thoughts is that in the West we might put together multistate alliances, possibly with Colorado as the focus. Wyoming, Montana, and Idaho don't have their own medical schools because their populations aren't sufficient to support one. Those states, together with Alaska, are part of a program that's allied with the University of Washington School of Medicine, the so-called WAMI (Washington,

Alaska, Montana, Idaho) program. Students do their basic science studies at the University of Washington and have their clinical experiences at clinics in their home states. Our hope is to develop an alliance program with WAMI on our way to developing collaborations in all fifty states.

The Sullivan Alliance has been up and running now for seven years. To this point most of our students have been African American, but some of our grantees have been Latino, and we are attempting to initiate programs for Native Americans. We want to involve all underrepresented minorities. The number of Native Americans who have come to us so far is very small, but the Universities of Colorado and North and South Dakota have special interests in Native American education, and we hope to collaborate with them to bring more of these students into the health profession pipeline.

A major hurdle we face in diversifying the field is the poor preparation a good percentage of these youngsters get in K through twelve. Many extremely capable young people are disadvantaged by that from the start. A lot of community colleges and universities have preparatory and enrichment programs for youngsters like that. But we ourselves do not yet have the resources to contribute to solutions in this area. What I foresee is that in the next several years we may be in a position to engage with this problem, potentially by identifying particularly effective college programs, setting up methods of evaluation, establishing best practices, and helping to disseminate them.

In the meantime we have now had more than 350 students go through the alliance program, many of whom are now in medical, dental, or nursing school. I think it's not too much to say that in seven years the Sullivan Alliance has become synonymous with national efforts to diversify the health care workforce. This is a long-term effort that is addressing absolutely critical needs. We have, I think, made a good start.

⸻

We've made a slower but decent start too on the National Health Museum, which I also became involved with as I began thinking seriously about retirement. Everett Koop initiated the idea of a national health museum when he was surgeon general. Back in the 1950s there was a medical museum on the Washington Mall, but toward the end of the decade it was moved to the Walter Reed Hospital to make room for other Mall museums. At that time the medical museum was designed to exhibit significant developments in the history of medicine. It contained more than a few oddities: photographs of wounds of soldiers in the Civil War, conjoined twins, the bullet that killed Abraham Lincoln. These were curious items, but they didn't draw large numbers of visitors, and when the museum was moved to Walter Reed even the attendance it previously had dropped off considerably.

Koop's idea was to update the exhibits and move the museum back to the Mall in an effort to increase the general public's interest in medicine and medical advances. Initially he thought it should be one of the Smithsonian Museums. The Smithsonian's board of regents didn't disagree. They thought it was a worthwhile idea, but they passed on it. "We have our hands full," they told Koop. "We're underfunded as it is." The idea of taking on another museum wasn't something that interested them.

Koop didn't give up, though. In 1995 or 1996 he recruited Bill Haseltine to head the museum project. Haseltine was a noted AIDS researcher at Harvard who had founded Human Genome Sciences, a biotech company that focused on developing drugs from DNA sequencing. Several years into his chairmanship Haseltine asked me to join his board (I subsequently recruited two other former HHS secretaries, Joe Califano and Tommy Thompson). But a year or so after I joined the bottom fell out of the biotech industry and Haseltine's company, which had seemed so promising, found itself in serious straits. Bill had to drop out of the museum chairmanship, and the board asked if I would step in.

By the time I came onto the board the idea of the project had shifted from a medical museum to a health museum. That's what had attracted me to it in the first place, and one of the reasons I was recruited was that during my tenure as secretary I had been extremely active in pushing the concept of health promotion. I had little interest in creating an old-fashioned museum of exhibits, but it seemed to me that if we could develop a venue whose purpose was to change health behaviors, that would be worthwhile.

The kind of project I had in mind would be a follow-on in a different genre to the *Healthy People 2000* report we had issued when I was secretary. The object of that report had been to instill the idea that people could to a large degree manage their own health. To accomplish that we needed to create awareness, show what could be done, and provide the information needed for people to change their behaviors for the better.

My hope for *Healthy People 2000* was that it would help transform the national psychology about "health care" from something the medical establishment was responsible for—that is, "sick care"—to something that people could in large measure take in hand themselves. During the twentieth century the health professions developed a tremendous capacity to treat disease. The first mitral valve repair operation, for example, was performed by Dr. Charles Bailey at Hahnemann Hospital in Philadelphia. Before that, rheumatic heart disease that affected the valve or other valve diseases would often lead to heart failure. Bailey found a way to go in and correct that, a tremendous discovery. We've continued to create innovations in treatment: new kinds of joint replacements, new stents, new drugs, new procedures.

We want to keep on track with that kind of progress. But whatever innovations we come up with, they miss the mark of what we more fundamentally need. Health care cannot be a sickness care system. We want it, rather, to be a wellness maintenance system. Wellness maintenance improves the nation's overall health and reduces the ever-higher price of new technology and procedures, which contribute so substantially to our out-of-control health costs. That's what the healthy people movement was about. I see that as the purpose of the National Health Museum as well.

I conceive the museum as a way of improving the health literacy of Americans so that increased knowledge would lead people to change their behavior. So many of our major problems have a significant behavioral component: obesity, diabetes, heart disease, cancer. Changing the way we eat, exercise, and take care of ourselves otherwise can make great inroads on the incidence of these and other diseases and conditions.

That's an almost universal understanding now, but thirty and forty years ago it seemed more in the realm of mysticism and witchcraft. In 1950 and well beyond the whole idea that behavior affects health seemed strange. Surgeon General Luther Terry's 1964 report on smoking and cancer generated a seismic shift in that cultural mindset. Then in 1979 the idea picked up momentum with Julius Richmond's *Healthy People* report, which went beyond smoking to subjects such as proper diet and exercise. Over the past thirty years or so many studies have shown that regular exercise lowers high blood pressure, decreases the incidence of heart attacks and strokes, and even helps prevent cancer. Extensive research has demonstrated the health effects of eating certain foods and not others. Childhood immunizations have almost eliminated the occurrence of a number of communicable diseases. Seat belt usage has become the norm, which has dramatically lowered the incidence of automobile injuries and fatalities.

What has happened is that over time the public has become convinced. We understand that behaviors have real consequences, that if we're to lead healthy lives we need to pay attention. But it's easy to forget the long-term history of this concept. Getting to this place has required a major change in orientation, the sort of change that takes time, the accumulation of evidence, and the constant pressure of education.

Even then progress can be hard. A full 47 percent of American adults smoked in 1964. Today, despite the plethora of information and warnings, it's still 20 percent. In terms of heart disease, high blood pressure, and deaths from cancer, either the curves have flattened out or indeed are coming down. On the other hand, we are losing the battle over obesity. Fifteen years ago an authoritative survey showed that the incidence of obesity was climbing. That has continued to the point where we now have a major problem on our hands. Ten or fifteen years from now the health consequences of obesity are going to create a massive impact. That's when today's obese twenty-five and thirty-year-olds will be dropping like flies from heart attacks and strokes.

Over the past years our focus in public health has been on improving the system, finding ways to cover more people without breaking the bank. That's a necessity, but the obesity problem is a prime example of why it isn't enough. We have to ensure access and train enough doctors and other health professionals, but along with that we have to change our health behavior. The purpose of the National Health Museum is to find ways to inform people more successfully than what we've been doing thus far, and not only to inform them but to motivate them to act.

When I took over as chairman, that was the concept. To make it a reality, we needed first of all to find a place. Starting in 2001 we began looking at sites in Washington. The Mall would have been ideal, but there was no more room there. We had competition too; the African American Museum was also searching. It took three years, but eventually we found what we were looking for, a site on Independence Avenue on top of the Twelfth Street underpass. The Agriculture Department building was just to the west, the Forrestal Building to the east. The vacant space was government property, but the General Services Administration (GSA), which manages federal properties, had no plans to use it.

The GSA thought the museum would be an excellent use of the land. But to sell the property to us they needed approval from Congress. To accomplish this we had a bill placed on the suspension calendar, which meant that if there were no objections it would automatically pass. We and our sponsors didn't foresee any problems. We were eager to acquire the site and forge ahead.

To our considerable surprise, the bill was stopped. It took us a couple of weeks to find out that the person who had done it was a representative from Lancaster, Pennsylvania, Joe Pitts. His problem was stem cells. He was concerned that the museum would be teaching people about stem cells, which was part of the abortion question. If we wanted to reverse his objection, he said, the museum would have to sign a pledge that we would never present anything on stem cells. The pledge would have to be written into the *Congressional Record*.

This wasn't something we could agree to. Doing such a thing would immediately eliminate our credibility in the scientific community. We are going to have doctors, nurses, and biomedical scientists around the country working with us. We could not under any circumstances be seen as a tool of political propaganda.

We tried to negotiate. I had supporters among antiabortion members of Congress, as well as other powerful allies such as Arlen Specter and Tom Harkin. I didn't talk with Pitts. I didn't have a relationship with him, and from my point of view he was so wrong and so far out of bounds that I didn't feel a discussion between the two of us would be productive. But others talked to him at length. "Look," they told him, "we're not going to be advocating for abortion. That's the last thing we want to do. We're not getting involved in that kind of issue; we're trying to build a health museum." But the man was impervious. We got nowhere.

Pitts's viewpoint had very little support in Congress. Had we been able to get an anonymous vote, almost no one would have favored his position. But you can't get an anonymous vote, and representatives are afraid that when they come up for reelection strange people will appear in their districts shouting that they are baby killers. They could just see it. "He voted for a government National Health Museum that teaches about killing babies." By the time you explain something like that you've lost the game.

Finally, after two years with no headway my board decided that Washington was a dead issue. We had to look elsewhere. What we needed was a city with a large enough population so that the traffic flow could support a museum. The locale we chose would also have to have a decent-sized corporate and philanthropic community. We started out with thirty-two cities and narrowed it down to four: New York, Chicago, Philadelphia, and Atlanta.

In the end we chose Atlanta, primarily because of the enthusiastic support from the mayor, the chamber of commerce, and the economic development council. The programmatic infrastructure was also strong enough there, with the Emory and Morehouse medical schools, a first-rate bioengineering program at Georgia Tech, and twenty-seven institutions of higher learning. Atlanta was also home to the CDC, a rich asset, plus the Atlanta airport, which would give us a global reach. So we chose Atlanta. Now we were ready to move ahead with constructing the museum and developing the kinds of programs and innovative displays that would accomplish our purpose.

The problem we need to solve is the disconnect between information and behavior. People have a great deal of information available now, yet the obesity rate keeps increasing, along with the diabetes rate, and tobacco use resists efforts to eliminate it. We don't have the answers yet as to how to get people to act on the information they're given, but that's what we hope to accomplish. We're going to have behavioral scientists and educational specialists, experts in the field of how learning takes place and what motivates people. What are the strategies we can use to reach people? How do we get people to adopt these behaviors as part of their daily lives? That's the great challenge.

To our frustration, I might say almost to our dismay, just as we were gearing up for this effort, the financial crisis of 2008 hit, and with it the deep and lasting recession that followed. At one point I thought back with a bit of a chill to Morehouse College president John Hope, who had initiated planning for a medical school back in the 1920s only to run into the brick wall of the 1929 stock market crash and the Great Depression that followed. Not that I really thought we were in for something similar, but who knew?

The recession meant we couldn't immediately raise the money for the physical museum, but we were still able to move ahead developing and rolling out programs. Genentech supported the creation of a science program for high school teachers. We created educational modules that we could deploy in specially designed kiosks for public use. GlaxoSmithKline supported that project, and we placed kiosks in several locations, including one in Lancaster, Pennsylvania (Glaxo happened to have a vaccine-production division there). We developed a kiosk module on heart disease, high blood pressure, strokes, diabetes, and STDs that we placed in Blakely. We wanted to see if having a kiosk in an area short on physicians would be of value, a place where people could get a lot of questions answered without necessarily seeing a physician. We received a grant from the Georgia Health Department for this endeavor.

We have begun designing the museum itself, even though we don't have land or a physical building yet. There will be exhibits on many aspects of how the body works—how the blood flows, how food is digested, how the body moves. We'll cover the body's interaction of nerves, bones, and muscles and what happens when heart disease or cancer develops. There will be five amphitheaters, the last one devoted to nutrition, which will lead directly to our cafeteria and our chefs, demonstrating how to make good, inexpensive, balanced, nutritious meals.

We want all of this to be easily understood and presented in an entertaining, exciting, interactive way so that people will not just be spectators. We want them to be involved and, we hope, motivated to incorporate what they learn into their lives. We think that can be done.

I don't regard the National Health Museum as something separate from the work that has motivated me for most of my professional life. I've been a clinician, a scientist, and an administrator, but what I've most strived for is to make a difference in the health of the poor, the minorities, the underserved. That's what Morehouse School of Medicine was and is about; that was the theme of my tenure as secretary; that's ultimately what I was after with the Sullivan Commission and now with the Sullivan Alliance. The Health Museum's great endeavor is to bridge the gap between information and action, and by far the hardest part of that challenge pertains exactly to the communities that I have always been most concerned for. They are the people with less education, fewer resources to eat well and less access to recreation or health clubs or even safe places to walk or jog or bicycle. They have less of a sense that they control their own lives. They find it more difficult to avoid the behaviors that lead to poor health. If we are successful, everyone will benefit, but they will benefit particularly.

So for me the Health Museum isn't a deviation from what I have always focused on. At the same time I have always felt that my commitment to those who have been excluded and marginalized was about something larger than that. My charge as secretary was to care for the health of everyone, not just the underserved, and I took that charge to heart. In point of fact, that was not different from what I have really been after all along.

Whatever I may have wished, my life has been inextricably tied to questions of race. As an African American man in a majority white society, especially growing up when I did and where I did, how could it have been different? The racial and minority problems I have lived through and witnessed are embedded in the history of our nation. Our American DNA includes enfolding refugees and outsiders of all kinds into our society and body politic. It includes the continual enlargement of our belief about who deserves to be covered by our most fundamental national values—that all people are created equal and endowed with the same inalienable rights. But at the same time our history is also replete with the suppression, exploitation, and relegation of minorities. That is part of our American DNA too.

The question is, how do you counter an orientation so hurtful and so deep dyed? To my way of looking at it, ingrained problems like this require countermeasures that are broad in scope, draw on the strength of many, and persist through time. Over the years my answer has been to build institutions that educate, create dignity, and fight for inclusion, even if progress on this road is a very long march.

I can't claim that I understood this when, together with Hugh Gloster, I undertook to build a medical school. But looking back, I can see that I was determined to do whatever I could to create these kinds of institutions: Morehouse School of Medicine, the Association of Minority Health Professions Schools, the Office (now Institute) of Minority Health, the Sullivan Alliance. The purpose of all these has been to bring minorities into the mainstream, to recognize that they are in fact inextricable from the mainstream, which every day becomes more and more true as we move on through the vast demographic changes of our new century.

Redefining what it is to be a full participant in this nation and its promises has been the challenge of my generation. It is an ongoing struggle, but one that has afforded us a distinctive sense of accomplishment and also, I think, of pride, which I feel as deeply as any.

EPILOGUE

In 2008 John Maupin invited me to lunch. Maupin had been president of the Morehouse School of Medicine for two years, and we talked frequently about school issues. But this lunch was not about Morehouse, at least not directly. It was about Grady Hospital, Atlanta's big public hospital that also served as a teaching hospital for Morehouse as well as for the Emory School of Medicine. Along with Emory's dean, Maupin was an ex officio member of Grady's board of trustees.

Grady, like many big city public hospitals, was in deep financial trouble. In its effort to figure out a way to survive, Grady had recently taken a major step. In Georgia, public hospitals are under the jurisdiction of their county governments, and since its founding in 1890 Grady had been run by appointees from Fulton and DeKalb, the two counties whose borders include the city of Atlanta. The Fulton-DeKalb Hospital Authority had identified political interference as a large contributing factor to Grady's mounting deficit crisis. Pressure from politicians often influenced how contracts were awarded and which people were hired, leading to overspending and inefficiencies. To tackle this, the authority had decided to turn the direction of the hospital over to a new, independent corporation and board of trustees. Maupin told me the new board's mission was, very simply, to save the hospital. Would I join?

I was noncommittal over lunch. But the fact was that I just didn't think I could do it. This wouldn't be a matter of lending my name; this would mean putting my shoulder to the wheel. A crisis this deep at such a major institution—Grady was the fifth largest public hospital in the country—would require a very large investment of time, and given the work I was already doing with the Sullivan Alliance, the Health Museum, and other boards and projects, I couldn't see how I could possibly fit it in.

So I said no. "I understand the gravity of it," I told Maupin. "But I simply am not able to make the time commitment."

Two weeks later I got a call from Pete Correll, one of Atlanta's leading businessmen. Pete was chairman and CEO emeritus of Georgia Pacific and was on various other major boards as well. I had served on the Georgia Pacific board when Pete was there, and he had played an important role in my fund-raising efforts for Morehouse. Pete was now chairman of the new Grady board. He wanted to talk further about the possibility of my coming on. When could we meet?

The truth was that by then I had thought more about it. I knew Grady fairly well. The hospital was important, maybe essential, for Atlanta, and especially for Atlanta's poor and minority populations. I myself had been born there, as had my brother, Walter—in Grady's segregated unit back in the days of Jim Crow. I was now seventy-three years old, nowhere near the end of my productive years, I hoped, but old enough to think that this place had helped with my coming into the world, and if I could take a hand in saving it now, it would be something like closing a circle.

Grady was also important for Morehouse. Most of the school's clinical teaching took place there. Here I am, I thought, the former secretary of Health and Human Services. What would it look like if I declined to help this hospital, if I were asked and said no? It didn't seem right. By the time Pete came to see me, my mind was made up. "I don't know if the hospital is going to survive," I told him. "Hopefully it will, and I might be helpful. But if it doesn't survive, I'd much rather be in there bailing water with everybody else instead of standing on the sidelines watching it go down."

Grady was significant to the Atlanta area in dozens of ways. The hospital had the only level one trauma center in a hundred-mile radius. It housed specialized burn and dialysis units, a poison center, and first-rate obstetric and infectious disease centers. It treated indigents and migrants. More than a quarter of Georgia's physicians had trained there. The list went on and on. But in addition to the services it provided, Grady Hospital was itself a living history of black-white relations in the city.

Grady had started off in 1892 with fifty beds for whites and fifty for blacks. Twenty-five years later separate facilities were built, and people began calling it not Grady but "the Gradies," which some old-time Atlantans still do. Even before then the Emory School of Medicine was using Grady as its primary teaching hospital.

As a segregated institution, Grady didn't allow black physicians to affiliate and had no beds at all for black private patients. But in 1952 the formidable Grace Hamilton led a fight that forced Fulton-DeKalb to build a hospital for black private patients across the street from Grady, called the Hughes-Spalding Pavilion. (Hamilton was the same powerhouse politician who had tried to stop the Morehouse medical education program in its tracks back in 1975 when she accused Gloster of violating the Atlanta University Center bylaws.) Hughes-Spalding's medical director was Dr. Asa Yancey, who played a leading role himself in the evolution of Atlanta's black-white medical scene.

Yancey was a trailblazer; he had attended the University of Michigan Medical School in the late 1930s, one of the extremely few blacks admitted anywhere other than Howard and Meharry in those days. When Grady integrated in 1962, Yancey became its first black attending physician, and in 1972 he was named Grady's medical director.

Nine years later Morehouse School of Medicine gained its full accreditation, which meant that we became a four-year rather than a two-year medical school, which in turn meant that we needed a hospital affiliation where our students could do their clinical training. Grady was the obvious place, really the only nearby possibility. But Emory was already there. They had been training their clinical students at Grady for more than half a century. Multiple medical schools sharing the same teaching hospital was always a problem, and putting a black school together with a white school in the same facility would likely magnify the inherent difficulties.

On the other hand, Yancey was Grady's medical director, and he was in favor. In a sense Yancey had a foot in both camps. He was a Morehouse College alumnus and also Emory's first African American medical professor. In addition, the Emory School of Medicine had been extremely helpful in establishing the Morehouse medical program. I had worked closely with Emory's dean, Arthur Richardson; two vice presidents for health affairs, Garland Hernden and Charles Hatcher; and other high-level Emory administrators. Over the years the two schools had maintained a warm, mutually respectful relationship. With that background I began discussions with Arthur Richardson, Hatcher, and Asa Yancey about a Morehouse affiliation with Grady.

Despite the good will, bringing Morehouse in to share the facility with Emory faced huge challenges. The first was that multiple medical school affiliations had proven problematic and economically untenable elsewhere; they were being phased out all over the country. I had seen that up close at Boston City Hospital, where the Tufts and Harvard medical schools had been asked to leave after they and BU hadn't been able to agree on combining their programs. The same scenario had played out in Philadelphia, where Philadelphia General Hospital had been home to five medical school affiliations. New York with Bellevue and other cities with public hospitals were going through the same kind of consolidations.

As a result, there was considerable skepticism that a joint affiliation at Grady would work; we were clearly going against a strong tide. As we expected, we ran into opposition from department chairs and leading clinicians who weren't happy with the idea of sharing resources and who didn't have the global perspective of an Arthur Richardson or Charlie Hatcher. Emory professors and students had a tendency to think, we're one of the top medical schools in the South, so why are we giving up some of our turf to these new people?

Asa Yancey played a key role in addressing these kinds of concerns and dealing with the egos involved. Persistent problems between chairs went to the deans, and if the deans couldn't resolve them they came to Richardson or Hatcher and me. "I am not going to stand in this hospital door," Charlie Hatcher said, "like George Wallace." And Emory didn't. Quite the opposite.

Early on the tensions came out in various ways, including incidents that reflected an ongoing racial bias. Morehouse had white as well as black students, and it wasn't that uncommon for one of our white students to be complimented by an attending physician—"Excellent job! You Emory students are so much better than those Morehouse students"—only to be told, "Well, doctor, thank you, but I *am* a Morehouse student."

There was a lot of that kind of attitude around, some of which I attributed to the inherent challenges in bringing together two schools like these, one old, one new; one rich, one not so rich; one black, the other white. Today, with Morehouse's many achievements—its graduates, its outreach, its ranking on social mission—and simply the passage of time, much of the racial discomfort has disappeared. After a quarter of a century Morehouse School of Medicine is recognized as an important institution in the community, a valuable asset not just for blacks but for the city and state as well.

Racial suspicions, of course, went both ways. When we had the public meeting about setting up an independent board, some in the room were up in arms. The black community had always looked to Grady for their care, and there were elements that saw the change of governance as an egregious "white takeover" of the hospital. This suspicion was aggravated when the board decided that the hospital needed different leadership and, after a search, we decided on a white applicant to replace the departing African American CEO.

Fortunately, people with that kind of racial perspective were in the minority. Most recognized that Grady needed the most effective leadership available, whether the person happened to be white or black. Also, in Atlanta there's a lot of pride in the black community in terms of its tolerance. We do not want to be the dispensers of bias in the same way that we have been the recipients of bias. So there's a significant effort to get beyond the racial divides—not that we're completely there yet.

Four years into the new board's operation, we've completed a major funding drive to upgrade Grady's facilities and equipment, and we have addressed some of the ongoing financial problems. The work has required a continual effort on the part of the board, which I anticipated before I joined. But it has been a worthwhile fight and an important one, and at this point it looks like it might come out positively. If we do succeed, Atlanta will benefit tremendously, and the efforts we've made may well prove helpful to other big city public hospitals fighting for their own lives.

———————

Grady Hospital has been so tied to my own life story that a good deal of the satisfaction I've gotten from my involvement is personal. I see Grady's history too as an illustration of Atlanta's racial evolution—institutional as well as emotional and psychological. What's happened with Grady, from its days as the segregated "Gradies" to Asa Yancey and Grace Hamilton, to Emory and Morehouse, has reflected the changes that the city and many of its citizens have also gone through.

Yet old ways and old conditioning do not leave quietly. They persist. Years ago, when our son Halsted was a young adolescent, we sent him to a YMCA summer camp near Talladega, Alabama, one of the first integrated camps in the region. The following winter Ginger came with me to Birmingham, where I was speaking at a medical conference. Halsted came too; he wanted to visit one of his camp friends who lived in the city.

Ginger spoke with the friend's parents, and we dropped Halsted off at their house, making arrangements for him to meet us at our hotel when the conference was over. After the conference Ginger and I were in the hotel lobby talking with friends when I saw Halsted come in with a white girl, their arms around each other's waists. The instant I spied them I jumped. My heart began racing. I caught myself quickly and glanced around. Thankfully, nobody seemed to have noticed.

A moment later Halsted was introducing us to his camp friend, both of them as relaxed as could be. For them, a white girl and black boy together was perfectly natural. But in the recesses of my own brain, something very different was going on. Down there things were churning: memories of the black kid who had fled

Blakely to save his life when it was discovered that he had a relationship with a white girl; similar stories from other places in Georgia, some with tragic endings; Emmett Till, who was murdered in Mississippi. All of that came together to shout "danger" the instant I saw Halsted and his friend.

It surprised and embarrassed me to realize that I harbored conditioning this deep. I kept that very private, but it warned me to be aware that while Halsted and his friend might be living in a new era, part of me was still down there in the old days. Intellectually, I've adjusted. But deep down, some of that emotional scarring is still there. And, of course, that's true not only of myself.

But the changes we're all living through today have also brought home to me how far we've come. Working for Grady's survival has helped do that for me. And for several years now the town of Blakely itself has once again become part of my life. Charles Barton Rice precipitated that. Charles Rice was the founder of Barton Security, a large national company that provided security for the 1996 summer Olympics and for many major companies around the country. About seven or eight years ago Charles sold the company, which made him a very wealthy man. I had never heard of either Charles or his company, but he called me and introduced himself. He was from Blakely, he said. He had known something about my family when he was growing up. Now he was involved in a project in Blakely. Might we talk?

Charles and I had lunch in Atlanta's Buckhead Club. There he described his plans to develop Blakely, to bring in businesses, housing, and infrastructure and make Blakely into a thriving rural center. To do this he had established a nonprofit foundation called Early County 2055. He was dedicating substantial resources to this effort, he said, and he wanted to be sure that the black community shared in its benefits equally with the white. He saw this as something for the entire community.

Charles Rice is five or six years younger than I am, and white. We had never run across each other growing up and wouldn't have even had we been the same age. Strict separation of the races had been the rule there, and black and white children rarely had anything to do with one another. Not untypically, though, Charles had had a black nanny. She had taken care of him for years, and in the way of these things, the family had become very attached to her. Charles himself had great affection for her. But as he grew older he also understood the huge discrepancies between his family and hers, how every aspect of her family's life was impoverished and limited compared to the ease and opportunities his family enjoyed. Eventually, he told me, he came to understand that the system was fundamentally unjust and inexcusable. Now that he had the means, he wanted to do what he could to change things.

He knew me, he said, because my family had been prominent in Blakely and, of course, because I had been HHS secretary. He wanted to share his thoughts with me to see if I might have any interest in getting involved. He thought I might be able to help ensure that the black community would participate and benefit.

Charles laid out his plans for me, which were already in the early stages of implementation. But he was running into doubts about his motives, from both whites and blacks. He was buying up land and tearing down long-empty buildings, which launched suspicions that maybe he was out to make a big financial killing. Why else would he be doing this? So his credibility had been challenged. Was he really trying to resurrect the town, or did he have some personal motive?

Some in the white community thought, Why is he stirring up trouble? Everyone here is happy with the way things are. And the blacks were thinking, Why aren't we part of this? There were a couple of African Americans on Rice's committee, but the locals were saying, "They're handpicked. They're not really representing us." Rice himself didn't have credibility in the black community. According to him, I would be respected in both communities. I could help people understand what he was trying to do and why. I could help bridge the tensions between the black and white communities. Did I think this was an effort I could get involved in?

Charles's plans made sense, as far as they went. And money wasn't an object with him. He was committed to developing this somnolent, stagnant town that he had grown up in and that he still loved. Now that he had made his fortune, this was what he wanted to do, and he thought he knew how to do it, or at least how to begin doing it. And while he was at it he could right some of the wrongs that had been part of this place when he was young, some of which still remained.

When I considered Rice's plans for Blakely the word "quixotic" came to mind. Blakely still looked pretty much as it had fifty years ago, only worse for wear. Many stores around the stately old courthouse were vacant and shuttered. What had been the center of the black community, where our vacant house and funeral parlor still stood, was broken down and decrepit. Unemployment was high, and the town was neither strategically located nor home to any large local company. Time has not treated Blakely kindly, as it hasn't many of America's small rural communities. On the other hand, Charles Rice was a smart, sophisticated man with a wealth of business experience and very substantial resources. He had not undertaken this challenge frivolously.

Never in my life would I have imagined that someone like Charles Rice might come along and put his hand to Blakely's well-being, nor that I would be asked to take part in the effort. Like him I had, and have, an emotional attachment to the town. If my roots are anywhere, Blakely (and Atlanta) is where they are. But my emotions were both positive and negative. Our family had made a life for ourselves there, and through my mother's and father's hard work we had thrived. But in many ways Blakely had been, as my brother, Walter, once put it, hostile territory.

Things were different now. I had been invited various times to speak at chamber of commerce meetings and other similar occasions. Blacks and whites were certainly doing better together than they had in earlier times. But those times weren't forgotten either. When I was in town with Walter once to give a high school commencement speech, there was a banner hung across the street that read, "Welcome Home, Mr. Secretary." But one elderly black gentleman pulled Walter's jacket and said, "Isn't this remarkable. They tried to kill y'all. And now it's welcome home."

I'm aware that in a way the life I've led has allowed me to get beyond that, which was why Charles Rice approached me. After thinking about it, I did say yes to him. Working for Blakely is a little like working for Grady Hospital—it's taken me back to something that was part of who I've been from the beginning. More than that, it's allowed me to confront some of the unresolved feelings I've carried with me deep in the recesses, as that situation with Halsted and his camp friend so surprisingly revealed to me. I have the sense too that in a minor way I'm helping to carry on the work that my father did, fighting to give the black community its share in the life of the town.

I hope we will be successful in Blakely. I want to be positive about the eventual outcome at Grady Hospital too, and I'm optimistic about the National Health Museum. But these are works in progress. Morehouse School of Medicine is something else, an established institution on the American scene that will continue to contribute to our national life on into the future. But Morehouse too was a quixotic enterprise at first, a risk-filled venture with extremely uncertain prospects.

When I think about these things I can't help remembering Benjamin Mays addressing us in the Morehouse College chapel when we were undergraduates. That was more than half a century ago, but in my head his voice rings as clear as it did in life. "It is not a sin to fail," Mays told us. "The sin is not to try." I've carried that message with me ever since. Like everyone else, I have failed from time to time, but I've always chosen to try, and that continues to give my life its very greatest satisfactions.

———————

When Barack Obama was inaugurated president on January 20, 2009, after defeating John McCain, Ginger and I were sitting in the reserved seats near the front. My government days were past but Georgia representative Phil Gingrey had been kind enough to get tickets for us. Obama was, of course, a Democrat, and I had been a Republican for many years who had served in a Republican administration. In addition, neither Ginger nor I were sure Obama was ready for the position of national and international leadership he was about to assume. He had, after all, been a senator for only part of one term. But those considerations took a distant second place to our feelings about being present at this historic moment. The significance of the inauguration affected us deeply. We both felt it as we sat there in the bitter eighteen-degree chill, thinking not about the weather but about what this event meant.

As monumental as it was—seeing an African American standing on the Capitol podium taking the presidential oath of office—I did not feel it was a turning point in America's struggle with its troubled past and still racially charged present. This was a great moment, a historic moment, but not one that was going to put an end to or even mark the beginning of the end of the county's racial divisions. It wasn't a turning point, I thought; it was more of a milestone in a still difficult, ongoing journey.

Sitting there on the rise I looked back toward the Lincoln Monument on the other end of the Mall and was carried back to the previous time Ginger and I had been on the Mall together, forty-six years earlier, on August 28, 1963, standing right up there near Martin Luther King Jr. as he gave his "I Have a Dream" speech. The mood then wasn't the electric joyfulness that surrounded the Obama inauguration. Instead it was a potent mix of anger and hopefulness and striving. The year 1963 was volatile. Bull Connor's fire hoses and attack dogs were on national television; sit-ins, marches, and protests seemed to be daily affairs. In April of that year Martin Luther King wrote his "Letter from Birmingham City Jail." It was only a few months later that A. Phillip Randolph and other civil right leaders called for a march on Washington.

Back then we—America's African Americans—were petitioning for equality and justice, demanding it, invoking America's ideals and deploring America's reality: 250 years of slavery followed by a century of discrimination, segregation, and unequal opportunity. The Kennedy administration was backing a civil rights act to correct some of those wrongs, but it seemed to be going nowhere fast in Congress. So that day in 1963 the anger and hope that pervaded the Mall was joined by a building tide of frustration.

But now, forty-six years later, Ginger and I were seeing an African American inaugurated as president. The two events, the March on Washington and this inauguration, were like bookends in our own life journeys. We were both thirty years old when Martin Luther King gave his speech. Forty-six years later we were well into our seventies. Bookends: not just for us but for our generation, white as well as black.

Ginger and I were elated to have seen these events in our lifetimes. We had high expectations for this new president who looked like us. It was of no concern to me that he was a Democrat. We are now into Obama's second term, and I've had some reservations about him. But those reservations fade next to the immense fact of his presidency. I suppose that means I can forgive him his shortcomings. No one is perfect. He is a black man trying his best to do what he thinks is right for America's poor and minorities. Against that, the fact that I might wish he were doing some of those things differently bears little weight.

Obama's second inauguration was almost as profoundly symbolic as his first. It meant that Americans did not think that having elected a black president was a mistake, that the first election hadn't been some strange, anomalous happening, never to be repeated. The second inauguration also had an extraordinary poignancy about it. The year 2013 marked the 50th anniversary of the March on Washington and the 150th anniversary of the Emancipation Proclamation. The inauguration also coincided with the celebration of Martin Luther King's birthday. Obama was sworn in at the Capitol end of the Mall, looking down toward the Lincoln Memorial, on whose steps King had given his famous speech. The confluence of Lincoln, King, and Obama's reelection intensified the sense of how elemental a role the struggle to achieve equality for all its citizens has played in the life of our nation.

Martin Luther King fought against a system that denied equality and equal opportunity to the country's African American citizens. We think of that struggle in terms of voting rights, access to employment, freedom to live where we wish, and other conspicuous rights obstructed by de jure and de facto discrimination. Most people are not aware, though, of the manifestation of injustice that to King was the most pernicious of all. "Of all the forms of inequality," he said, "injustice in health is the most shocking and inhumane."

I would not have been able to articulate that when I was growing up, but I saw it firsthand, and I felt as if I needed to do something about it, at least in whatever small sphere I could—by becoming a doctor for people suffering from that inequality. For various reasons I never realized that early aspiration. But becoming the founding dean of Morehouse School of Medicine gave me a second chance to do that on a larger scale than what I might have accomplished as a physician in private practice. Being nominated and confirmed as secretary of Health and Human Services gave me a chance to try to achieve that goal on a national level.

The health care system I found in place when I arrived in Washington was in some ways the best in the world. The United States had, and has, what is probably the world's most rigorous and advanced education system for health professionals, demonstrated by the fact that people from all over come here for special training, often not available elsewhere. We invest more dollars in biomedical research than any other nation. American scientists win more Nobel prizes in physiology and medicine than do those from elsewhere.

The United States also spends more of our GDP on health care than any other nation. But in spite of all this we have a shorter life expectancy and higher infant mortality rates than many other Western countries. On a whole range of health indices we are simply below par. Our problem is not in our medical training system; it's not in our biomedical advances; it's not in the funds we allocate to health care. It's in what I call our distribution system. The benefits of our system are not equitably available to all segments of our society. Dr. King called this kind of inequality "shocking and inhumane." That is exactly what it is.

When I came in as secretary thirty-seven million of our fellow Americans had no health insurance. These uninsured, underserved people were major contributors to our shameful national health care statistics. Because so many of their health problems went unaddressed until they became emergencies, their treatment was far more costly and less effective than their care would have been if they had access to primary care physicians and standard basic practices such as mammograms, pap smears, colonoscopies, cardiovascular screenings, and vaccinations for influenza and other communicable diseases.

At that time—in 1989—we were spending $1 trillion on health care, 11 percent of our GNP. By 2010 that figure had spiraled to $2.4 trillion, 18 percent of our GNP. Yet during that same period the number of our uninsured rose from thirty-seven to forty-seven million people. As I write this, in the winter of 2013, the Affordable Care Act measures have only partially kicked in to help address the failings of a system that is almost as broken now as it was when I took office.

During George H. W. Bush's presidency we attempted to fix this broken system. According to the actuaries, the proposals that were part of our health reform proposal would have reduced the numbers of uninsured from thirty-seven million to five million in the eight years it would have taken for full implementation. At the same time we included mechanisms that would have reduced costs substantially. But although our reform plan included key features that appealed to both Republicans and Democrats, the legislation went nowhere. The political stars were not aligned. When President Obama's Affordable Care Act passed in early 2010, they were aligned, though barely. The act passed the Democratic-controlled House by only seven votes.

Obamacare is legislation I support because, while it isn't perfect by any means, it does represent an important beginning. By providing coverage for most of the uninsured it will improve the overall health of our citizens. Reducing illness and injury will improve economic productivity and lessen the need for social supports. More people will be earning wages and paying taxes rather than being disabled by illness and weighing down the system with costs.

One way it will make insurance coverage available is through state insurance exchanges that will create transparent and competitive markets in which individuals and small businesses can buy health care coverage. These state insurance exchanges are similar to the small group purchasing cooperatives that we had in our legislation, which were meant to enable small businesses to purchase reduced-cost health insurance by spreading the risks and administrative expenses over a pool of buyers. This was an idea that had its origins in the Heritage Foundation and was considered a conservative concept at the time. With the dramatic rightward shift of the Republican Party, these exchanges have become controversial. But the controversies here are ideological rather than pragmatic.

But while the Affordable Care Act moves toward covering a large percentage of the uninsured, it does little to address some of the significant cost drivers. Medical malpractice reform, for example, is not included in the ACA, because trial lawyers make fortunes representing malpractice litigants, and trial lawyers are perennially among the heaviest contributors to Democratic candidates. Malpractice suits and threats of suits may be healthy for lawyers' pocketbooks, but they burden the health care system with huge costs by forcing doctors and hospitals to order unnecessary testing to protect themselves from suits. The cost of litigation itself, as well as exorbitant jury rewards, drive doctors' malpractice insurance costs into the stratosphere.

In our legislation we proposed malpractice arbitration panels, with experts to determine if indeed an outcome was the result of poor medical care and, if so, how much the penalty or reimbursement should be. Our legislation also incorporated no-fault malpractice insurance. Altogether we would have saved many billions of dollars. At today's costs malpractice reform would save many tens of billions, probably between 5 and 10 percent of the country's total health care bill.

But overall I believe the Affordable Care Act is a good start, one that can be tweaked and amended over time to address deficiencies and the unintended consequences that health care laws are prone to. I am especially pleased that the act allocates more resources to prevention and health promotion than before. The numbers are still woefully insufficient—only $4 billion—but it is a start in an area that I believe is perhaps most important of all in making the country healthier and lowering our health care costs.

We have other ways of lowering costs. They run the gamut from malpractice reform to bringing down the price of drugs, equipment, and procedures to changing the fee for service models to raising Medicare age criteria. But none of them comes anywhere near the cost-reduction potential of simply keeping ourselves healthier through prevention and education. We must, in other words, do everything we can to convert our approach from the sick care system we have now to a wellness maintenance system. And to do that we have to allocate adequate resources.

A large-scale shift in behavior is necessary if we are to significantly improve the nation's health. The factors that drive behavioral shifts are complex, but we have now reached a point where we at least have clear and convincing evidence of which health-conducive behaviors actually work. Twenty-five years ago there was still a good deal of skepticism and disbelief about the benefits of exercise and diet. People knew in a general way that exercise was a good habit and that certain foods were "good for you" while others weren't. But these assumptions were presumptive rather than proven. There weren't enough large, well-conducted studies to generate the kind of broad understanding that leads to real changes in behavior.

We now have those studies. We know for certain that exercise helps to reduce the incidence of heart attacks and strokes, that it increase bone and muscle strength, that people who exercise live longer. Alzheimer's disease even seems to be less severe or less frequent in people who have regular programs of exercise. The benefits of a Mediterranean-type diet for the prevention of cardiovascular disease are no longer in doubt. We also know that exercise in conjunction with dietary measures will help address the problems of obesity and diabetes, which are at epidemic levels in our country and which represent a dramatic challenge to our health care resources.

But prevention is a difficult concept to implement. Procedures and medications that fix problems are easier to see and to assess. Behaviors that prevent problems from developing in the first place are far more difficult. Psychologically, it's hard for many people to grasp that preventive measures are real and to see that they save significant dollars.

But recent studies have been conducted that conclusively demonstrate the financial savings. Some companies (Pitney Bowes is a leading example) have put in place exercise, diet, and health education programs that have significantly lowered health care costs for both the company and its employees. Various workplace studies have shown that by reducing their weight, employees have lowered incidences of heart attacks, strokes, and diabetes, which have decreased the concomitant costs. Johnson & Johnson has achieved a significant reduction in health care costs by promoting healthy diets, exercise, and other healthy behaviors.

So those studies are coming on line. But we've yet to develop the necessary level of understanding, commitment, and support for prevention, because we are as a society focused on acute problems, and that mindset will change only if resources are focused on strategies to help it change. The Obama health care legislation has started that with $4 billion dedicated toward prevention and health promotion. But that figure needs to be a lot more. We also need to have the active participation of private sector companies to complement and reinforce the public effort.

When I was secretary I wanted the department itself, with its 124,000 employees, to be a model for change. We had our food vendor in Washington create healthy menus. (Ginger actually precipitated this after she had lunch in the department cafeteria one day and was appalled by the amount of fried food being served.) The company that ran our food service was so reluctant to revamp its offerings that we had to guarantee them against income loss due to the menu changes. But when we implemented "The Secretary's Healthy Diet" sales went up instead of down. We also established an exercise program that provided access to gyms, and we monitored blood pressure and weight levels for department employees who volunteered. But this was twenty plus years ago, and it was indicative of the times that Congress criticized me for wasting taxpayer money on such things.

But now we know for certain that diet and exercise work and that they have positive economic consequences. The prevention of sickness through lifestyle change is a critical element in cutting through the Gordian knot of spiraling health care costs and subpar health outcomes. But to get there we need to do a far better job at educating people and improving health literacy. My hope is that the National Health Museum, whose chairman I now am, will play a leading role in that effort.

Obamacare will provide many of the reforms we so badly need. But finding out how to effectively present the facts about how people can keep themselves healthy and then, even harder, how to bridge the gap between knowledge and action—those are the keys to making our nation's health care system truly affordable.

ACKNOWLEDGMENTS

There are many individuals who have served as role models for me during various periods of my life. There are others who provided support, advice, and direction, which was most helpful at specific times and places.

First are my three children (now adults), Paul, Shanta, and Halsted, who inspired me to become the best father I could be, and with whom I spent many joyous hours at play and in exploring the wider world at home and abroad. Paul and his lovely wife, Laura, have given Ginger and me the precious gift of two handsome grandsons, Paul Jr. and Brent, who continually master the latest electronic marvels almost instantly, to my amazement.

My big brother, Walter, always gave me friendly advice as well as helpful criticism and support when needed, particularly during my younger years.

In Blakely, the small town in southwest Georgia, my family had many friends in the black and white communities who were appreciative of my father's efforts to improve the lives of those who were poor and were the victims of legally sanctioned segregation, discrimination, and unequal opportunity. I am grateful to the Reverend Fred Daniels and to Mr. George Brown for their help in organizing meetings for David Chanoff and me with current residents of Blakely to review, recall, and discuss those times from 1937 to 1957.

In Booker T. Washington High School in Atlanta, Walter and I had many outstanding and dedicated teachers who exhibited a love of learning and inspired us to do the same. They included Laura Woods (eighth-grade biology), Joseph Martin (ninth-grade geometry), X. L. Neal (tenth-grade chemistry), A. R. Phillips (eleventh-grade English), and Earl F. Starling (band director and music teacher). My high school classmates were, simultaneously, inspiring supporters and academic competitors, including Mattie Goodrum (Taylor), Emily Morrow, Bill Jones, Bill Allison, and E. B. Williams.

At Morehouse College I quickly learned that there are a lot of bright, hardworking people in the world—including my college classmates and my instructors. I was challenged to be as successful as they were. My classmates Ezra Davidson,

243

Donald Moore, Henry Foster, and Rowan Sanders all became successful physicians after their college years at Morehouse. Among my role models at Morehouse was President Benjamin E. Mays, a brilliant, articulate, and challenging leader who inspired us all to "reach for the stars and grasp the moon." Dr. James Birnie, my premed adviser, was a rigorous scientist who exemplified excellence in his teaching and research.

At Boston University School of Medicine, my transition to professional school while working and living in an integrated environment for the first time was made easier by my classmates Barry Manuel and Jerry Rosenfeld and by supportive faculty, including Elizabeth Moyer (anatomy), Isaac Asimov (biochemistry), Chester Keefer (medicine), and Franz Ingelfinger (medicine).

In 1958 Dr. E. Hugh Luckey, chairman of medicine at New York Hospital–Cornell Medicine Center, chose me for a medical internship at that prestigious institution, the first African American in a period when such appointments were rare. Chief medical resident Jim Strickler and senior nurse Meta Buehler were great teachers for me and were very supportive at NYH-Cornell. Drs. Benjamin Castleman, chief of pathology at Massachusetts General Hospital, and William Castle, director of the Thorndike Memorial Laboratory (Harvard Medical Unit) at Boston City Hospital, gave opportunities to me for specialty training in hematology and research.

President Hugh Gloster of Morehouse College provided me with the unique opportunity to become the founding dean of Morehouse School of Medicine and was a great supporter. Helping in this undertaking were Morehouse College faculty Joseph Gayles, Thomas Norris, and Alice Greene, joined later by board of overseers members Edgar Smith, Sarah Austin, and Monroe Trout, among others. Dr. William Bennett of the U.S. Bureau of Health Manpower (then based at the National Institutes of Health) provided valuable guidance and support.

During my years at Morehouse School of Medicine, I was superbly supported by a dedicated series of executive assistants—including Allie Clift, Shirley Desaussure, Debra Francis, and Gayle McDaniel—who helped me manage the continually changing kaleidoscope of activities of my office.

Of the many talented administrators who have worked with me, I salute my three chiefs of staff during my four years as U.S. secretary of Health and Human Services: Everett Wallace, Michael Calhoun, and Robin Carle. At MSM, Stanley Olson gave me wise guidance and counsel, gained from his years of serving as dean at three medical schools. Also at MSM, Ronny Lancaster was outstanding with innovative ideas and a passion for finding ways to implement them. Eli Phillips was a superb financial manager; Chris Metzger managed our facilities creatively, efficiently, and economically.

Over the years we gained many friends for MSM who gave generously of themselves in our fund-raising efforts: Barbara Bush, Donald Keough, Bob Froehlke, Dick Gelb, Bill and Sally Hambrecht, Donald Clark, Desi Di Simone, Sidney Feldman, Jerry Tamkin, Lew Platt, Nancy Rabstinek Nichols, Bill Taylor, Gerry Blakely, and many more.

Among the congressional supporters of MSM were U.S. representatives Andy Young, John Lewis, Louis Stokes, Charlie Norwood, and Paul Rogers, plus U.S. senators Arlen Specter, Tom Harkin, Orrin Hatch, Herman Talmadge, and Sam Nunn. Georgia governors who supported our efforts included George Busbee, Joe Frank Harris, Zell Miller, and Speaker of the House Tom Murphy. Members of the Georgia Legislative Black Caucus, led by Ben Brown and Calvin Smyre, were strong supporters. Fulton County commissioners who supported our MSM efforts were J. T. Wyatt and Harold Dodson. Others to whom I am grateful are the late Rev. Leon Sullivan and Asa Yancey, MD, who served as role models, inspirers, and supporters.

To all of these and many more, I say thank you for helping me along the way.

Some of those who were so significant to me in various phases of my life also contributed specifically to writing this book, providing their recollections of events we experienced together. They include former first lady Barbara Bush; former president George H. W. Bush; Barry Manuel; my brother, Walter; and my wonderful wife, Ginger. Others who were kind enough to help sharpen and broaden my own memories are Connie Newman, Rev. Joseph Lowery, Yvonne Gloster, Jim Story, Edgar Smith, Bill Toby, Gail Wilensky, Beverly Allen, and Mattie Taylor. I want to express my special thanks to each of them.

My gratitude also goes to Ms. Marcie Wynn, teacher and archivist at Atlanta's Booker T. Washington High School, and Mr. Henry Goodgame, director of Alumni Affairs at Morehouse College, for providing me with photographs from my years as a student at both institutions.

Finally, I would like also to thank my friend Dr. Augustus White, who introduced me to my collaborator, David Chanoff, and my assistant, Gayle McDaniel, whose competence and hard work were so important in every phase of writing and production. The Honorable Andy Young knows how much I have to thank him for over the years, which now includes the gracious foreword to *Breaking Ground*.

INDEX